Strategies for Career-Long Teacher Education

Teacher Education Yearbook

Volume 6 *Founded 199.*

Editors

D. John McIntyre, *Southern Illinois University at Carbondale*

David M. Byrd, *University of Rhode Island*

Editorial Advisory Board

Strategies for Career-Long Teacher Education

Teacher Education Yearbook VI

Editors
D. John McIntyre
David M. Byrd

Association of Teacher Educators

CORWIN PRESS, INC.
A Sage Publications Company
Thousand Oaks, California

For information:

Corwin Press Inc.
2455 Teller Road
Thousand Oaks, California 91320
E-mail: order@corwin.sagepub.com

SAGE Publications Ltd.
6 Bonhill Street
London EC2A 4PU
United Kingdom

SAGE Publications India Pvt. Ltd.
M-32 Market
Greater Kailash I
New Delhi 110 048 India

Printed in the United States of America

Library of Congress Cataloging-in-Publication Data

ISSN: 1078-2265
ISBN: 0-8039-6673-3 (Hardcover)
ISBN: 0-8039-6674-1 (Paperback)

98 99 00 01 02 03 10 9 8 7 6 5 4 3 2 1

Editorial Assistant:	Kristen L. Gibson
Production Editor:	S. Marlene Head
Typesetter/Designer:	Andrea D. Swanson
Indexer:	Mary Kidd
Cover Designer:	Marcia M. Rosenburg
Print Buyer:	Anna Chin

Contents

96025

Introduction: The Quest for Career-Long Teacher Education

D. John McIntyre

David M. Byrd

D. John McIntyre is Professor and Director of Professional Education Experiences at Southern Illinois University at Carbondale. He is past president of the Association of Teacher Educators and has received ATE's award for Distinguished Research in Education. He has nearly 100 publications in the area of teacher education. He is a graduate of Otterbein College, Ohio State University, and Syracuse University.

David M. Byrd is Associate Professor and Director of the Office of Teacher Education at the University of Rhode Island. He has a long-term professional and research interest in the preparation of teachers, preservice through inservice. He is a graduate of the doctoral program in teacher education at Syracuse University. He has authored or coauthored nearly 30 articles in professional journals.

It was not too long ago that the concept of teacher education was confined to the 4 years that a prospective teacher spent studying at an institution of higher education. Once prospective teachers were hired by school districts, their professional development often consisted of a series of 1-day workshops focusing on potentially relevant topics or of graduate courses in their teaching areas. However, the recent resurgence in educational reform and excellence has created a reexamination of professional development and a realization that a teacher's development as an educator spans an entire career.

Sparks and Hirsh (1997) have suggested that three powerful ideas are currently shaping the schools within the United States and, consequently, the professional development of teachers that occurs within them. The first of these ideas is results-driven education. This concept focuses on what a student should know or be able to do at the various grade levels, and the skills and knowledge that teachers must possess to facilitate students learning the identified knowledge and skills. Thus, the success of professional development is based not on the number of attended workshops or courses but rather on the improved performance of students and staff.

The second idea that is shaping career-long teacher education is "systems thinking." Rather than seeing individual events, systems thinkers view the interconnectedness of all events and understand that causality is circular rather than linear. The authors state that because most educators have not approached educational reform in a systematic manner, that reform has been implemented in a more piecemeal fashion. Approaching staff development from a systems perspective encourages all people within the organization—administrators, staff, teachers, students, parents—to see how, if working together in a systematic way, they can change the system.

The third concept that is influencing staff development is constructivism. Constructivists believe that learners construct their own knowledge structures rather than merely receiving them from others. To facilitate constructivism, teachers must model the skills and behaviors necessary for students to construct their own knowledge scheme rather than relying on telling and directing the students.

Although much recent attention has been devoted to career-long teacher education, recent statistics released by the National Center for Education Statistics (1997) indicate that during the 1993-1994 school year, 50% or more of full-time public school teachers participated in professional development on topics such as the uses of educational technology for instruction, methods of teaching in their subject field, student assessment, and cooperative learning in the classroom. Also, 48% of full-time public school teachers received release time from teaching, and 41% received scheduled time for professional development. Twenty-two percent received none of the available types of support. Finally, elementary and secondary teachers in their first 3 years of teaching were more likely to have participated in a formal professional development program than were teachers with 4 or more years of experience.

Interestingly, the same data indicate that full-time public school teachers were more likely to participate in activities on all types of professional development topics than were full-time private school teachers. Full-time public elementary school teachers were more likely to participate in professional development activities than were their secondary school counterparts. Full-time public school teachers were more likely to receive professional growth credits and released and scheduled time from teaching than were their private school counterparts. However, private school teachers were more likely to receive tuition and/or fees than were than were public school teachers.

These statistics raise several serious questions about the status of career-long teacher education for our nation's teachers. Clearly, the fact that only slightly more than half of our classroom teachers participated in any kind of teacher education activity during the 1993-1994 school year is troubling. As knowledge rapidly expands and classroom demographics change, teachers must continually update their knowledge, skills, and areas of expertise. In addition, it is clear that many school districts do not support the continued development of their teachers through release time from teaching or through any scheduled time for professional development. Both of these findings should be unacceptable to the educational community. A medical doctor who failed to update herself on the latest knowledge, trends, and procedures in her field would eventually jeopardize the welfare of her patients. The same can certainly be said for a teacher who fails to update his knowledge and skills on receiving an initial teaching license.

The purpose of this yearbook is to shed further light on the notion of career-long teacher education. The chapter authors and respondents have examined the teacher education continuum from a variety of perspectives and points of view. For example, several authors examined how teachers learn about teaching and learning and how they develop their own educational schemata through the areas of teacher cognition, constructivist teacher education, cases and case methods, and inquiry-oriented teacher education. Others have looked at how universities and schools can collaborate through professional development schools and other avenues to further the education and development of both novice and experienced teachers. Still others have focused on how teacher education courses are offered and what actually occurs in a teacher education course.

Burke (1985) has stated that the history of teacher preparation has evolved into a phase that emphasizes career-long education. The most recently reported data on the numbers of teachers participating in professional development activities seem to refute that notion. What is more likely is that the practice of career-long teacher education has not yet caught up with the theory of career-long teacher education. It is hoped that this yearbook will help shed light on the education of a teacher as a career-long venture. We hope that it will also encourage you to reflect on your role as a teacher educator.

References

Burke, P. (1985). The history and development of teacher education. In P. Burke & R. Heideman (Eds.), *Career-long teacher education* (pp. 3-24). Springfield, IL: Charles C Thomas.

National Center for Education Statistics. (1997). *Teachers' participation in professional development.* Washington, DC: U.S. Department of Education, Office of Educational Research and Improvement.

Sparks, D., & Hirsh, S. (1997). *A new vision for staff development.* Alexandria, VA: Association for Supervision and Curriculum and Development.

TEACHER COGNITION, CONSTRUCTIVIST TEACHER EDUCATION, AND THE ETHICAL AND SOCIAL IMPLICATIONS OF SCHOOLING: OVERVIEW AND FRAMEWORK

Edith M. Guyton

Edith M. Guyton, Associate Professor of Early Childhood Education, was guest editor for a special issue (Summer 1996) of *Action in Teacher Education* on constructivist education. She is an editor of the 1996 *Handbook of Research on Teacher Education* and was editor of the Georgia Association of Teacher Educators journal for 6 years. She has served on the Executive Board of the Association of Teacher Educators, was president of the Georgia and Southeastern Association of Teacher Educators, and recently was elected President of the Association of Teacher Educators (1999-2000). She has published numerous articles in the leading teacher education journals. Her current writing and research focus is on constructivist teacher education, teacher change, and cultural diversity.

It seemed important that an overview suggest some common ideas for the reader to consider. At first, that task seemed defined by the fact that all three chapters deal with case studies. In the Nierstheimer, Hopkins, and Dillon chapter, though, the case study is the research method used rather than the subject of the research. At first, this fact seemed to be problematic for developing an overview for all three chapters, for developing a framework that might serve for reading all three chapters. Fortunately, this was not the case. After reading the chapters, four domains of thought in teacher education seemed to be relevant: teacher cognition, constructivist teacher education, the use of cases and case methods in teacher education, and inquiry-oriented teacher education that includes ethical and social implications of schooling. The individuality of the chapters will be honored more in my reflections, but I offer the following ways of thinking across the chapters.

There is a growing acceptance of the belief that teaching performance is a function of complex intellectual processes. Sprinthall, Reiman, and Thies-Sprinthall (1996) summarized findings from a research program/ study of inservice teacher education (Griffin, 1986):

> Effective teacher education programs are based on a conception of teacher growth and development; acknowledge the complexities of classroom, school, and community; are grounded in a substantial and verifiable knowledge base; and are sensitive to the ways teachers think, feel, and make meanings from their experiences. (p. 667)

The authors then advocate a model for cognitive-developmental instruction that includes role taking, taking on a more complex role, reflection (journals, demonstrations, case studies for dialogue on the meaning of experience), balance of role taking and reflection that forms an interactive praxis, continuity, and a balance between support and challenge (Sprinthall et al., 1996, p. 693). They advocate working on the development of programs that promote more efficient cognitive problem solving by teachers and on developing authentic assessments to judge the effectiveness of the interventions (p. 673).

The work of Vygotsky (1978), Blumer (1969), and others underscores the centrality of social interaction in learning to teach. Vygotsky defined the "zone of proximal development" as the level at which a person can perform intellectually with the support of a more competent person. The expert scaffolds the novice's development by sensitively adjusting the level of support to the novice's emerging understanding. This conception clarifies the importance to teacher education of meeting the teacher where he or she is. Vygotsky emphasized the importance of learning as a social interaction, which includes discussion, reflection, and growth.

Teachers' thought processes have been a subject for study for some time (Clark & Peterson, 1986). Many studies have shown some connection between teacher cognition and student outcomes (Fennema, Franke, Carpenter, & Carey, 1993; Kennedy, 1991; Knapp & Peterson, 1991; McKibbin & Joyce, 1981; Miller, 1981; Peterson, Fennema, Carpenter, & Loef, 1989; Sprinthall et al., 1996). All of the studies support the need for an emphasis on developing teachers' cognitive development.

The literature also indicates that cognitive development is not automatic. This growth does not happen as a result of age or experience; it requires a stimulating and supportive environment along with appropriate interaction (King & Kitchener, 1994; National Center for Research on Teacher Education, 1991). These studies strongly suggest that intervention is needed to promote teachers' cognitive growth. There must be ways of drawing meaning from experience. Much theoretical support exists for developing the reflective ability of teachers (Reiman & Parramore, 1993; Ross, 1988; Schön, 1983, 1987; Sprinthall, Reiman, & Thies-Sprinthall, 1993). Johnson (1996) advocated "cognitive apprenticeship" models of teacher education. But as Richardson (1996) reported, despite many calls for reflection-in-action, there are few programs of this sort. The chapters in this section are exceptions to that statement. Morine-Dershimer uses the cognitive apprenticeship framework for developing her class structure and her research. In all the chapters, reflection is the primary method used in the teacher education courses described.

One current focus of change in teacher education involves developing constructivist teacher education programs designed to prepare teachers who base their teaching on constructivist principles and theories. The philosophy of John Dewey undergirds constructivist education, and Dewey (1938) differentiated this philosophy from traditional education:

> To imposition from above is opposed expression and cultivation of individuality; to external discipline is opposed free activity; to learning from texts and teachers, learning through experience; to acquisition of isolated skills and techniques by drill is opposed acquisition of them as means of attaining ends which make direct vital appeal; to preparation for a more or less remote future is opposed making the most of opportunities of present life;

to static aims and materials is opposed acquaintance with a changing world. (pp. 19-20)

Dewey insisted that the competent educator "views teaching and learning as a continuous process of reconstruction of experience" (p. 87). Dewey also emphasized the "importance of the participation of the learner in the formation of purposes which direct his activities in the learning process" (p. 67).

The literature on constructivist theory and its implications for education is extensive. The particular aspects of this body of literature pertinent to this discussion can be summarized as follows:

- Learning involves construction of concepts, ideas, and beliefs (Cannella, 1992).
- Learning is interactive and social (Belenky, Clinchy, Goldberger, & Tarule, 1994; Cobb, 1994; Cochran, DeRuiter, & King, 1993; Vygotsky, 1978).
- Learners play an active role in their own learning (Cobb, 1994; Condon, Clyde, Kyle, & Hovda, 1993; Grinberg, Goldfarb, & Martusewicz, 1994; Mosenthal & Ball, 1992). ·

In two of the chapters in this section, case studies are used as vehicles for active construction of knowledge. In the case studies of the teacher education students, the authors assume that students are constructing their own knowledge about literacy teaching and learning and at-risk children. All three chapters are closely related to notions of constructivist teacher education. Morine-Dershimer frames her work around collaborative learning and cognitive apprenticeship. Sibbett, Wade, and Johnson emphasize the importance of dialogue and interaction as means for students' reflecting on, refining, and reconstructing knowledge. Niersfheimer, Hopkins, and Dillon explore the effects of previous school experiences and perceptions of selves as teachers on students' development of understandings about teaching at-risk literacy learners. The chapters reject a transmission view of teaching and learning and emphasize the importance of active construction of knowledge.

The interest in teacher cognitions and constructivist teacher education has been paralleled by a growing interest in using cases and case methods in teacher education. Merseth (1996) delineated three categories of purposes for case studies: using cases as examples of theory, instructional technique, or some other form of propositional knowledge about teaching;

providing opportunities for decision making and problem solving based on content that embodies the complexity of the teaching process; and using cases to stimulate personal reflection on educational practice and issues. The latter two categories are directly related to affecting teachers' cognitions. Case studies also are a form of pedagogy that encourages more active learning and knowledge construction by students.

Merseth (1996) stated that "the extent to which individual writers assert the benefits of cases and case methods far outweighs the empirical work that confirms these benefits" (p. 729). Two of the three chapters in this section provide much needed empirical work focused on using cases and case methods in teacher education. Sibbett et al. explore the dialogue generated by a case discussion and categorize reflections as technical, contextual sensitivity, and critical reflection. Their work looks at the issue of what case content might promote critical dialogue and stimulate critical reflection. Morine-Dershimer analyzed the small group discussions of students about a case to determine what students attend to in these discussions and how what they attend to affects their thinking about the issues inherent in the case. Her work extends beyond the question of whether case studies can affect teachers' thinking to examine how students learned from case discussions.

Another common thread among the chapters is a commitment to social justice in education, to the notion that teacher education should develop teachers with beliefs and attitudes compatible with a commitment to teach all children, teachers who are both committed to the ideals of multicultural education and competent in their practice of it.

Awareness of the need for multiculturally adept teachers has increased over the years due to continued demographic and teacher recruiting trends. James Banks reported in 1991 that children of color will make up more than 30% of all public school students and more than half of the student body in 25 of the 50 largest school districts in the United States by the year 2000 (cited in Zeichner, 1993). The Children's Defense Fund reported that these same students are also more likely to be children of poverty, to have poorer health care, to come to school hungry, and to eventually drop out of school than their mainstream counterparts (cited in Zeichner, 1993).

In contrast, only 12% to 14% of our nation's teaching force is nonwhite, and 67% to 68% is female—a percentage that is increasing (Grant & Secada, 1990; Valencia, 1995). Zeichner (1993) stated that "teacher education students are overwhelmingly white, female, monolingual, from a rural (small town) or suburban community; and they come to their teacher education program with very limited interracial and intercultural experience" (p. 4).

As long ago as 1983, Carl Grant, a leading voice in the multicultural education arena, called for a comprehensive philosophy of multicultural education to be pervasive throughout the teacher education process:

> If teacher educators don't work out their philosophy as it relates to human diversity, their "old" philosophy will be guiding the program and, I would argue, multicultural education will not happen if that is the case. . . . Thus, I argue, teacher education students need multicultural philosophy, practice, and content throughout their program in order to implement multicultural education. (p. 30)

Lifelong attitudes can be amazingly resistant to change (McDiarmid, 1992; Sia & Mosher, 1994; Vavrus, 1994). Sparapini, Abel, Easton, Edwards, and Herbster (1995) measured 832 preservice teachers' attitudes toward children with exceptional needs and/or cultural diversity. Throughout their teacher education program, they acquired a general understanding of the issues involved in multicultural education but experienced little change in their attitudes from the beginning to the end of their program. Some studies have shown raised levels of sensitivity and cultural awareness after multicultural education courses (Chiang, 1994; Hadaway, Florez, Larke, & Wiseman, 1988; Martin & Koppleman, 1991). All of the chapters in this section are examples of teacher education designed to affect attitudes about teaching diverse children. The chapters add to the literature about what may and may not be effective, even though that is not the main focus of any of the chapters.

Sibbett et al. make a commitment to social justice explicit in their theoretical framework, and the intended purpose of their use of case methods is to promote critical reflection, which "moves beyond the classroom context of action to the ramifications of the wider society in which the action of the classroom exists. It requires more than introspection, it means questioning, deciding, analyzing, and considering alternatives within an ethical and political framework" (p. 28). Morine-Dershimer uses a case study for the purpose of getting teachers to move beyond concern focused solely on children's academic needs to a consideration of their social needs and what school and community resources are available for dealing with this complex myriad of needs. NiersTheimer et al. express a clear desire to instill in their students in a literacy methods course a belief that "they will be able to reach and teach all children."

This overview provides one framework for thinking about the connections among the chapters in this section. The areas addressed in these research reports are current and significant.

References

Belenky, M. F., Clinchy, B. M., Goldberger, N. R., & Tarule, J. M. (1994, Summer). The teacher as midwife. *Hands On Teacher Reader,* pp. 59-62.

Blumer, H. (1969). *Symbolic interactionism: Perspective and method.* Englewood Cliffs, NJ: Prentice Hall.

Cannella, G. S. (1992). *Constructivist approaches to learning: New directions for learning style theorists.* Paper presented at the annual meeting of the Association of Teacher Educators, Orlando, FL.

Chiang, L. H. (1994, October). *A study of the prospective teacher's attitudes toward social diversity.* Paper presented at the meeting of the Midwestern Educational Research Association, Chicago.

Clark, C., & Peterson, P. (1986). Teachers' thought processes. In M. C. Wittrock (Ed.), *Handbook of research in teaching* (3rd ed., pp. 255-296). New York: Macmillan.

Cobb, P. (1994). Where is the mind? Constructivist and sociocultural perspectives on mathematical development. *Educational Researcher, 23*(7), 13-20.

Cochran, K. F., DeRuiter, J. A., & King, R. A. (1993). Pedagogical content knowing: An integrative model for teacher preparation. *Journal of Teacher Education, 44,* 263-272,

Condon, M. W. F., Clyde, J. A., Kyle, D. W., & Hovda, R. A. (1993). A constructivist basis for teaching and teacher education: A framework for program development and research on graduates. *Journal of Teacher Education, 44,* 273-278.

Dewey, J. (1938). *Experience and education.* New York: Macmillan.

Fennema, E., Franke, M., Carpenter, T., & Carey, D. (1993). Using children's mathematical knowledge in instruction. *American Educational Research Journal, 30*(3), 555-584.

Grant, C. A. (1983). Multicultural teacher education—Renewing the discussion: A response to Martin Haberman. *Journal of Teacher Education, 34*(2), 29-32.

Grant, C. A., & Secada, W. G. (1990). Preparing teachers for diversity. In W. R. Houston (Ed.), *Handbook of research in teacher education: A project of the Association of Teacher Educators* (pp. 403-422). New York: Macmillan.

Griffin, G. (1986). Clinical teacher education. In J. Hoffman & S. Edwards (Eds.), *Reality and reform in clinical teacher education* (pp. 1-24). New York: Random House.

Grinberg, J., Goldfarb, K., & Martusewicz, R. (1994, Summer). Paulo Friere's legacy to democratic education. *Hands On Teacher Reader,* pp. 63-64.

Hadaway, N. L., Florez, V. E., Larke, P., & Wiseman, D. (1988, February). *Multicultural education: What educators know, what they need to know.* Paper presented at the meeting of the American Association of Colleges for Teacher Education, New Orleans, LA.

Johnson, K. E. (1996). The vision versus the reality: The tensions of the TESOL practicum. In D. Freeman & J. C. Richards (Eds.), *Teachers learning in language teaching*. Cambridge, UK: Cambridge University Press.

Kennedy, M. (1991). *An agenda for research on teacher learning* (Technical report). East Lansing: Michigan State University.

King, P. M., & Kitchener, K. S. (1994). *Developing reflective judgement: Understanding and promoting intellectual growth and critical thinking in adolescents and adults*. San Francisco: Jossey-Bass.

Knapp, N., & Peterson, P. (1991, April). *What does CGI mean to you? Teachers' ideas of a research-based intervention four years later*. Paper presented at the annual meeting of the American Educational Research Association, Chicago.

Martin, R. J., & Koppleman, K. (1991). The impact of a human relations/multicultural education course on the attitudes of prospective teachers. *Journal of Intergroup Relations, 18*, 16-27.

McDiarmid, G. W. (1992). What to do about differences? A study of multicultural education for teacher trainees in the Los Angeles Unified School District. *Journal of Teacher Education, 43*, 83-93.

McKibbin, M., & Joyce, B. R. (1981). Psychological states. *Theory Into Practice, 19*, 248-255.

Merseth, K. K. (1996). Cases and case methods in teacher education. In J. Sikula, T. J. Buttery, & E. Guyton (Eds.), *Handbook of research on teacher education* (pp. 722-744). New York: Macmillan.

Miller, A. (1981). Conceptual matching models and interactional research in education. *Review of Educational Research, 51*(1), 33-84.

Mosenthal, J. H., & Ball, D. L. (1992). Constructing new forms of teaching: Subject matter knowledge in inservice teacher education. *Journal of Teacher Education, 43*, 347-356.

National Center for Research on Teacher Education. (1991). *Final report*. East Lansing: Michigan State University.

Peterson, P., Fennema, E., Carpenter, T., & Loef, M. (1989). Teachers' pedagogical content beliefs in mathematics. *Cognition & Instruction, 6*(1), 1-40.

Reiman, A. R., & Parramore, B. M. (1993). Promoting preservice teacher development through extended field experience. In M. O'Hair & S. Odell (Eds.), *Teacher education yearbook I: Diversity and teaching* (pp. 11-121). Fort Worth, TX: Harcourt Brace Jovanovich.

Richardson, V. (1996). The role of attitudes and beliefs in learning to teach. In J. Sikula, T. J. Buttery, & E. Guyton (Eds.), *Handbook of research on teacher education* (pp. 102-119). New York: Macmillan.

Ross, D. (1988). Reflective teaching: Meaning and implication for preservice teacher educators. In H. Waxman, H. J. Freilberg, J. Vaughan, & M. Weil (Eds.), *Images of reflection in teacher education* (pp. 25-26). Reston, VA: Association of Teacher Educators.

Schön, D. (1983). *The reflective practitioner*. New York: Basic Books.

Schön, D. (1987). *Educating the reflective practitioner*. San Francisco: Jossey-Bass.

Sia, A. P., & Mosher, D. (1994, February). *Perception of multicultural concepts by preservice teachers in two institutions.* Paper presented at the annual meeting of the Association of Teacher Educators, Atlanta, GA.

Sparapini, E. F., Abel, F. J., Easton, S. E., Edwards, P., & Herbster, D. L. (1995, February). *Pre-service teacher education majors' understanding of issues related to diversity and exceptionality.* Paper presented at the annual meeting of the Association of Teacher Educators, Detroit, MI.

Sprinthall, N. A., Reiman, A. J., & Thies-Sprinthall, L. (1993). Roletaking and reflection: Promoting the conceptual and moral development of teachers. *Learning and Individual Differences, 5*, 283-299.

Sprinthall, N. A., Reiman, A. J., & Thies-Sprinthall, L. (1996). Teacher professional development. In J. Sikula, T. J. Buttery, & E. Guyton (Eds.), *Handbook of research on teacher education* (pp. 666-703). New York: Macmillan.

Valencia, C. (1995, April). *Teaching for all—The preparation of student teachers to work with diverse populations in the elementary school.* Paper presented at the annual meeting of the American Educational Research Association, San Francisco.

Vavrus, M. (1994). A critical analysis of multicultural education infusion during student teaching. *Action in Teacher Education, 16*(3), 46-57.

Vygotsky, L. (1978). *Mind in society.* Cambridge, MA: Harvard University Press.

Zeichner, K. M. (1993). *Educating teachers for cultural diversity* (NCRTL Special Report). East Lansing: Michigan State University, National Center for Research on Teacher Learning.

1 Perceptions of Self as Teacher

Case Studies of Three Preservice Literacy Teachers

Susan L. Nierstheimer

Carol J. Hopkins

Deborah R. Dillon

Susan L. Nierstheimer is Assistant Professor of Literacy Education at Illinois State University.

Carol J. Hopkins is Associate Professor of Literacy and Language Education at Purdue University.

Deborah R. Dillon is Professor of Literacy and Language Education at Purdue University.

Their shared research interests are studying pre- and inservice teachers' belief systems and how these evolve as a result of study and reflection about how children learn to read and the role of the teacher in facilitating literacy abilities.

ABSTRACT

Case studies of three elementary education students enrolled in a literacy methods course were generated. The study examined preservice teachers' beliefs about at-risk literacy learners and their perceptions of themselves as teachers before, during, and after participating in a tutoring practicum. A central theme that emerged across the case studies was that throughout the course and practicum experiences, the abilities of the three preservice teachers to confront tensions and challenges were closely tied to their own K-12 school experiences and perceptions of themselves as teachers.

As teacher educators, we believe in the importance of addressing preservice teachers' beliefs about teaching at-risk literacy learners as well as their perceptions about themselves as teachers as they enter an undergraduate literacy methods course. When students participate in course experiences, such as tutoring children experiencing difficulty learning to read, they are challenged to confront previously held beliefs (Cole & Knowles, 1993; Nierstheimer, Hopkins, & Schmitt, 1996; Roskos & Walker, 1993) as well as to confront their confidence in their capabilities to meet children's needs. These novice teachers face some of the same challenges that practicing teachers face as they work with the hardest-to-teach children (Allington & Walmsley, 1995; Soodak & Podell, 1994) and question their own self-efficacy (Bandura, 1977, 1986, 1993; Ross, Cousins, & Gadalla, 1996; Soodak & Podell, 1996). Preservice and inservice teachers alike question whether they will be able to reach and teach all children.

We have witnessed how difficult it is to help students confront previously held beliefs about teaching and learning in general, and at-risk literacy learners in particular, and how tightly interwoven those beliefs are with their prior experiences as learners (Nierstheimer et al., 1996). As we have provided innovative learning opportunities for our undergraduates, certain preexisting notions seem to remain steadfast, whereas others seem amenable to change (Hopkins, Schmitt, Nierstheimer, Dixey, & Younts, 1995). For example, we found that preservice teachers gained new understandings about how at-risk literacy learners could be helped as they observed peers tutoring children behind a one-way mirror (referred to hereafter as behind the glass) and engaged in simultaneous discussion. However, certain beliefs, such as why some children have reading problems, seem more difficult to challenge (Nierstheimer et al., 1996) and appear linked to undergraduates' prior understandings and school experiences.

Each semester, as we see our students struggle with planning and enacting tutoring lessons, we have hypothesized about the impact of their perceptions of themselves as teachers on their abilities to meet the needs of the children they tutor. Our persistent questions concerning students' perceptions of children and their perceptions of themselves, and how those beliefs might be interrelated, caused us to systematically study three preservice teachers in depth. Thus, the purpose of this study was to examine how prospective teachers' perceptions of themselves as teachers influenced their teaching of at-risk literacy learners and how their self-perceptions were challenged through course experiences.

Our data collection was guided by the following research questions: (a) How do preservice teachers see themselves as teachers of at-risk literacy learners before, during, and after a tutoring practicum? (b) What changes and shifts occur in preservice teachers' perceptions of themselves as teachers during and after the course? and (c) If students' perceptions change, what is the nature of those changes and what experiences seem to influence changes or shifts?

Methodology

Qualitative methodology was chosen for this study because of the purpose as well as the guiding research questions; this methodology helped us understand how people perceive, understand, and interpret the world (Patton, 1990). Phenomenology was the framework that under-pinned our research and guided the data collection, analysis, and inter-pretation. Phenomenology allowed us to understand the nature of our preservice teachers' beliefs from their emic perspectives (Patton, 1990) and to study the structure and essence of the lived experiences of these students (van Manen, 1990) to gain a deeper understanding.

The three key informants purposively selected to be the subjects of these case studies (Miles & Huberman, 1984) were elementary education students enrolled in a literacy methods course that includes a practicum in the university reading clinic where students tutor one child weekly. In addition to other course experiences, students participate in behind-the-glass teaching sessions where students tutor their children on one side of the glass while peers engage in small-group discussion led by the course professor on the other side of the glass.

Data Collection and Analysis Strategies

The primary data collected from one male and two female key informants were four semistructured interviews that were audiotaped and transcribed for later analyses. Data analyses of interview transcriptions proceeded from holistic and selective approaches (van Manen, 1990) to uncover thematic aspects from each of the three students across the four interviews. These themes became the substance of the narratives we created. We used cross-case analysis (Patton, 1990) as we looked across the case studies to identify patterns as well as variance that occurred in the students' responses. However, each case was treated as a holistic entity (van Manen, 1990) that could stand alone because of the unique perspectives of each student. The experiences of these developing practitioners as they dealt with the challenges of literacy teaching and learning throughout a semester are documented in the case studies below.

Ryan

Ryan entered the university as an aeronautical engineering major because "that's the closest thing I could come to being an astronaut." However, he was not far into his engineering course work when he decided to change his major to education. During the first interview, prior to any course content or experiences, when asked, "Why do you think some children have trouble learning to read?" he replied:

> I think . . . there's too many reasons. One is they physically can't. They have a problem reading or they have a mental problem. The physical problems they can't help. They may want to read but they can't read and they get so frustrated that they don't want to. Mentally there might be something at home or something at school that distracts them and breaks their concentration. They worry about that more than the reading.

Like many of his classmates, Ryan targeted physical problems as the main reason for reading difficulties. He asserted that it was the teacher's job to "get them [children] into, I don't want to say an imaginary world, but get them into a world where they have no other worries. Where they're having fun and they're enjoying themselves and then they can focus on the reading."

Ryan then offered several possibilities for what could be done to help children who experience difficulty learning to read. He suggested that children who were having a hard time be placed with other children who were successful readers because this would scaffold the struggling readers toward more success without singling them out as low-achieving pupils.

Ryan was assigned to tutor 11-year-old Jimmy, who had been coming to the reading clinic for 2 years and was struggling with reading and writing. Ryan created engaging lessons that built on Jimmy's keen interest in sports. We observed one lesson that Ryan taught behind the glass for his peers, and one that he taught in a separate tutoring room. True to Ryan's stated beliefs, he provided a safe learning environment that encouraged Jimmy to take risks and explore sports through literacy activities.

Having looked at how Ryan initially saw himself as a teacher of children who are experiencing difficulty learning to read and his beliefs about what can be done to help such children, as well as observing Ryan's teaching practices, we looked for evidence of changes and shifts in his knowledge and beliefs during and after participating in the course. At the beginning of the semester, Ryan expressed confidence in his abilities to help at-risk literacy learners. At the end of the semester, we asked him what he knew and believed now about at-risk literacy learners that differed from his ideas at the beginning of the semester. His response seemed focused more on challenges he would face as a teacher. Ryan acknowledged that literacy teaching was much more difficult than he thought it was going to be. He cited the example of trying to teach Jimmy to use conventional spelling in his writing. Ryan was frustrated that he was unable to move Jimmy past the invented spelling stage.

Another challenge Ryan acknowledged was difficulty integrating course assignments and course readings into his teaching. It appeared that as Ryan focused on teaching, he was unable to deal with the complexity of simultaneously applying course readings, interpreting the results of informal assessments, and tutoring. We were concerned that perhaps Ryan had suffered a crisis in confidence. On the contrary, Ryan believed that his experiences in the course had helped him value his teaching and what he had accomplished with Jimmy:

> I learned that I'm a better teacher than I think I am. . . . I just hope that my classroom goes as well as this semester did, because we got a really great relationship going. . . . It just seemed like we weren't doing any reading, any writing, anything educational, but we were! And that's the best kind of teaching.

We characterized the changes and shifts in Ryan's perceptions of himself as a teacher of at-risk literacy learners in the following ways. First, prior to his experiences in the course, Ryan believed that children had physical or mental problems that kept them from being able to read and that perhaps these would impede his ability as a teacher to help such children. Before meeting Jimmy, Ryan said that he expected the worst in terms of Jimmy's limited capacities to learn after reading Jimmy's file:

> It took me an hour to read the file thoroughly and I'm just sitting there like, "Oh, this is going to be fun!" [said sarcastically]. . . . I didn't know what to expect at all. . . . He was one of the older ones and I had no idea of what to expect. It seems like the file and the child are just two totally different things! . . . He was a lot better than that.

Earlier, Ryan noted that by creating the right learning environment a teacher could move the child forward. Later, Ryan determined that his earlier view may have been too simplistic, especially as reflected in his comments concerning Jimmy's lack of progress in spelling, as well as outside pressures for Jimmy to do better. Perhaps Ryan was also confronting some previously held unrealistic notions of teaching and learning. Bound together with the complexities of teaching and unrealistic expectations for students' learning was his difficulty with balance as he worked to complete the variety of course assignments.

One belief that seemed to remain constant for Ryan throughout the semester was that the classroom teacher is responsible for reaching every child in his or her care. And despite challenges throughout the semester, Ryan remained confident that he could succeed as a teacher and that children in his future classrooms would succeed.

Glenna

As a contrast to Ryan, who exuded confidence in himself as a learner and teacher, we present a portrait of Glenna. Glenna was a second-semester junior who had arrived at the university with an undeclared major and decided late in her studies to become a teacher. During the first interview when Glenna was asked why she thought some children had difficulty learning to read, she drew almost exclusively on her own childhood literacy experiences:

> My brother used to read all the time. I mean he always had a book in his hand but I, my parents never read. I don't remember them reading to us very much, and I didn't grow up with a reading background. . . . I came into this [course] and I'm like, "Oh! I don't

know anything about this kind of stuff." But I think it has to start in the home . . . because I know I was in the low reading program until like third grade, and it's kind of like you feel like you're dumb because I had hearing problems so I was slower. Because I didn't start talking 'til late either, and I had to go to summer school, too, for reading.

As we studied the transcriptions of our multiple conversations with Glenna, we found it interesting that Glenna often interchanged the pronoun *I* for the pronouns *you* and *they* to describe why some children had difficulty learning to read and what could be done to help them. It seemed that as she told of her own frustrations in school, she generalized them to include other children's experiences and frustrations.

Glenna continued to feel "not smart" during her elementary school years even after she was moved to a higher reading group. She expressed that she still did not enjoy reading or consider herself a skilled reader. She called herself a "perfect case" (with a touch of irony in her voice) in reference to fitting a profile of children with reading difficulties.

When we asked Glenna what could be done to help children who are at risk of failing to learn to read she seemed perplexed. She told of her experiences in an elementary education observation class as she listened to a struggling reader read and did not know what to do or what the teacher could do. One solution she thought might work was one-on-one tutoring. However, she was adamant that this tutoring take place after school hours, preferably away from the school site. She questioned special reading pullout programs and believed that they reinforced a child's low self-esteem. "I know they need special help but . . . I hate it when they do that! Take them out of class like that. I don't know. I just don't know if that's right."

When Glenna predicted what her tutoring experience in the course might be like, her comments reflected excitement about the possibility of helping a child coupled with the fear of making mistakes that might be damaging.

I'm kind of scared . . . but I'm kind of excited like I might help. I am kind of afraid that I'm going to do something wrong and screw up their reading for the rest of their life, or something. Or scare them away or something. But I just hope that I can take what I learn and encourage them to do better.

After Glenna met with her pupil, she reported that even though she was extremely nervous, her first session had gone well with Andrea, a fourth grader. Glenna reiterated her concern that she might not be able to help Andrea as much as she would like, but as she explained a teaching idea for her next session she seemed encouraged.

In a videotape of Glenna's tutoring, she seemed at ease in her interactions with Andrea as she was observed by her peers behind the glass. In this lesson, we saw a developing teacher who was prepared and organized and who responded to the child's needs. When we asked Glenna her reactions to teaching that lesson, she said that she and her peers thought it had gone well. However, in that same interview, Glenna told us that compared to peers in the class, she felt her teaching fell short. "Well, everyone has all these different things that they're doing and these different kinds of activities and I feel like I'm so boring because we do the same things."

She also reported that when her supervisor asked her to identify goals for herself and her pupil she was perplexed. "I didn't really know what to say. . . . I knew what goals I had for her but I didn't know for me. . . . One of them was self-confidence, that I need to work on."

The self-confidence issue emerged again as Glenna observed and discussed her peers' teaching of their pupils. Out of six behind-the-glass observation sessions, only once did Glenna contribute to the class discussion. She explained:

I'll be like, I don't want to say something because I feel like it's just gonna be totally stupid or something. But I mean, I have said things before but I think a lot of times, it's more that, I just don't know.

As we observed Glenna's lack of participation, we often witnessed behaviors that signaled engagement. Even though she did not contribute to the conversation, she usually sat close to the course professor, nodded in agreement or shook her head in disagreement when other people ventured a guess about a child's reading behavior, sat forward and occasionally stood up to get a better view of the lesson, and took notes about what was occurring in the lesson.

During our last interview, Glenna discussed what she had learned and now believed about at-risk literacy learners and herself as a teacher. First, she was convinced that children with reading challenges needed one-on-one instruction as did other children in school settings. She acknowledged that giving individual attention to all children was probably impossible, but that teaching should be different from that which she had experienced.

Second, Glenna stated that keeping children "on task" was essential to learning. "If you can do more one-on-one or more targeted stuff to different kinds of kids, then they're going to be able to stay on task . . . and want to do it."

Third, Glenna noted that she had learned about the importance of ongoing assessment and designing instruction to meet the needs of children. "I think I'll be able to assess them better because I've never done anything like that . . . and be able to focus more on what's wrong and be able to give them more things to help. . . . I think if I hadn't had this class, I would have been like, I don't know what to do!"

As we interacted with Glenna throughout the semester, we characterized her as a complex individual with contradictions and incongruities. She struggled with issues of low self-esteem and lack of confidence, yet she volunteered to be a key informant for this study as well as to teach in front of her peers. She often referred to not knowing what to do, yet she was able to provide successful learning experiences for her pupil and to articulate her beliefs about at-risk literacy learners. She almost never participated in the behind-the-glass discussions, yet she was seemingly engaged. Additionally, she drew on what she learned from observing others behind the glass to inform her teaching. When asked during the last interview if she felt more confident at the end of the semester than she had at the beginning, her responses indicated growth in her confidence as a teacher. "I mean, I'm still scared about it, but I think I know more what I want to do and what needs to be done."

It is our prediction that her empathy for at-risk literacy learners, drawn from her own school experiences, may move her toward her goal of being an effective teacher. Her challenge will be to overcome some of the ways she sees herself as a result of those same experiences.

Erica

Erica, a first-semester senior, came to the university knowing that she wanted to be a teacher. A high school church trip to an Appalachian school convinced her that teaching was the career that she wanted to pursue. When asked why some children experience difficulty learning to read, Erica responded:

> I think a lot of it is just because they're not read to when they're young and they don't have any books around the house or their

older brothers and sisters are off doing something. . . . I know that was a big influence on me, just being read to when I was young, and that made me want to read and it made me learn to read. . . . Parents are busy now. . . . No one is teaching them [children] how, and then they're already behind when they get to school.

Erica's solutions for what could be done to help children who are at risk of failing to learn to read focused on early intervention. She felt that one-on-one tutoring "right away" was essential and that early intervention could eliminate future problems. She also noted that for children who were at risk of failing to learn to read, it was important to build up self-esteem through encouragement to "keep on trying."

When asked to predict what she believed her course practicum tutoring experiences would be like, Erica was enthusiastic and energetic as she stated that although she was slightly nervous about being observed, she felt that the experience would be good for her. Additionally, she anticipated that she would be successful because "I think it will be a confidence builder."

When we asked Erica about her first tutoring session with Caleb, a fourth grader, Erica said that they were off to a good start but that the books she had chosen were too difficult for Caleb and she needed to select easier texts. She cited goals of helping him feel less frustrated as he read, having him depend less on her for help, and improving his attitude about writing.

We asked Erica what worried her the most about tutoring Caleb and what she was most confident about. She worried that she would not be able to help Caleb or that she would concentrate her teaching on "the wrong things." She was most confident that "whatever activity I have planned for him, he will do it." Based on their first interaction, she believed that Caleb would be a willing, compliant learner. However, Caleb missed tutoring sessions, and whether these absences caused a lack of continuity in lessons, or other factors were involved, it seemed that Caleb became increasingly disinterested in Erica's lessons and Erica became increasingly discouraged about her teaching.

Erica's assessment of the situation was that she had not yet been successful in selecting appropriate texts for Caleb and that her lessons were boring and needed to include more hands-on activities. However, despite Erica's sincere desire to employ teaching strategies that encouraged Caleb's engagement, she was not successful. Erica was able to articulate what she needed to do. She was able to observe peers' tutoring experiences and write about why their lessons "worked well." But she was not able to apply what she knew to what she did. During our final interview, Erica related her most memorable course experience:

> Well, probably the most memorable was one day when I couldn't get Caleb to do anything at all. And he wouldn't sit up straight, you know. He wouldn't look up. He wouldn't look at anything that I was trying to do to get him focused on reading. And he started telling me how much he hated reading and writing. And [my supervisor] came in with a lot of different books and in just, in that one session I just saw Caleb totally transformed because she was doing a lot of creative activities with him. Like getting him to change his voice to pretend to be the characters in the book and we sat on the floor instead of sitting at the desk, and she just really gave him a new perspective on reading. And he was smiling at the end of that lesson and said that he had fun that day and everything. And I just remember that, because then it clicked, "Oh, this is what this child needs, you know, more active activities, and more creative games or something like that to make reading fun and just easier-level books to make him feel successful and things that he's able to read." And I mean, I think that's just really when it hit me: That's what my lessons needed to be like! And so, I'll just always remember that because I just saw him change, you know, drastically from the beginning to the end!

It was this most difficult lesson that proved to be an epiphany for Erica, a moment where all the things that she understood at a cognitive level were now understood at a much deeper, internalized level. When we asked Erica to identify new understandings from the course she responded:

> I've had this one-on-one experience with a child. And I've seen him act in different ways, and I'll be able to pick up easier on behavior of children in the classroom. And, "What else can I do to reach this student?" . . . and confidence. I think I've felt like [I've gained] a lot of confidence just because things didn't work for me, at first, like I was hoping they would. But I learned so much from that.

This statement showcases Erica's developing maturity as a reflective practitioner; she was able to take a difficult situation and use it as a learning experience. Erica noted that she could "pick up" on students' behavior more easily and that it was her responsibility to reach a student and help him or her learn. Erica's earlier prediction that tutoring would be a confidence builder turned out to be different than she had expected. Still, at the end of the semester, she was able to say, "I'm glad that everything happened the way it did."

Results and Discussion

A central theme that emerged across the three case studies was that students can and do shift their beliefs about their responsibility for teaching at-risk students if they work closely with one child over time. Tutoring a child enables preservice teachers to closely observe a child's growth while they learn literacy teaching strategies through one-on-one interactions with supervisors, observations and discussions of peers' teaching, and reading books and articles that support the notion that literacy for all children is every teacher's responsibility. The students we studied acknowledged the complexity of teaching at-risk readers, and they noted that it was the teacher's responsibility to work one on one with these students to help them succeed. Our students believed that teachers must work to carefully observe children to learn about their interests and reading problems and then design engaging activities to help meet their needs.

Second, preservice students' own K-12 experiences and their observations of and discussions about teaching, as well as their tutoring experiences, seemed to bring about changes and shifts in what the students stated could be done to help children with reading problems. Third, students who began the class confident in their abilities as teachers remained confident; the one student who was insecure about her abilities did not appear to gain confidence. For example, Erica came into the tutoring experience confident in her ability to teach and reach at-risk learners. As the semester progressed, she encountered great difficulty in her teaching. However, at the end of the experience, she still expressed faith in herself as a prospective teacher. Ryan entered this course experience full of confidence in himself as a future teacher and left full of confidence. Glenna entered the course unsure of her ability to teach, largely based on her negative experiences as a student. Even though she encountered many positive experiences in her tutoring and positive support from supervisors, Glenna still lacked self-confidence at the end of the semester. Each student's view of self as teacher seemed tied to his or her prior life and school experiences and was influenced less by his or her immediate experiences as a practicing teacher. Furthermore, the preservice teachers' assessments of their tutoring experiences were seen through the lenses of their beliefs in themselves.

Our goal was to provide observation, discussion, and teaching opportunities to challenge preservice teachers' beliefs about at-risk literacy learners. Several documented experiences appear to have helped preservice teachers reconsider their roles in helping the lowest-achieving children. However, as we gained deeper understandings of the three prospective teachers, we discovered that challenging their beliefs about children wasn't enough. We also had to consider each student's prior life experiences, especially her or his experiences as a learner. Our research resonates with Kagan's (1992) report that the content and experiences of methods courses are screened through preservice teachers' prior beliefs and practices. Furthermore, the perceptions of preservice teachers about themselves as teachers appear to be firmly grounded in their images of themselves as learners. As Bean and Zulich's (1992) case studies of preservice teacher development indicate, a student's personal background is a crucial factor that influences an individual's path toward becoming a teacher.

We believe the findings of this study underscore the importance of accommodating and respecting the backgrounds of teachers in preparation (Knowles, 1992) and follow Broaddus's (1995) advice to take into account each preservice teacher's uniqueness. Just as we teach and encourage prospective teachers to treat children as individuals, we must also address the individual needs of our students at the university level.

What remains a question is whether students' views of themselves and their abilities to succeed as teachers can be altered after they have reached adulthood, and what specific experiences students need to facilitate such change. If, as Bullough (1991) suggests, novices who enter teaching experiences without clear images of themselves as teachers are doomed to failure, we must provide opportunities for undergraduate students to try on the role of teacher, have successful experiences, and begin to see themselves as teachers. We agree with Knowles's (1992) statement that university preservice teacher preparation programs should meld with students' previous life experiences, particularly the negative aspects of previous learning experiences, in an effort to move our students toward an "I can do this!" attitude.

References

Allington, R. L., & Walmsley, S. A. (1995). Redefining and reforming instructional support programs for at-risk students. In R. L. Allington & S. A. Walmsley (Eds.), *No quick fix: Rethinking literacy programs in America's elementary schools* (pp. 19-44). New York: Teachers College Press and International Reading Association.

Bandura, A. (1977). Self-efficacy: Toward a unifying theory of behavioral change. *Psychological Review, 84*, 191-215.

Bandura, A. (1986). *Social foundations of thought and action: A social cognitive theory.* Englewood Cliffs, NJ: Prentice Hall.

Bandura, A. (1993). Perceived self-efficacy in cognitive development and functioning. *Educational Psychologist, 28*(2), 117-148.

Bean, T. W., & Zulich, J. (1992). A case study of three preservice teachers' beliefs about content area reading through the window of student-professor dialogue journals. In C. K. Kinzer & D. J. Leu (Eds.), *Literacy research, theory, and practice: Views from many perspectives* (pp. 463-474). Chicago: National Reading Conference.

Broaddus, K. (1995, December). *Scratching the surface: Researching the cultural contexts of literacy as a preservice teacher.* Paper presented at the 45th annual meeting of the National Reading Conference, New Orleans, LA.

Bullough, R. V. (1991). Exploring personal teaching metaphors in preservice teacher education. *Journal of Teacher Education, 42*, 43-51.

Cole, A. L., & Knowles, J. G. (1993). Shattered images: Understanding expectations and realities of field experiences. *Teaching and Teacher Education, 9*, 457-471.

Hopkins, C. J., Schmitt, M. C., Nierstheimer, S. L., Dixey, B. P., & Younts, T. (1995). Infusing features of the reading recovery professional development model into the experiences of preservice teachers. In K. A. Hinchman, D. J. Leu, & C. K. Kinzer (Eds.), *Perspectives on literacy research and methods* (pp. 349-357). Chicago: National Reading Conference.

Kagan, D. M. (1992). Professional growth among preservice teachers. *Review of Educational Research, 62*, 129-169.

Knowles, J. G. (1992). Models for understanding pre-service and beginning teachers' biographies: Illustrations from case studies. In I. F. Goodson (Ed.), *Studying teachers' lives* (pp. 99-152). New York: Teachers College Press.

Miles, M. B., & Huberman, A. M. (1984). Drawing valid meaning from qualitative data: Toward a shared craft. *Educational Researcher, 13*(5), 20-30.

Nierstheimer, S. L., Hopkins, C. J., & Schmitt, M. C. (1996). "But I just want to teach regular kids!": Preservice teachers' beliefs about teaching children experiencing difficulty learning to read. *Literacy, Teaching and Learning: An International Journal of the Early Literacy, 2*(1), 15-24.

Patton, M. Q. (1990). *Qualitative evaluation and research methods.* Newbury Park, CA: Sage.

Roskos, K., & Walker, B. (1993). Preservice teachers' epistemology in the teaching of problem readers. In C. K. Kinzer & D. J. Leu (Eds.), *Examining central issues in literacy research, theory, and practice* (pp. 325-334). Chicago: National Reading Conference.

Ross, J. A., Cousins, J. B., & Gadalla, T. (1996). Within-teacher predictors of teacher efficacy. *Teaching and Teacher Education, 12,* 385-400.

Soodak, L. C., & Podell, D. M. (1994). Teachers' thinking about difficult-to-teach students. *Journal of Educational Research, 88,* 44-51.

Soodak, L. C., & Podell, D. M. (1996). Teacher efficacy: Toward the under-standing of a multi-faceted construct. *Teaching and Teacher Education, 12,* 401-411.

van Manen, M. (1990). *Researching lived experience.* Albany: State University of New York Press.

2 Preservice Teachers' Reflective Thinking During a Case Discussion

Joyce Sibbett

Suzanne Wade

Larry Johnson

Joyce Sibbett is Adjunct Clinical Professor at the University of Utah, where she teaches courses in teacher education and supervises student teachers. She recently completed her dissertation, "Reflection in Practice: An Exploratory Study of Student Teacher Reflection," in which she analyzed student teachers' self-authored cases, the case discussions in peer groups, and journals.

Suzanne Wade is Associate Professor of Education in the Department of Educational Studies at the University of Utah. She received her Ed.D. in 1984 from the Harvard Graduate School of Education. She has been supported in her work in reading research and case pedagogies by a National Academy of Education Spencer Fellowship and the Joseph P. Kennedy, Jr. Foundation. She and her colleagues are currently writing a two-volume book, *Preparing for Inclusive Education.*

Larry Johnson is Adjunct Instructor, Department of Educational Studies, University of Utah, where he teaches courses on the historical, philosophical, and social foundations of education. His current research interests include the creation and development of community colleges, the ideology of vocationalism, and the creation of antiracist, antisexist, and anticlassist pedagogy.

ABSTRACT

Efforts to promote critical reflection in the literature have achieved mixed results. Often, preservice and inservice teachers offer simple, technical solutions to complex problems without challenging assumptions, reframing problems, or raising social issues of race, class, or gender. This research project sought to promote critical reflection by using previous research to restructure a course about inclusion and to reformat a case discussion on the dilemmas faced by a secondary ESL teacher. The data, drawn from the transcript of that discussion, were analyzed using a framework Sibbett (1996) developed to categorize reflection into three categories—technical, contextual, and critical. Results show that prospective teachers engaged in all levels of reflection as they connected to and challenged one another's ideas.

Reflection is a concept in teacher education that is widely accepted as a means to help student teachers refine and improve their teaching ability. It is generally thought of as a process by which teachers think and rethink a specific teaching episode. Beyond this generalization, different scholars of reflection hold widely disparate views of exactly what reflection entails.

Three distinct perspectives stand out with identifiable goals for what reflection should accomplish (Sibbett, 1996). The first perspective is technical reflection, usually associated with Cruikshank's (1985) program of reflective teaching, which views reflection as a means to improve teaching strategies. Teachers with the help of their peers consider their teaching performance and look for ways to improve specific practices by refining teaching strategies or incorporating new ones. Many educators have criticized this approach as being teacher oriented, too reliant on research and theory, generic across contexts and subject matter, and unidirectional as opposed to dialogic (cf. Gore, 1987; Grimmett, MacKinnon, Erickson, & Riecken, 1990; Zeichner, 1992). Tom (1985) has criticized the technical focus on strategies as lawlike, and Munby and Russell (1993) contend that reflection that is used to reach a definite end focuses on answers rather than questions that might broaden teachers' perspectives and suggest alternative courses of action.

A second and more broadly accepted view of reflection is Schön's (1987) dual concepts of "reflection-in-action" and "reflection-on-action," both of which are intended to help teachers become transformed as more aware, sensitive, and capable individuals. Embedded in the classroom context, reflection-in-action is a process wherein the practitioner consciously interacts with a problematic situation and experiments with it at the time. Reflection-on-action occurs as a retrospective analysis of a teaching experience, usually through journal writing, whereby teachers rethink their experience and analyze the complexity of the embedded action, seeking ways to enhance future experiences.

Schön (1983, 1987) suggests that reflection should promote growth that will move prospective teachers from recognizing and applying standard rules to helping them think like professionals and enabling them to develop new forms of understanding and action. He emphasizes that the key ingredient of reflection is action, which situates a problem in an authentic environment with an awareness of students and a sensitivity to their needs. The goals for teachers as they reflect on their teaching experiences is to frame and reframe a situation to gain greater insight into the purpose of teaching and learning.

A third distinguishable perspective of reflection is critical inquiry, the purpose of which is to achieve social justice. Gore and Zeichner (1991) suggest that at the preservice level, teacher educators should be attempting to create learning environments that reflect a commitment to certain fundamental values (e.g., equality and social justice, which incorporates an ethic of caring for the needs and representing the interests of each student). Critical reflection moves beyond the classroom context of action to the ramifications of the wider society in which the action of the classroom exists. It requires more than introspection; it means questioning, deciding, analyzing, and considering alternatives within an ethical and political framework (Adler, 1993). Henderson (1992) advocates that teachers should have a historical awareness that drives them to recognize problems that require a transformation of society. Others (Elliot, 1990; Liston & Zeichner, 1990) argue that reflective practice must include both self-critique and institutional critique. Proponents of critical reflection see action research as a primary means of facilitating reflection on practice.

Research examining the effectiveness of each of these perspectives in achieving the goals of reflection has been mixed (Sibbett, 1996). One reason may be their lack of emphasis on shared reflection, which has the potential to move teachers beyond their personal understandings of a problematic issue. As Cinnamond and Zimpher (1990) contend, without an emphasis on dialogue, methods such as journal writing or action research may limit teachers' ability to achieve the goals of reflection.

Case pedagogies are becoming recognized as means of fostering reflection because they emphasize dialogue (Easterly, 1992; Grossman, 1992; Laboskey, 1992, 1994; Richert, 1992; J. Shulman, 1992; L. Shulman, 1992; Sykes & Bird, 1992). By analyzing, articulating, and possibly challenging the arguments presented during case discussions, teachers become creators and definers rather than simply dispensers of knowledge (Harrington & Garrison, 1992; Richert, 1992).

Drawing on Sykes and Bird (1992) in the present study, we hypothesized that case discussions would encourage reflection by providing preservice teachers with opportunities to analyze, interpret, frame, and reframe situated teaching problems from multiple perspectives, to challenge stereotypes and assumptions, and to generate and evaluate a variety of possible solutions that are highly contextualized. Theoretically, dialogue—or shared inquiry—enables teachers to transcend the limitations of their own experiences and values by allowing their values to be heard, acknowledged, and possibly challenged by others (Harrington & Garrison, 1992).

Nevertheless, the potential for case pedagogies to promote reflection is not always realized. In a study of case discussions, Moje and Wade (in press) found that neither preservice nor inservice teachers questioned the school curriculum or their own assumptions about the nature of teaching, knowledge, and ability; in addition, they never raised issues related to race, class, or gender. Moje and Wade argued that cases and case discussions must be carefully crafted to highlight certain issues and to challenge assumptions.

We came to similar conclusions in our earlier analysis of case discussions that preservice teachers had posted on the electronic notice board in a course on inclusive education. The results of these case discussions looked much like what has been reported in Moje and Wade (in press)—that is, participants rarely questioned the case writers' assumptions or attempted to reframe the issues or problems that were implicit in the cases or in the questions posed at the end of the cases. Similar to Bird, Anderson, Sullivan, and Swidler's (1993) findings, we found that the peer commentaries were oriented toward relatively simple, technical solutions without much analysis given to the situation. Furthermore, there was little evidence that peers connected their comments to broader social issues such as race, culture, language, or power—even when they were central in the case. These findings motivated us to think about how we might structure whole-class case discussions in future sections of the course to promote the sort of reflectivity that is thought to be theoretically possible.

The present study is part of a larger project funded by the Joseph P. Kennedy, Jr. Foundation to prepare regular educators for inclusive settings.

In this chapter, we analyze results of a whole-class case discussion that we structured in a way that might encourage reflective, critical dialogue. Because the course in which the discussion occurred focuses on issues of inclusive education, equity issues permeate the course. We therefore thought that the potential of case discussions to encourage reflection might be more readily realized in a course with issues of inequality at its center.

Method

Study Participants and Context of the Study

Participants in the study were 28 preservice teachers enrolled in a required secondary teacher education course at a large research university in a city in the western United States. Participants were majoring in a variety of disciplines including English, science, math, art, physical education, French, social studies, and health. All had just completed student teaching, and most were planning on graduating at the end of the academic year. Of the 28 students, 17 were female and 11 were male. Most were European Americans, although one was a Native American and one had immigrated from France.

The case discussion that is the focus of this study occurred in the middle of the course on inclusive education, which is taught every spring quarter after students have completed student teaching. While focusing on individuals with disabilities, advocates of inclusion seek to change the philosophy and structure of schools to ensure the education of all students who might otherwise fail for reasons related to differences in language, culture, ethnicity, economic status, gender, and ability. Because general education teachers are likely to be teaching diverse students in inclusive classrooms, the purpose of the course was to examine instructional, curricular, and policy issues related to inclusive education.

To examine the complex issue of inclusion, the course relied on a variety of teaching cases that were used for different purposes—from video cases used to introduce issues to teaching cases in a text format used to discuss issues in depth. In addition to the cases, students were assigned readings that covered issues of inclusion, multicultural education, curricular and instructional strategies for inclusive settings, strategies for adapting instruction to meet specific needs, and collaborative teamwork and problem solving among professionals and parents. Students were also asked to draw on their readings from previous classes, which included multicultural education and critical analyses of schools and of teaching. By the time students engaged in the case discussion that is examined in this chapter, they had read (or viewed) and discussed six cases and participated in two role-playing activities.

In the present study, we examined the dialogue that occurred during a whole-class discussion of one of the student-authored cases written the previous year by a preservice teacher. Based on the case author's experience during student teaching and subsequent interviews with a number of content area teachers and with the school's ESL teacher, this case described the attitudes of teachers in a junior high school toward ESL students. The case study also provided information about the composition of the ESL group, which consisted of exclusively Spanish-speaking Mexican or Mexican American students during the year the case was written.

In planning the structure of the case discussion and the questions that the instructor would ask, we employed several different forms of representation (Conquergood, 1993)—namely, whole-group case analysis, small-group work, role playing, and debriefing. We hoped that these activities and questions would encourage critical inquiry in a relatively risk-free environment. The resulting teaching notes consisted of two parts. The first part was designed to focus students' attention on "constructing" and analyzing the case. The second part of the discussion involved role playing. We hoped that role playing would further students' ability to understand multiple perspectives—specifically, the assumptions, beliefs, and attitudes that underlie the positions to which they were assigned. Furthermore, we hoped that the way we structured the role playing would encourage students to challenge the assumptions that were expressed—both those of their peers and those of the individuals whose roles they were playing.

To structure the role playing, we divided students into three groups of 8 to 10 students. Each group was given a different case discussion sheet, which asked participants to assume the role of one of the three groups of teachers described in the case—those who opposed the ESL program and advocated mainstreaming without accommodation; those who advocated a self-contained classroom for ESL students; and those who were receptive to mainstreaming and collaborating with Sarah,[1] the ESL teacher. Participants prepared for the role play by discussing the underlying beliefs and attitudes of the teachers they were assigned to role play and the kinds of strategies Sarah might employ in dealing with them. Then, each of the three groups was divided into those who would role play the teachers and those who would take Sarah's part in the ensuing discussion. After each group engaged in the role play in front of the whole class, the discussion was opened up for debriefing. The case discussion was concluded by a short wrap-up by the instructor.

We recognize that the context of the course had a profound influence on what would occur during this particular case discussion. The context included (a) students' prior experience with case discussions and role playing; (b) the course's emphasis on the topic of inclusion, which focused students' attention on broad social issues such as equity; and (c) the tools students had available to analyze the case, which consisted primarily of their own experiences during student teaching and the knowledge and language from readings assigned in the course and previous course work.

Data Sources and Analysis

To collect data that would yield information about students' thinking and interaction in the whole-class discussion, we tape-recorded the interaction among participants as they analyzed the case and engaged in role playing and debriefing. To identify patterns in the data, we relied on methods of within-case content analysis (Patton, 1990). We began with the classification system derived from the literature on reflection and modified during preliminary analyses of the data. The resulting categories that guided our analyses are described below.

Technical Reflection. These are comments that offer generic, teacher-centered strategies without indicating sensitivity to the needs of students.

Contextual Sensitivity. These are indications that the study participants are sensitive to the needs of students, teachers, and other contextual factors that are relevant to the case; a sympathetic awareness of cultural differences and of the disconsonance between students' cultures and the culture of the school; a willingness to examine issues from multiple perspectives and to rethink and reframe the problems they see in the case.

Critical Reflection. These are indications that participants are contextually sensitive and willing to look critically at the status quo; to challenge assumptions, beliefs, and stereotypes that are based on race, class, gender, language differences, and abilities/disabilities; to recognize differences in power relations among individuals and groups; to show an underlying concern for issues of equity and social justice; to advocate change that would bring about equity, especially at the systemic or societal level; and to challenge solutions that maintain the status quo and marginalize underrepresented groups.

Results

In presenting results of our analysis, we focus on two aspects of the case discussion: (a) study participants' construction and analysis of the case, and (b) the solutions that they offered and evaluated.

Preservice Teachers'
Construction and Analysis of the Case

At the beginning of the case discussion, as the preservice teachers were asked to describe the key players in the case, several described the ESL students in these ways: "They kind of make a mockery of the system" (Ross), "manipulate the system" (Katy), "manipulating" (Rob), and "they just had no motivation either" (Katy). When the class was asked by the instructor if they agreed with this, other class members challenged these characterizations in these ways: "not all of them," "Are you saying all?" (Bryce), "You have to take them on a case-by-case individual matter when it comes to that" (Sam), "They seem to be grouped together or pegged [by the teachers in the case] . . . I think [the case] said that not all the ESL students were sloughing, taking advantage, you know, not showing up. Some of them, I'm sure, were good students but they're all being treated as one kind of person; stereotyping them" (Rita). This was the beginning of students' challenging their peers' stereotypes.

In the comments that directly followed this interchange, we began to see some examples of both contextual sensitivity and critical reflection. In the first of the comments below, Will focused on the only ESL student mentioned in the case who was not Chicano (this was a student from a previous year). Will's comment seemed to differentiate ESL students on the basis of race, language, and culture (i.e., Polish from Mexican American) without addressing the stereotyping of Chicano students. Note that although his comment reflects an attempt to be sensitive to cultural differences, it also espouses a deficit theory. However, Nick's comment that followed indirectly challenged the deficit theory by offering an analysis of the disconsonance between the culture of the ESL students of Mexican heritage and the "culture of school":

Will: She [the case author] makes the point of one Polish student who had gone to a private or Catholic school, and that student picked up English right away because they compare Latin to English. But also, in that home, education had been seen as something that was vitally important in that culture . . . for other ESL students, that may not be a part of their culture.

Nick: I think one other way to compare the Polish student with the Spanish students is that he was used to the culture of school where they weren't.

At a later time in the discussion, study participants raised issues of racism and blame in ways that reveal both contextual sensitivity and critical reflection. Some of their comments focused on the racist attitudes of the teachers, whereas others critiqued the methods and attitudes of the teachers in the case that placed blame for failure on the student. Below is one data exemplar:

Mike: It's like they put blame on the student. Where they're saying the student is not trying to learn, rather than saying the teacher is not finding a different teaching method that will help the students. It's like all the blame is on the student and none of the blame came back to the teachers.

Later in the discussion, several participants continued to reflect critically by advocating schoolwide goals of inclusion (Leah) and by describing how some of the assumptions underlying the stereotypes were racist (Doug):

Leah: Just the whole subject of diversity and how do you—if you have all these different types of students, which you could have in every school, how do you include everybody in one classroom and make everybody feel celebrated?

Doug: It's almost out-and-out bigotry if you're saying it's a whole group of kids and then one year they're all Hispanics and saying none of them have the ability to make it to AP courses for whatever reason. I mean, [the AP teachers] don't even expect to see them because none of them can make it [in the AP classes].

Generating and Evaluating Solutions

Although analysis of this case discussion suggests that participants did spend a good deal of time discussing the issues in the case before moving to solutions, they also offered technical solutions during the analysis phase of the discussion. Below is a data clip in which two participants offered a similar solution to a problem that one of them had experienced during student teaching. This excerpt followed a lengthy discussion among participants about how the Chicano students in the case had been stereotyped by teachers and negatively compared to a successful ESL student from Poland. Just before this data clip, participants had discussed the issue of cultural differences and the dissonance between the culture of school and the culture of some minority groups:

Will: In relationship to the culture of school, I mean, I had students who were good students but they seemed to feel that on taking a test, it wasn't a bad thing to discuss back and forth what was going on. And they weren't Hispanic—they were Bosnian. So, I mean, it's not just the Hispanic culture that's teaching that.

Zack: Well, and that's where Delpit[2] comes in and would say, once again, all the implicitness that's going on and not being explicit about your expectations and saying, "Look, you have your culture and I understand and appreciate that, but we are now in this school and here's what my expectations are and here's what I'm giving over to you. You need to do this and if you don't, you'll fail."

Will: Yeah, and that's what I did is I pulled them aside and said, you know, I understand that it might be something in your culture and that's all right. But here, that's not something I can allow in the class, and I never had a problem with it later.

We characterized these solutions as technical because they offer a "quick fix" that ignores Delpit's (1988) emphasis on "the culture of power" and the transformation of schools and society. The danger is that were this solution to fail, blame can then be placed on the students because the teacher had "done the right thing."

After further analysis and participation in the assigned role plays, we found numerous instances of critical reflection in which participants proposed changes at the institutional level to address the problems that they saw as central in the case. Below is a data clip in which preservice teachers suggested fundamental changes in school policy related to tracking and team teaching:

> *Will:* I think that when the schools allow the teachers to begin to just teach the honors classes and that their whole area is the honors curriculum, then it is easy for them to begin to develop an elitist attitude.
>
> *Leah:* That is why teaming would help with that because you are working with other teachers who are coming in contact with ESL students, whether you are or not.

In addition, participants frequently problematized and challenged one another's solutions. Below is an excerpt from a lengthy discussion regarding ways to evaluate students' learning. We view some (but not all) of this dialogue as critical reflection for a number of reasons. First, some of the study participants suggested fundamental changes in the school's evaluation policy and challenged the idea of ability as fixed and unchangeable. Second, solutions to abolish grades or base grades on improvement were offered as ways to accommodate students in the mainstream classroom. Third, both the solutions and the challenges that others made to alternative evaluation were based on issues of equity:

> *Sam:* Another issue that kind of goes with curricular ideas, I guess, is the idea of evaluation. The one teacher was giving the students the benefit of the doubt and giving them a higher grade because they were ESL—grading them on their improvement and what they could do rather than holding them to the same standards other students had.
>
> *Katy:* If they are resource kids, if they are special ed kids, if they are mainstreamed—you know, if you are going to make exceptions, you need to grade someone on an individual basis, and that is a really hard thing to do in a class. . . . They find out. What about students who don't have disabilities or who you are not going to put in any of these categories? So, that is an issue that we really need to address.
>
> *Cari:* Future teachers, though, they go back and check grades. I know that math teachers I've worked with—they will go look at the grades and expect a level of competency, and the grades don't reflect that. So, if you're padding grades, you're not giving future teachers a clear idea of what the students are capable of, either.

Sam: I don't think future teachers should hold grades as expectations, though. They should form their own ideas based on what the student can do in their own class.

Cari: Exactly, but you don't know what level to start your teaching.

Jim: I think that it has a lot to do with integrity, too. I think if you as a teacher give somebody an A and they are in high school, you are giving that person the opportunity to get a scholarship that maybe another student is not going to be able to get because you gave them an A for maybe what is less work than another student who gets a B. So, I think it has to do with teacher integrity, and although you can help these students, I think that eventually there has to be some type of level playing field.

Eve: But isn't that just a basic problem with grades? . . . You are never going to have completely objective grades no matter how you do it.

This discussion continued, with different participants problematizing grades as biasing future teachers against students who have gotten poor grades in the past. Participants also suggested that grades could be a manifestation of a teaching approach that did not work rather than the abilities of a student, which suggests that they view ability as malleable. For example, in response to the challenge that "in math you have to have a certain criteria for moving to the next level" (Cari), participants offered additional solutions, such as "You have to communicate with that teacher where it was that you left off in the curriculum, not where so and so was at" (Pam). Others suggested that grades should be eliminated altogether and that teachers should rely instead on preassessments.

In sum, we were encouraged by the overall result of the dialogue in this case discussion. We believe that teaching cases have the potential to allow prospective teachers to push issues in many different directions, to open their minds to diverse possibilities, to challenge some of the unexamined assumptions they may hold, and to move them toward a more comprehensive understanding of the complex nature of problems and issues associated with teaching and learning.

Discussion

This study contributes to our understanding of reflectivity in teacher education courses, increases our knowledge of how to use teaching cases as a means to promote critical dialogue, and demonstrates the value of action research to improve teacher education. It provides some of the much needed empirical data on what dialogic reflection sounds like and how the reflective process unfolds. Furthermore, we believe the study adds to our knowledge of prospective teachers, indicating that they are capable of engaging in many levels of reflection as they connect to and challenge one another's ideas through dialogic exchange.

In comparison to the commentaries on the electronic notice board and the results of Moje and Wade (in press) and Bird et al. (1993), which consisted of isolated, solution-oriented comments that were strictly technical in nature, the case discussion in this study was an exploration of thoughts and beliefs of many different participants that included much more than technical solutions. The dialogic format allowed participants to express their ideas and add to and challenge some of the assumptions, views, and solutions of their peers. In many instances, participants indicated a conscientious effort to understand the perspectives of students with limited English proficiency and to analyze how teachers' roles affect the teaching and learning context, which exemplifies contextual awareness. In still other instances, participants challenged stereotypes that were explicitly or implicitly stated by raising issues of justice and equity that affect the teaching and learning conditions of the classroom context, which represent critical reflection. Although the dialogue included examples of unchallenged technical solutions that applied a quick fix to difficult problems, later in the discussion far more solutions were based on critical reflection.

The topic of inclusion may have encouraged critical reflection because equity is central to its goals. Similarly, the quality and focus of the particular case was undoubtedly important. Issues of race, culture, language, and power are central to the case used in this study. The organization and structure of a case discussion was also a factor. Specifically, the assigned roles in the role play may have fostered critical reflection because the roles provided an opportunity for participants to explore beliefs that they may not have personally held and thereby take risks and express unpopular positions. This is similar to what Copeland, Birmingham, De La Cruz, and Lewin (1993) recommend for self-examination: "a teacher stepping out of the situation and exploring its ins and outs as an outsider without a vested interest in his or her own advantage" (p. 352). Most important, the role play and debriefing sessions provided the opportunity for participants to listen to a variety of viewpoints and to analyze and challenge the rationales for various positions. Their reflection moved from a teacher-centered urgency to solve the problem to an open-minded, responsible, and whole-hearted approach (Dewey, 1909/1933), in which they were willing to grapple with the complexities of the problems and issues they saw in the case.

Additional research is needed to examine how high levels of critical reflection can be fostered by the selection and crafting of the cases, the structure of the case discussions, and the choice and use of assigned readings. In addition, other factors may be influential as well—for example, the organization of the course as a whole, the familiarity of the discussants with one another, and the developmental level and experience of the participants.

Notes

1. All names of teachers in the case and participants in the study are pseudonyms.
2. Zack was referring to Delpit (1988).

References

Adler, S. A. (1993). Teacher education: Research as reflective practice. *Teacher and Teacher Education, 9*, 159-167.

Bird, T., Anderson, L. M., Sullivan, B. A., & Swidler, S. A. (1993). Pedagogical balancing acts: Attempts to influence prospective teachers' beliefs. *Teacher and Teacher Education, 9*, 253-267.

Cinnamond, J. H., & Zimpher, N. L. (1990). Reflectivity as a function of community. In R. T. Clift, W. R. Houston, & M. C. Pugach (Eds.), *Encouraging reflective practice in education* (pp. 57-72). New York: Teachers College Press.

Conquergood, D. (1993). Storied worlds and the work of teaching. *Communication Education, 42*, 337-348.

Copeland, W. D., Birmingham, C., De La Cruz, E., & Lewin, B. (1993). The reflective practitioner in teaching: Toward a research agenda. *Teaching and Teacher Education, 9*, 347-359.

Cruikshank, D. R. (1985). Uses and benefits of reflective teaching. *Phi Delta Kappan, 66*, 704-706.

Delpit, L. D. (1988). The silenced dialogue: Power and pedagogy in educating other people's children. *Harvard Educational Review, 58*, 280-298.

Dewey, J. (1933). *How we think.* Boston: Heath. (Original work published 1909)

Easterly, J. L. (1992). Classroom management in elementary school. In J. Shulman (Ed.), *Case methods in teacher education.* New York: Teachers College Press.

Elliot, J. (1990). Teachers as researchers: Implications for supervision and teacher education. *Teaching and Teacher Education, 6*, 1-26.

Gore, J. M. (1987). Reflecting on reflective teaching. *Journal of Teacher Education, 38,* 33-39.

Gore, J. M., & Zeichner, K. M. (1991). Action research and reflective teaching in preservice teacher education: A case study from the United States. *Teaching and Teacher Education, 7,* 119-136.

Grimmett, P., MacKinnon, A., Erickson, G., & Riecken, T. (1990). Reflective practice in teacher education. In R. T. Clift, W. R. Houston, & M. C. Pugach (Eds.), *Encouraging reflective practice in education* (pp. 20-38). New York: Teachers College Press.

Grossman, P. L. (1992). Teaching and learning with cases. In J. Shulman (Ed.), *Case methods in teacher education* (pp. 227-239). New York: Teachers College Press.

Harrington, H. L., & Garrison, J. W. (1992). Cases of shared inquiry: A dialogical model of teacher preparation. *American Educational Research Journal, 29,* 715-735.

Henderson, J. G. (1992). *Reflective teaching and becoming an inquiring educator.* New York: Macmillan.

Laboskey, V. K. (1992). Case investigations. In J. Shulman (Ed.), *Case methods in teacher education* (pp. 175-193). New York: Teachers College Press.

Laboskey, V. K. (1994). *Development of reflective practice.* New York: Teachers College Press.

Liston, D. P., & Zeichner, K. M. (1990). Reflective teaching and action research in preservice teacher education. *Journal of Education for Teaching, 16,* 235-254.

Moje, E., & Wade, S. E. (in press). What case discussions reveal about teacher thinking. *Teaching and Teacher Education.*

Munby, H., & Russell, T. (1993). Reflective teacher education: Technique or epistemology? *Teaching and Teacher Education, 9,* 431-438.

Patton, M. Q. (1990). *Qualitative evaluation and research methods.* Newbury Park, CA: Sage.

Richert, A. E. (1992). Writing cases. In J. Shulman (Ed.), *Case methods in teacher education* (pp. 155-174). New York: Teachers College Press.

Schön, D. A. (1983). *The reflective practitioner.* New York: Basic Books.

Schön, D. A. (1987). *Educating the reflective practitioner.* San Francisco: Jossey-Bass.

Shulman, J. (1992). *Case methods in teacher education.* New York: Teachers College Press.

Shulman, L. (1992). Toward a pedagogy of cases. In J. Shulman (Ed.), *Case methods in teacher education* (pp. 1-32). New York: Teachers College Press.

Sibbett, J. (1996). *Reflection in practice: An exploratory study of student teacher reflection.* Unpublished doctoral dissertation, University of Utah, Salt Lake City.

Sykes, G., & Bird, T. (1992). Teachers education and the case idea. In G. Grant (Ed.), *Review of research in education* (Vol. 18, pp. 457-521). Washington, DC: American Educational Research Association.

Tom, A. R. (1985). Inquiring into inquiry-oriented teacher education. *Journal of Teacher Education, 36*(5), 35-44.

Zeichner, K. M. (1992). Conceptions of reflective teaching in contemporary U.S. teacher education program reforms. In L. Valli (Ed.), *Reflective teacher education* (pp. 161-173). Albany: State University of New York Press.

3 Tracking Salient Comments in Case Discussions

Greta Morine-Dershimer

Greta Morine-Dershimer is Professor of Curriculum and Instruction at the University of Virginia. Her research interests focus on pupil and teacher cognitions during classroom interaction. Most recently, she has been investigating change in the cognitions of preservice teachers.

ABSTRACT

Case discussions are presumed to promote learning by encouraging prospective teachers to confront their own beliefs and values as they analyze issues associated with realistic, problematic educational events. A key factor is the interaction that occurs as students share perceptions and realize that their peers have perceptions and interpretations different from their own. This study examines peer impact on the learning of prospective teachers engaged in a case discussion, tracing the comments reported as heard by participants, and relating these to changes in students' interpretations of the case revealed by pre- and post-written reactions. Three patterns of peer impact in small discussion groups are identified; characteristics of pre- and postreactions associated with these different patterns are discussed. Results are interpreted in terms of a cognitive apprenticeship model.

Case discussions are presumed to promote learning by encouraging prospective teachers to confront their own (often tacit) beliefs and values as they analyze issues and suggest strategies for dealing with realistic, problematic educational events. A key factor is the interaction that occurs as prospective teachers share perceptions and realize that their peers have perceptions and interpretations that are different from their own. This study focused on that interaction by examining comments of peers that were salient to prospective teachers during a case discussion and exploring relationships between these salient comments and changes that occurred in participants' identification of key issues in the case under discussion.

Background

In an earlier study (Morine-Dershimer, 1996), I found "outcome" differences between students in classes that participated in large- versus small-group discussions of the same case. Students engaged in small-group discussions were more attentive to comments of their peers than those engaged in large-group discussions, and their final statements describing key issues in the case were more complex and more specific with regard to the substantive content of the case. These results piqued my interest in the role that small-group discussions might play in the learning occurring during case discussions. In particular, these findings raised questions about the nature of "peer impact" on the thinking and learning of prospective teachers in these two different formats for case discussions. I wondered what and how students were learning from their peers as they participated in case discussions.

Barbara Rogoff's work on cognitive apprenticeship provides some useful insights about the role of peer impact in learning from collaborative problem solving. She notes that

> the apprenticeship model has the value of including more people than a single expert and a single novice; the apprenticeship system often involves a group of novices (peers) who serve as resources for one another in exploring the new domain and aiding and challenging one another. Among themselves, the novices are likely to differ usefully in expertise as well. . . . Hence the model provided by apprenticeship is one of active learners in a community of people who support, challenge, and guide novices as they increasingly participate in skilled, valued sociocultural activity. (Rogoff, 1990, p. 39)

Of particular importance in relation to the methodology of this study are Rogoff's (1990) conclusions that "it is within social exchanges that we should look for the advances in individuals' ways of thinking and acting" (p. 195). She argues that in collaborative learning,

> information and skills are not transmitted but are transformed in the process of appropriation. . . . For as individuals participate in social activity, they choose some aspects for attention and ignore others, and they transform what is available to fit their uses. (p. 197)

This study attempted to trace the social exchanges chosen for attention by prospective teachers engaged in small- and large-group case discussions (i.e., salient comments), to identify the transformations that occur as they appropriate certain ideas (i.e., changes in interpretation from initial to final reactions), and to explore the factors associated with both saliency and change (i.e., peer impact).

Procedures

Setting

The setting for this study was a "Special Topics" seminar for prospective teachers in the fall of their final year. Concurrently, students were engaged in a full semester's student teaching and participating in a weekly subject-area seminar. In the Special Topics seminar, students met for 2 hours once a week for 4 consecutive weeks to discuss cases of at-risk pupils. The cases focused on issues of classroom diversity and mental and physical health. Cases used in the course came from a variety of sources (researchers, classroom teachers, student teachers) and were presented in film as well as written form. A variety of relevant supplementary reading/ resource materials were provided to students after each case discussion.

There were four sections of the course, two for elementary and special education students and two for secondary education students. The discussion sections were each led by a teacher education faculty member. Doctoral students in counseling and educational administration acted as teaching assistants in each section to provide varied perspectives on the cases discussed.

Participants

Participants in the study were students in the two discussion sections that I led. Four doctoral students served as teaching assistants in these two sections. They were selected to provide diversity of perspectives by ethnicity and gender as well as by professional expertise and included two African American women and two white males.

The Case

The study was conducted in Week 2 of the course, when the case for discussion focused on problems experienced at home and in school by a young gay male. The "Alston" case (Sears, 1993) had several unique features that made it particularly appropriate for this study. It was told primarily from the pupil's perspective and in the pupil's voice, it introduced a variety of issues for possible consideration, and it described Alston's experiences from early elementary school through high school. Thus, students at both elementary and secondary program levels could recognize aspects of the case as relevant to their own experience, and individual students had ample opportunity, in their initial reactions to the case, to select an issue that most concerned them.

Alston described a variety of difficulties that he faced during these years, including an abusive father, repeated harassment by peers because of his effeminate behavior, public ridicule from teachers who quickly voiced expectations that he would be "just like" his older siblings, and a school tracking system that relegated him to the "B" group, even after he clearly demonstrated that he was capable of A work. The one bright spot in Alston's life was Miss Langston, his fifth-grade teacher, who motivated him to study and continued to encourage him even after he moved on to sixth grade. Alston's early academic performance was "lackluster," and by third grade he was earning Ds and Fs, but with Miss Langston's support his grades steadily improved, so that by seventh grade he was a solid B student. Of all the difficulties he described, Alston was most bothered by the peer harassment, saying, "If there had not been such a taboo on being gay or being feminine, if people had not ridiculed me for it as much, it would have been a lot easier" (Sears, 1993, p. 165).

There were several possible ideas that I, as course instructor, hoped students might develop or explore in relation to this case:

1. The impact of children's social problems and family situations on their ability to learn
2. Teachers' responsibility to consider children's family background and social needs/problems, as well as their academic strengths or weaknesses
3. Teachers' responsibility for establishing and maintaining a supportive and accepting classroom environment
4. School and community resources available to assist children and their families, with information on how teachers might access these resources

Data Collection

Students read the Alston case before coming to class. As class began, students seated themselves in small groups and wrote their initial reactions to the Alston case. Color-coded paper provided at each seat facilitated tracking of responses by small discussion group membership. All responses were anonymous to reduce the probability that students would report what they thought the instructor wanted to hear.

After their initial reactions to the case were recorded, I invited students to share these reactions in their small discussion groups. After about 40 minutes, using a data collection technique developed in several prior studies (Morine-Dershimer, 1991, 1996), I told students, "Please write down on your colored paper two things that you heard anyone saying in your small-group discussion, and then write down what you think is a key issue in this case."

The class then shifted into large-group discussion. I asked each small group to share the ideas and issues the members had raised in the discussion, and students from other groups commented or raised questions in response. After 45 minutes, I invited the four teaching assistants to present their own reactions to the case, and to the students' commentary on it. Finally, I told students, "Please write down two things you heard anyone saying in the large-group discussion, and then write your final reactions to this case."

Immediately following each class session, I read students' records of comments they heard in the large-group discussion and, from my recall of the conversation, noted on their papers the names of the students or teaching assistants who had made the comments.

Data Analysis

I coded all initial reaction papers using four major categories of response (issues identified, feelings expressed, associated experiences noted, and principles/action plans stated). Next, I examined the data from each small discussion group, comparing the comments reported as heard to the issues identified in initial reaction papers for that group and noting any changes from the initial reaction to the key issue stated by each group member at the close of the small-group discussion. I observed different patterns of relationships among these three sets of data for different small groups, and I sorted the groups into three categories based on these different patterns.

I then examined the comments reported as heard in each of the two large-group discussions to identify the content and source of each comment, and I counted the number of students who reported hearing each particular comment or interchange. I designated any comment that was heard by more than 20% of the students as "salient" and determined the content and source of each salient comment.

Finally, I coded the final reaction statements of all students, using the four major categories developed for coding of the initial reactions. When all data were coded, I compared the initial reactions to the final reactions for all students who were present throughout the class session to identify general patterns of change in perceptions or interpretations of the case. In addition, I compared the patterns of response by category of small discussion group.

The numbers of students involved at different stages in the case discussions varied. Due to student teaching responsibilities, a few students in each section arrived late to class, and others left early. Results reported here are based on the following numbers: types of initial reactions and patterns of peer impact in small-group discussions, $n = 50$; patterns of peer impact in large-group discussions, $n = 38$; and patterns of change from initial to final reactions, $n = 36$. Results are reported as frequency percentages, based on numbers of students reporting at each phase of the case discussion.

Results

Preliminary data analysis showed that most students' perceptions or interpretations of the Alston case changed during the course of the 2-hour discussion. At the end of the discussion, rather than merely expressing sadness about the problems faced by Alston and others like him, and viewing Miss Langston's efforts to assist as an anomaly, most students acknowledged that as teachers they would have a responsibility to address pupils' social as well as academic problems, and many indicated awareness of the school and community resources available to assist them in this task.

But it is not enough to identify what prospective teachers have learned from discussion of a given case. To really understand the process of case-based teacher education, we need to know more about how they learned. In Rogoff's (1990) terms, it is appropriate to ask how peers served as resources to each other, and what types of social exchanges served to advance students' thinking. By tracking comments in the discussion that appeared to be salient to students, we can begin to address these questions.

Patterns of Saliency in Small-Group Discussions

Types of Peer Impact. One of the expectations for case discussions is that participants will expand their own understanding by exposure to the varied perspectives of other participants. A careful comparison of initial written reactions, comments of peers reported as heard, and key issues identified within each group at the close of the small-group discussion phase revealed three different types of peer impact on students' perceptions of the Alston case. I have labeled these types *generative, interactive,* and *influential* to describe critical differences in the direction of peer impact.

The most frequent form of peer impact (observed in 8 of 12 small groups) resulted in generative discussion. In these discussion groups, the salient comments reported, and the key issues identified by individuals at the close of the small-group discussion, included ideas, concerns, and issues that had not been mentioned in the initial written reactions of any members of the group. The students in these groups built on each others' initial reactions and moved beyond them to generate new perceptions of the situation presented in the case.

A less frequent form of peer impact (observed in three small groups) resulted in interactive discussion. In these groups, the salient comments reported indicated that students heard ideas that their peers had expressed in their initial written reactions, whereas the key issues they identified at the close of the small-group discussion demonstrated that they had adopted some of these ideas. Furthermore, the impact was distributed among several members of each group, such that "A" heard and adopted some of "C's" initial views, and "C" heard and adopted some of "B's" initial perceptions. However, no entirely new perceptions of the case were generated during the discussions of students in these interactive groups.

The least frequent form of peer impact (observed in only one group) resulted in influential discussion. In this form of discussion, the salient comments reported, and the key ideas stated at the close of the small-group discussion, showed that one student's initial views had been adopted by all other members of the group. In the course of this discussion, the diversity of issues identified in the students' initial written reactions (Alston's sexuality, teacher ridicule, peer harassment, family neglect, and Miss Langston's support) was narrowed considerably to a single focus on Alston's "awful home life" as the "root cause" of his problems in school.

Factors Associated With Types of Peer Impact. One interesting difference between students who participated in interactive versus generative small-group discussions was the type of issue identified in initial written reactions to the Alston case. Students in interactive discussions identified issues outside a teacher's control more frequently than students in generative groups. They commented particularly on Alston's sexuality (50% compared to 26%), on the school's tracking system (50% compared to 21%), and on the peer harassment described by Alston (42% compared to 21%). In contrast, students in generative discussions focused more strongly on the teachers' responsibility for Alston's difficulties and successes than students in interactive groups. They referred particularly to Miss Langston's encouragement of Alston (71% compared to 17%) and to the negative expectations of Alston's other teachers (24% compared to 8%). Another difference was that students in interactive discussion groups stated principles or action plans (solutions) more frequently than those in generative discussion groups (42% compared to 9%).

Perhaps the students in the interactive groups, having located Alston's problems in areas outside a teacher's control, and having already identified some solutions to the problems (e.g., "Teachers are often the ones held responsible for so many factors that occur outside the school. We have got to start reaching these kids in their homes and communities, and not necessarily leave all of it for school."), felt less compelled to explore the case issues in more detail in their small-group discussions. Students in the generative groups, on the other hand, having identified teachers as centrally responsible for Alston's problems, and having identified very few solutions, may have had much more reason to explore the case in more depth, thereby developing new perspectives.

Because only one group of four elementary/special education students engaged in an influential group discussion, it seems inappropriate at this time to attempt to identify relationships between initial reactions to the case and patterns of peer impact in this type of small-group discussion.

Patterns of Saliency in Large-Group Discussions

Elementary/Special Education Class Discussion. In the elementary/special education section, four events during the large-group discussion proved to be particularly salient to students (i.e., were reported as heard by more than 20% of the participants). The first such event occurred very early in the discussion. The first group to volunteer to share their perceptions of the case happened to be the small group that had engaged in the sole influential group discussion. Alicia,[1] a white student who had influenced her small group to adopt her view that Alston's home life was the "root of the problem," reported that view to the class and elaborated a bit by commenting on his abusive father. Carol, an African American student in another group, interjected an admonition to be careful about interpreting Alston's family's behavior as indicative of a lack of love for Alston, because different cultural groups have different styles of family interaction. Carol's comment was reported as heard by 47% of the students participating in the large-group discussion.

A later interchange among students occurred when someone asked what difference schools could be expected to make, given the strong effect of children's home environments. Several students responded to this, asserting that teachers could foster attitudes of respect for others, as well as teaching social skills to pupils. They asserted that this process was most successful with young children, but could also work with pupils in middle school. Examples of activities observed in their field placements were offered as evidence of this point. Comments made in this interchange were reported as heard by 47% of discussion participants.

Comments made by two of the graduate teaching assistants late in the discussion were also recognized as salient by students. Bob, a white doctoral student in counselling with prior experience as a teacher and school counselor, advised students that they should recognize and accept the fact that there are limits to a teacher's influence on a child's life, and he urged them to seek out other resources in the school (counselors, administrators) to help them. His comments were noted by 32% of participants in this large-group discussion. Tracey, an African American doctoral student in educational policy who had experience as a teacher and school administrator, suggested quietly that it was important for teachers to be aware of their own biases, because most people find behaviors or beliefs that are different from their own rather difficult to deal with. Her comments were recorded by 37% of discussion participants.

To summarize, students in the elementary/special education large-group discussion reported salient comments made by their peers that referred to the strong influence families can have on children's opportunities for a productive school experience, and to the constructive role that teachers can play in promoting social skills and fostering respect for others. The students who made these comments could be seen as more knowledgeable by their peers, either because of their experience as a member of a minority group, or because of their experience serving with teachers who were actively working to develop a positive classroom climate. Students in this class section also reported salient comments made by two of the graduate teaching assistants, who were clearly seen as more knowledgeable about the issues that they addressed, based on their personal and professional experience.

The impact that these salient comments in the large-group discussion had on students' final reactions to the Alston case was reflected in excerpted statements such as these:

> I liked the point about using your resources and not relying completely on yourself to make a difference for a child.

> Respect and tolerance can be taught—even to middle school children.

> I need to continually make sure I'm not being unfairly biased against a certain child for their differences.

Secondary Class Discussion. Three events in the large-group discussion held in the secondary section were reported as salient by participants.

Derek was a white student in social studies education with strong convictions about the dangers of prejudice. He initiated a discussion of the issue of peer harassment by commenting that it was imperative for teachers to teach pupils to accept each others' differences. This was reported as heard by 37% of discussion participants, and it was reported most succinctly by one of his peers as "intolerance is intolerable." As students discussed how teachers might best deal with the type of peer harassment that Alston encountered, Annette, an African American student in foreign language education, described her use of strong negative sanctions when pupils in a class she was teaching called a fellow pupil a faggot. Derek then warned Annette and the class that it was crucial for teachers to know the values held by the local community when they were addressing controversial issues in the classroom, or they could find themselves in serious trouble with parents. This comment by Derek was reported as salient by 26% of discussion participants.

The third salient contribution to this discussion came from Barry, a white doctoral student in educational administration with experience as a special education teacher and administrator. He advised students about the legal requirements for teachers to report cases of suspected parental abuse, and he described typical school policies for making such reports, as well as noting how schools interacted with community agencies in dealing with such pupil problems. Barry's comments were reported as heard by 58% of discussion participants.

It seems clear that students would regard Barry as having very specialized knowledge about policies for dealing with issues of parental abuse, which could well explain their attentiveness to his contribution. The reasons for the impact of Derek's comments are not so clear. Although he spoke with quiet conviction, he claimed no personal experience relative to the issues he addressed. One might speculate that his comments carried weight because, as a social studies major, he was perceived by his peers as more knowledgeable about these types of social issues.

All three of the salient comments identified by participants in this large-group discussion had some impact on students' final reactions to the Alston case, as reflected in these excerpts:

> I now view this as a tolerance/intolerance issue. As a teacher, I must advocate tolerance and acceptance of others—across all issues.

> The discussion about knowing the community in which you teach when confronting controversial issues was useful. It was also helpful to begin considering our roles and obligations to students who experience abuse at home and in the classroom.

> As teachers we need to be aware of our legal responsibilities as well as resources that can help our students both inside and outside of school.

Comparing Patterns of Saliency for Interactive and Generative Discussion Group Members. Patterns of saliency in large-group discussions were apparently influenced by the preceding small-group discussions. Students who were members of interactive small groups exhibited somewhat different patterns of attention to comments in the large-group discussions than did students who were members of generative small groups. Results reported here are consolidated across the two class sections, so only general patterns are considered, not specific salient comments.

During large-group discussions, students from generative small groups were more attentive to comments of their peers than to comments made by graduate teaching assistants (62% vs. 38% of comments reported). In particular, they heard more of their peers' comments about teacher role and responsibility than did students from interactive small groups (60% compared to 27% reported hearing such comments). Their focus on this topic was consistent with their initial reactions to the case, in which they emphasized teachers' responsibility for Alston's difficulties and successes.

Students from interactive small groups were slightly more attentive to contributions of graduate teaching assistants in the large-group discussions than they were to comments of their peers (54% vs. 46% of comments reported). In particular, they heard graduate assistants' comments about support services for pupils more than did students from generative small groups (91% compared to 36% reported hearing these comments).

In light of these patterns, it is especially interesting to note the differences in the final reactions of students from these two types of small discussion groups. Although students from interactive groups reported hearing more large-group discussion comments about outside resources like support services for pupils, students in the generative groups, in their final reaction papers, referred more often to teachers' use of outside resources in addressing the problems of at-risk pupils (32% compared to 9%). It would appear, therefore, that students in the generative small discussion groups continued to incorporate new ideas and expand their thinking related to the case throughout the various phases of the case analysis. In contrast, students in the interactive groups were somewhat limited in developing new ideas in their small-group discussions, and somewhat limited in appropriating ideas expressed in the large-group discussions.

The results of this study indicate that several important factors can influence the direction and extent of peer impact on changes in prospective teachers' perceptions and interpretations of a case, including the types of issues identified and the tendency to suggest solutions in initial reactions

TABLE 3.1 Summary of Group Patterns

Type of Data	Generative Discussion Groups	Interactive Discussion Groups
Initial written reactions to the case	Focus was on teacher responsibility as a central issue; few principles/solutions stated.	Focus was on factors outside teacher's control; principles/solutions frequently stated.
Small-group discussion	Salient comments and key issues stated included ideas not mentioned in any member's initial reaction statement.	Salient comments and key issues identified were limited to ideas stated in initial reaction statements.
Large-group discussion	Salient comments were peers' comments about teacher's role and responsibility for helping pupils.	Salient comments were graduate assistants' references to outside support services for pupils that teachers could access.
Final written reactions to the case	Final reactions referred frequently to teacher use of outside resources in responding to pupils' needs.	Final reactions rarely referred to outside resources in addressing pupils' needs.
Typical change from initial to final reaction	Initial focus on teacher responsibility expanded to include awareness of resources available to assist teacher in serving pupils.	Initial focus on outside factors as responsible for pupil problems shifted to emphasis on teacher responsibility to be aware of and address these problems.

to the case. Of particular interest were the differences in responses of students in the generative and interactive discussion groups as they progressed through the various phases of the case discussion. These patterns are summarized in Table 3.1.

Conclusion

The study reported here is a small-scale, exploratory, descriptive investigation, and it would be premature to suggest implications for practice in conducting case discussions based merely on the results summarized here. However, several of the findings do appear to be generally reflective of Rogoff's (1990) views on cognitive apprenticeship.

The study demonstrates, as Rogoff has argued, that by examining the social exchanges selected for attention by participants in these discussion groups, we can see the advances in individuals' ways of thinking, in this instance by tracing the gradual transformation of novice teachers' interpretations of a case as they engage in collaborative analysis. Also, the data from this study show, as the cognitive apprenticeship model would predict, that novice teachers are differentially attentive to peers who have more specific knowledge relative to the issues or problems being discussed. Furthermore, although the group data here show "common" patterns of attention to the social exchanges, it was also clear from individual differences noted in final reaction statements that individuals transformed what was available to fit their own uses, as Rogoff has anticipated. One of the findings here, however, speaks to a factor that is not addressed explicitly in the cognitive apprenticeship model described by Rogoff. In this study, the ideas that participants brought to the group, as presented in their initial reaction papers, influenced the degree of transformation that occurred during the collaborative activity of small-group discussion. This is a factor that may be more influential in collaborative activities of adults than in the types of activities of young children considered by Rogoff.

In addition to identifying characteristics of case discussions that fit well with the cognitive apprenticeship model, the results of this study lend themselves to suggestions of questions for further research. Of particular concern to researchers interested in case-based teacher education might be questions about use of open-ended versus structured questions/directions to prompt initial reactions; use of different types of cases to provide the stimulus for discussion; and the role of students' individual variation in "expertise" relative to the issues/events in the case under discussion. Answers to questions such as these would provide teacher education researchers and advocates of case-based teaching with a clearer understanding of the process by which collaborative case analysis contributes to prospective teachers' development of professional knowledge. This could serve to assist teacher education practitioners in their attempts to improve the learning that occurs in case discussions.

Note

1. All names of students are pseudonyms.

References

Morine-Dershimer, G. (1991). Learning to think like a teacher. *Teaching and Teacher Education, 7*, 159-168.

Morine-Dershimer, G. (1996). What's in a case—And what comes out? In J. A. Colbert, P. Desberg, & K. Trimble (Eds.), *The case for education: Contemporary approaches for using case methods* (pp. 99-123). Boston: Allyn & Bacon.

Rogoff, B. (1990). *Apprenticeship in thinking: Cognitive development in social context.* Oxford, UK: Oxford University Press.

Sears, J. T. (1993). Alston and Everetta: Too risky for school? In R. Donmoyer & R. R. Kos (Eds.), *At-risk students: Portraits, policies, programs, and practices* (pp. 153-172). Albany: State University of New York Press.

PERCEPTION OF SELF, REFLECTION, AND PEERS AS RESOURCES: REFLECTIONS

Edith M. Guyton

This section does not attempt to summarize each chapter. It reports some of what I believe are the more interesting findings in each study and some common findings among the studies. Then it states some implications for teacher education.

Nierstheimer, Hopkins, and Dillon addressed the influence of biography and prior beliefs on what is learned from experiences in teacher education. They found that the conception of self as learner is tied to the conception of self as teacher. A teacher education student's view of self was more influenced by prior life and school experiences than on immediate current teaching experiences.

They also found students can and will shift their beliefs about at-risk students if they work closely with one child, although the experience did not affect students' confidence levels. Their work indicates that challenging beliefs has to take into consideration the biography of students.

Sibbett, Wade, and Johnson found that case discussions led to more than technical reflection, to deeper and more meaningful reflection. Their work indicates what is needed for case studies to promote critical reflection:

an appropriate topic, appropriate structures, dialogue, use of role play, and discussion.

Morine-Dershimer's study went beyond the effects of a particular set of experiences in teacher education on students' beliefs. She analyzed classroom discussions to determine what comments were salient to students and how they influenced students' perceptions or interpretations about the case. Her work indicates how peers serve as resources to each other, an empowering conception for teacher education because it does not rely on direct contact with the professor.

Morine-Dershimer also categorized small discussion groups as generative, interactive, or influential. This strategy assumes that all small group discussions are not the same and thus may not have the same effects on students. It provides much richer information for teacher educators in terms of how they might structure discussion groups.

One of the findings reported in this chapter is particularly interesting. Whether students identified issues as within or beyond the teacher's control influenced their discussion of the issues. If they felt efficacious, the discussion was more likely to be generative. Many other studies have found teacher efficacy, the belief that teachers can have an influence regardless of the situation, to be a powerful factor in teaching performance (Ashton & Webb, 1986; Gibson & Dembo, 1984; Tracz & Gibson, 1986).

Implications and Conclusions

All three chapters deal with methods of teacher education. In each case, the authors were clear about the purposes they hoped to achieve in teacher education and then chose a method to achieve that purpose. This clarity of purpose is not always evident in teacher education. Also, teacher education has been prone to rely on generic "one size fits all" methods, rather than acknowledging the complexity of the process of teacher education. These chapters represent research that takes into account the processes of teacher education and the cognitions and interactions among participants in teacher education experiences. They produce richer descriptions and deeper understanding to inform practice in teacher education. They do not just report that teacher education students learned when exposed to a certain methodology; they create knowledge about how people learn. As we go about the business of teacher education, it is important that we be purposeful and that our research reflect the complexity of the process.

The three chapters also confirm the importance of dialogue in teacher education. They support constructivist views of teaching and learning, that students constructing their understandings in social settings and that the knowledge they develop will be influenced by previous beliefs and experiences. The findings in these studies highlight the personal and the interpersonal aspects of teacher education. It is important that we take into consideration where our students are when they enter teacher education programs and courses and that we provide opportunities for them to interact with other people in ways conducive to achieving purposes identified as crucial in teacher education.

The Morine-Dershimer and the Sibbett et al. chapters indicate that using case studies in teacher education may be particularly powerful in dealing with students' beliefs, because they involve taking on a perspective different from one's own and exposure to others' ideas. The importance of beliefs and attitudes in learning to teach has been indicated by many studies, as has the difficulty in changing beliefs and attitudes (Richardson, 1996). Teacher education can benefit from more studies that explore not only what techniques affect beliefs but also how these techniques affect students' attitudes.

This section of the yearbook creates new insights into the process of teacher education and also poses questions and indicates the need for further research. Teacher educators need to know more about the influences of teachers' backgrounds and about how to structure teacher education programs to take into account individual differences. The studies generate questions about what influences teachers' thought processes and how they are affected. They raise the issue of what are appropriate and achievable goals for teacher education. These chapters address questions at the very essence of teacher education—what are our purposes and how do we achieve them?

References

Ashton, P. Y., & Webb, R. B. (1986). *Making a difference: Teachers' sense of efficacy and student achievement.* New York: Longman.

Gibson, S., & Dembo, M. (1984). Teacher efficacy: A construct validation. *Journal of Educational Psychology, 57,* 569-582.

Richardson, V. (1996). The role of attitudes and beliefs in learning to teach. In J. Sikula, T. J. Buttery, & E. Guyton (Eds.), *Handbook of research on teacher education* (pp. 102-119). New York: Macmillan.

Tracz, S. M., & Gibson, S. (1986). *Effects of efficacy on academic achievement*. Paper presented at the annual meeting of the California Educational Research Association. (ERIC Document Reproduction Service No. ED 281 853)

DIVISION II

SCHOOL-UNIVERSITY COLLABORATION AND CAREER-LONG PROFESSIONAL DEVELOPMENT: OVERVIEW AND FRAMEWORK

Nancy Fichtman Dana

Nancy Fichtman Dana is Assistant Professor of Education in the Department of Curriculum and Instruction at Pennsylvania State University, University Park. Her research interests include issues in teacher education, school-university collaboration, teacher research, and qualitative research. Her publications have appeared in the Association of Teacher Educators' *Teacher Education Yearbook II* and *Action in Teacher Education*.

Traditional images of career-long teacher education have been characterized by three distinct phases in teacher development (e.g., Sikula, Buttery, & Guyton, 1996). Phase 1 is termed *initial teacher preparation* or *preservice teacher education* where teachers are trained, largely at universities, in theory and methods of teaching with field or clinical experiences culminating in a semester-long student teaching experience where new teachers must prove competent in a number of technical skills. Phase 2 is termed *teacher induction* where beginning teachers obtain their first teaching job and are mentored into the profession through beginning teacher programs mandated by a school district or states to keep certification. Phase 3 is characterized by *inservice teacher education* where veteran teachers attend conferences or districtwide inservice days to receive training in the latest educational innovation. This traditional organization has limited the ways we understand and define career-long teacher professional development as something that is done to teachers by experts in the field: administrators and university faculty.

However, with the host of educational changes witnessed in the past decade, including the advent of school-university collaboration, career-long teacher professional development has a new definition. No longer are teachers being viewed as technicians to be trained, and no longer are administrators and university faculty charged with the sole responsibility for training and evaluating the work of teachers. Each chapter in this section of the yearbook is characterized by stories of teachers taking charge of their professional development, and the changing roles of teachers, administrators, and university faculty within the context of a school-university collaborative partnership. The purpose of this overview and framework is to provide a brief background on school-university collaboration and the roles the participants play to set the stage for the three chapters that appear in this division.

Definition of School-University Collaborative Partnerships

A school-university partnership is a collaborative consisting of practicing teachers, administrators, university faculty, and prospective teachers (Ball & Rundquist, 1993). Within a collaborative framework, university and schools unite to make the connection between theory and practice. Partnerships designed collaboratively between school systems and schools, colleges, and departments of education provide a context for facilitating the integration of preservice classroom instruction with experience in the field; contribute to the professional development of practicing teachers, administrators, and teacher educators; and allow university classroom instruction to be more sensitive to current issues in public education (Beacham, 1992; Book, 1996; Darling-Hammond, 1994).

School-university collaborative partnerships often involve school and university faculty teaching and researching together to further develop and examine curricular changes in public schools and teacher education programs (Green, Baldini, & Stack, 1993). Historically, universities and public schools have worked independently. Recently, however, "attention has been focused on the idea of the two institutions working together on an ongoing and equal basis to solve problems and improve practice in both the schools and at the university" (Russell & Flynn, 1992, p. 8). Collaborative partnerships are an example of how schools and universities are seeking one another's professional wisdom and expertise to combat the problems existing in public education. Notwithstanding, university personnel attempt to improve their teacher education program by linking their practices and sharing their educational beliefs with those of public school educators. Goodlad's *Teachers for Our Nation's Schools* (1990) and *Tomorrow's Teachers: A Report of the Holmes Group* (Holmes Group, 1986) have served as catalysts to the formation of contemporary school-university partnerships.

Tomorrow's Teachers (1986) was written by The Holmes Group, "a consortium of education deans and chief academic officers from the major research universities in each of the fifty states" (p. 3). Their primary purpose was to come together as a group to improve the quality of their teacher education programs. Although The Holmes Group (1986) has evolved significantly in the past 10 years, one of the original goals of the group is still strong:

> If university faculties are to become more expert educators of teachers, they must make better use of expert teachers in the education of other teachers and in research on teaching. In addition, schools must become places where both teachers and university faculty can systematically inquire into practice and improve it. (p. 4)

After the publication of this initial report, which emphasized the need for teacher education reform, many universities sought collaborative partnerships with public schools. These partnerships allow for experimentation, reflection, and open discussion to take place among practicing teachers, administrators, teacher educators, and student teachers (Pugach & Johnson, 1995). The Holmes Group has evolved to The Holmes Partnership, where public schools and universities apply for a joint membership in the organization. The first meeting of the expanded organization occurred in January 1997 and was characterized by equal participation of deans of schools, colleges, and departments of education (SCDEs); teachers and administrators from public schools; and university faculty. One of the highlights of this meeting was the Role-A-Like sessions, where those who played similar roles in university-school collaborative partnerships came together to discuss the promise and problems associated with each of the participants in school-university collaboratives.

Role of Participants in Collaboratives

Practicing teachers may serve various roles during a school-university collaborative partnership. Teachers become researchers themselves by observing, collecting data, experimenting with new methodologies, and reflecting on their past experiences. Rather than "supervise," school practitioners serve as mentors and facilitators in guiding student teachers to reflect on the day's events, seeking deeper understanding of teaching problems and possibilities (Olson, 1990). Practicing teachers "are one of the first contact points for students' initial field experiences; they open their doors to enable teacher education students to get a sense of what teaching is about" (Pugach & Johnson, 1995, p. 207).

By providing a comfortable, nonthreatening environment, practicing teachers may help their prospective teachers understand the importance of developing their own philosophy of education and matching that philosophy with instruction. In addition, practicing teachers may contribute to teacher education programs by team-teaching methods courses, leading teacher education seminars, or engaging in professional research projects.

By relating what they are learning in their methods classes with what is actually happening in classrooms in the field, teacher education students are "learning by doing" and are better able to decide what is most appropriate for children and youths. They may also have an opportunity to team teach with their practicing teacher and/or a university faculty member. This, in turn, gives them a different perspective on teaching and on collaboration, for prospective and practicing teachers alike "are simultaneously learners and teachers to each other" (Pugach & Johnson, 1995, p. 207).

The university researcher's role may be to "facilitate individual teacher roles, disseminate ideas on research process, link research to practice, and suggest alternate approaches and solutions" (Oja & Ham, 1984, p. 182). Furthermore, teacher educators collaborate with practicing teachers in investigating methodologies that make a difference in the instruction of all areas for children. As teachers construct a system of meaning and critically examine current strategies and practices, the university researcher's role may be to "facilitate the development of teachers' reflective capacities" (Dana, 1994, p. 14). Professors of education also have an opportunity to experience what it is like to be in the classroom once again and close the chasm between theoretical knowledge and exemplary practice.

Benefits of Collaborative Partnerships

School-university collaborative partnerships should first and foremost benefit the children attending the school. In addition, practicing teachers, administrators, prospective teachers, and teacher educators also benefit from the synergetic relationships created between all members of the collaborative. According to Russell and Flynn (1992, p. 15), some of the benefits for school practitioners and administrators participating in a collaborative include

- Involvement in joint research, evaluation, planning, and inservice efforts
- Better access to latest research findings on effective practices
- Visible response to calls for educational reform
- Collegial interactions with professionals who may have different perspectives regarding common problems
- Input into the university's professional preparation programs
- Involvement of school personnel as clinical or adjunct faculty at the university
- Influencing university research efforts to focus on current school problems

Some of the more obvious benefits Russell and Flynn (1992, p. 16) found for universities include

- Access to the concerns and needs of students, teachers, and administrators in public schools

- Input from experienced practitioners for improving the College of Education's professional preparation programs
- Direct impact on pre-K through adult education programs at the point of delivery
- A chance to apply theory to practice

The most intensive type of school-university collaboration, and one of the intended outcomes of The Holmes Partnership, is the establishment of professional development schools (PDSs; McIntyre, 1994).

Professional Development Schools

"Professional development schools are public schools that are structured, staffed and supported to develop and use research-based knowledge to improve K-12 teaching and learning" (Rosaen & Hoekwater, 1990, p. 144). Darling-Hammond (1994) characterizes PDSs as "a special case of school restructuring: as they simultaneously restructure schools and teacher education programs, they redefine teaching and learning for all members of the profession and the school community" (p. 1). Research is an essential and ongoing part of PDSs, in which university faculty and school practitioners work as colleagues in examining issues such as teacher education, professional growth, school research, and the improvement of teaching. Developing interpersonal and working relationships, undertaking genuine problem-solving skills to work toward common goals, and developing a common vocabulary and knowledge base are some of the intended facets of PDSs (Rosaen & Hoekwater, 1990). PDSs grant "multiple opportunities for collaborative relationships between those who are planning to teach and those who are in the profession already" (Pugach & Johnson, 1995, p. 207). Over and above, these schools promote an environment conducive to teaching and learning for understanding; form a learning community among university and school personnel; and inform teachers, administrators, and teacher educators of the importance of pursuing educational research as a continual learning process.

According to the Holmes Group (1990), six general guiding principles exist for creating PDSs. PDS sites must include a commitment to

- Teaching for understanding (rather than a factual recall) so that students learn for a lifetime
- Organizing classrooms and schools as learning communities

- Setting ambitious goals for everybody's children
- Establishing an environment that supports continuing learning for all adults as well as children
- Making reflection and inquiry the central feature of the school
- Inventing a new organization

In the past decade, "a remarkable flurry of effort has produced hundreds of school-university collaborations across the country that call themselves PDSs" (Darling-Hammond, 1994, p. 2). Yet relatively little systemic research has been completed on PDS development and implementation. One of the major outcomes of The Holmes Partnership national meeting was to develop and launch a national research agenda focused on understanding and assessing PDSs.

Three Research Reports

This section of the yearbook includes three studies that address career-long teacher development in the context of school-university collaboration. Frankes, Valli, and Cooper compare the professional development goals of PDSs to current research findings through a comprehensive review of the literature on PDSs. They focus on the expanded role of the teacher from solely classroom teacher to researcher, decision maker, teacher educator, and political activist. Their review can lay the foundation for others answering The Holmes Partnership's call for a program of national research on PDSs.

Johnson and Brown tell the story of a large elementary school that had a PDS partnership with a university. Within this PDS, peer supervision and the organization of collegial support teams (CSTs) replaced traditional supervision practices. Their research supports that the CST process fostered collegiality and experimentation—two guiding principles of PDSs.

Finally, the chapter by Zuelke and Nichols tells the story of two professors' efforts over 3 years to assist a high school in doing action research on school climate. Along with providing the procedures and results of the research project, the authors speculate as to why the findings from the study were not implemented at the high school.

Each of these chapters contributes to a reconceptualization of career-long teacher professional development and the meanings that has for the roles of teachers, administrators, and teacher educators.

References

Ball, D. L., & Rundquist, S. R. (1993). Collaboration as a context for joining teacher learning with learning about teaching. In D. K. Cohen, M. W. McLaughlin, & J. E. Talbert (Eds.), *Teaching for understanding: Challenges for policy and practice* (pp. 13-42). San Francisco: Jossey-Bass.

Beacham, B. G. (1992). *A university and public school collaborative approach to preparing elementary teachers.* East Carolina University, Wilmington, NC. (ERIC Document Reproduction Service No. ED 357 621)

Book, C. L. (1996). Professional development schools. In J. Sikula, T. J. Buttery, & E. Guyton (Eds.), *Handbook of research on teacher education* (pp. 194-212). New York: Macmillan.

Dana, N. F. (1994). Building partnerships to affect educational change: School culture and the finding of teacher voice. In M. J. O'Hair & S. J. Odell (Eds.), *Partnerships in education: Association of Teacher Educators' teacher education yearbook II* (pp. 11-26). Fort Worth, TX: Harcourt Brace College.

Darling-Hammond, L. (1994). Developing professional development schools: Early lessons, challenge, and promise. In L. Darling-Hammond (Ed.), *Professional development schools: Schools for developing a profession* (pp. 1-27). New York: Teachers College Press.

Goodlad, J. I. (1990). *Teachers for our nation's schools.* San Francisco: Jossey-Bass.

Green, N., Baldini, B., & Stack, W. M. (1993). Spanning cultures: Teachers and professors in professional development schools. *Action in Teacher Education, 15*(2), 18.

Holmes Group. (1986). *Tomorrow's teachers: A report of the Holmes Group.* East Lansing, MI: Author.

Holmes Group. (1990). *Tomorrow's schools: Principles for the design of professional development schools.* East Lansing, MI: Author.

McIntyre, J. (1994). Partnerships and collaboration in the contexts of schools and teacher education programs. In M. J. O'Hair & S. J. Odell (Eds.), *Partnerships in education: Association of Teacher Educators' teacher education yearbook II* (pp. 1-8). Fort Worth, TX: Harcourt Brace College.

Oja, N. S., & Ham, M. C. (1984). A cognitive-developmental approach to collaborative action research with teachers. *Teachers College Record, 86*(1), 171-191.

Olson, M. W. (1990). *Opening the door to classroom research.* Newark, DE: International Reading Association.

Pugach, M. C., & Johnson, L. J. (1995). *Collaborative practitioners, collaborative schools.* Denver, CO: Love.

Rosaen, C. L., & Hoekwater, E. (1990). Collaboration: Empowering educators to take charge. *Contemporary Education, 61*(3), 144-151.

Russell, J. F., & Flynn, R. B. (1992). *School-university collaboration.* Bloomington, IN: Phi Delta Kappa Educational Foundation.

Sikula, J., Buttery, T. J., & Guyton, E. (Eds.). (1996). *Handbook of research on teacher education.* New York: Macmillan.

4 Continuous Learning for All Adults in the Professional Development School

A Review of the Research

Lisa Frankes

Linda Valli

David H. Cooper

Lisa Frankes has been pursuing postdoctoral studies as a professional development school network coordinator at the University of Maryland. Her research interests include teacher education, democratic schooling, and school-university partnerships. She has accepted a position in teacher education at Eastern Michigan University.

Linda Valli is Associate Professor in the Department of Curriculum and Instruction at the University of Maryland. She serves as Associate Dean for Professional Studies. Her research interests include learning to teach, cultural diversity, professional development, and school reform.

David H. Cooper is Associate Professor of Special Education at the University of Maryland. His research interests include factors that place young children at risk of school failure.

AUTHORS' NOTE: This chapter is based on a comprehensive review of research on professional development schools presented at an American Educational Research Association annual meeting and published in *Review of Research in Education*, Vol. 22, 1997.

ABSTRACT

Professional development schools (PDSs) are touted as new types of institutions that simultaneously prepare new teachers, provide ongoing professional development for experienced educators, and support research on teaching and learning. This chapter compares the professional development goals of PDSs to research findings. These goals encourage teachers to assume four significantly new areas of responsibility. In addition to classroom teacher, the PDS teacher would be a researcher, decision maker, teacher educator, and political activist. These new roles need changed institutional norms and structures to support them. Review of the research indicates that more changes have occurred for the proposed roles of decision maker and teacher educator than for researcher and political activist. To facilitate lasting change in each of these four areas of professional development, schools and universities need to provide more support through participation structures, fostering collaboration, and rewards and incentives.

A promising educational reform, *professional development schools* (PDSs) are defined as schools created "for the development of novice professionals, for the continuing development of experienced professionals, and for the research and development of the teaching profession" (Holmes Group, 1990, p. 1). The PDS is a monumental undertaking that entails the creation of a new institution. If this vision is realized, teachers, administrators, and university faculty would see their roles transformed.

This chapter provides a description of the professional development goals promoted in The Holmes Group (1990) report, *Tomorrow's Schools: Principles for the Design of Professional Development Schools,* and matches these goals with evidence of accomplishments described in the PDS research literature. The following questions guided this segment of our inquiry:

1. What does the literature say about aspirations for professional development within the PDS? What do proponents claim these new organizational structures can accomplish?
2. What do research studies of professional development within PDSs say has been accomplished?

To match claims with actual achievements, we conducted a review of the literature. Our primary source of data was Abdal-Haqq's (1993) annotated bibliography of resources on professional development schools, which yielded 23 studies. An ERIC search of "professional development schools" and "research" from 1992 to 1996 provided 36 sources, many of which overlapped with the Abdal-Haqq list. Others were added from a search of ERIC technical reports and a hand search of 11 academic journals from 1994 to 1996.

The Vision

The Holmes Group calls for the continuous learning of all adults within the PDS: teachers, teacher educators, administrators, and support staff. The importance of professional development opportunities for teachers is addressed in the greatest detail, however, and the vision promoted in *Tomorrow's Schools* is of teaching as a political act of leadership (Holmes Group, 1990, p. 10). By exercising responsibility and authority, empowered teachers seek to establish inclusive "democratic communities of learning" (p. 29) and "press the claims for justice on the larger society" (p. 33).

Teachers' roles extend across four primary areas. As teacher researchers they contribute to the development of the knowledge base; as teacher educators they participate in the clinical supervision and development of novice teachers; as activists they collaborate with others in seeking justice and equity in the greater society; and finally, as decision makers, they determine school goals and instructional decisions.

In the following sections, these four roles are explored more closely. We begin each section by outlining the vision espoused by The Holmes Group followed by a description of documented reform efforts.

Teachers as Researchers

Schools have seldom been organized as centers for teachers' own reflection and inquiry. The Holmes report encourages research that develops from teachers' daily work, employs strategies of inquiry that reveal the complexity of teaching and learning, and values teacher knowledge. Moreover, teachers and university professionals would collaborate in ways that promote the leveling of hierarchical distinctions typically embedded in traditional research designs.

Research evidence indicates that PDS partnerships support school-based inquiry and encourage a greater degree of peer observation and feedback. Teachers have taken advantage of research opportunities (Snyder, 1994), studied teaching as a means of school improvement (Lemlech, Hertzog-Foliart, & Hackl, 1994), and participated in action research projects and courses (Berry & Catoe, 1994; Rosaen & Lindquist, 1992). Teachers have also shared their research publicly (Jett-Simpson, Pugach, & Whipp, 1992). However, the depth with which these activities are described in the research literature varies widely (Boles & Troen, 1994; Grossman, 1994; Jett-Simpson et al., 1992; Rushcamp & Roehler, 1992; Schack & Overturf, 1994).

For example, Rushcamp and Roehler (1992) examined a school that historically promoted teacher inquiry. With the advent of the PDS, research was extended to 11 classrooms. Not stated, however, is whether research was conducted systematically or if results were used to inform teaching beyond the teacher researchers' classrooms. In contrast, teachers of the Learning/Teaching Collaborative (Boles & Troen, 1994) have conducted formal research with the intent of disseminating results. One teacher stressed the importance of inquiry by stating his commitment to developing a "voice for the teacher researcher in the context of the larger research world" (p. 19). From "deliverers of knowledge" to creators of knowledge, teachers' roles were transformed (p. 19). Engaging in work traditionally considered the university's domain, teachers expanded their sphere of influence.

Another common feature of inquiry within the PDS is the prominence of individual or small-group projects. Schoolwide involvement is rare. Schack and Overturf (1994), for example, worked with four middle school teachers and a group of preservice students to examine their impact as a professional development team. One project they undertook involved the creation of a heterogeneous setting for gifted, learning disabled, at-risk, and nonlabeled students. To determine the effectiveness of their effort, team members surveyed students and parents, and the professor also conducted interviews with six student teachers and four participating teachers. Participants presented at conferences and published articles in collaboration with the researchers.

In another instance, two teacher researchers formed a yearlong collaboration to explore the use of writer's workshop in one fifth-grade classroom (Rosaen & Lindquist, 1992). They collaborated through planning, teaching, and researching. As a result, the classroom culture was transformed from one of workplace to a learning place where knowledge was socially constructed.

Unfortunately, the nature of research and inquiry remains one of the least elaborated areas of PDS work, and research is still perceived as peripheral to teachers' work (Moore & Hopkins, 1993). Moreover, research within the PDS still remains the primary domain of university personnel. As centers of inquiry, PDSs are still in an early stage of development.

Teachers as Decision Makers

The Holmes Group (1990) criticizes top-down organization that isolates teachers, compartmentalizes knowledge, and renders teachers powerless (p. 42). The Holmes Group cautions that many administrators perceive certain expanded roles for teachers as threatening (p. 83); new forms of leadership are tentatively advanced that portray teachers as empowered decision makers who create school goals and policies, promote new standards of practice, and further the creation of an inclusive and just school community.

In accordance with the preceding goals, studies indicate positive changes have occurred in the area of teacher decision making. These changes primarily involve redefinition and creation of new roles that provide teachers with more authority. Within the PDS, participatory governance and collaborative teams were the most common structures used to build democratic relationships, and many initiatives were guided by the discourse of teacher empowerment. "Every leader is a teacher and every teacher a leader" (Whitford, 1994, p. 77). Top-down approaches to decision making were replaced with more democratic approaches as teachers engaged in strategic planning alongside principals and university professionals (Francis, 1992).

The position of teacher leader coordinator (TLC), for example, was a newly created role for middle school teachers participating in a partnership with the University of Washington (Romerdahl, 1991). A list of TLC responsibilities included attending planning meetings and meetings with the PDS director, leading site meetings, overseeing PDS site budgets, screening and interviewing prospective student teachers, and involving other teachers in PDS activities. Only one teacher, however, was provided with release time from her regular duties (Gehrke, Young, & Sagmiller, 1991). Gehrke et al. (1991) describe the need to find mechanisms for distributing leadership tasks more evenly.

Within the PDS, teachers have also engaged in decision making about important curricular and instructional issues. For example, a 3-year study conducted by Michigan State University researchers yielded a portrait of one PDS teacher who learned to change classroom discourse patterns and authority relations through her involvement in an intensive mathematics study group (Gross, 1993).

Finally, teachers have assumed active roles in designing and delivering college courses, often as co-instructors with university professors (Lemlech et al., 1994; Miller & Silvernail, 1994; Snyder, 1994). A primary theme among these studies involves the blurring of status boundaries and the nurturing of trust and role shifts for the purposes of creating a new culture.

Teachers as Teacher Educators

Within the PDS, according to The Holmes Group (1990), classroom teachers who assume new roles as teacher educators would help bridge the "enormous disjunction" between university instruction and the actual problems of schools (p. 34). Greater continuity of purposes and the interweaving of theory and practice would be accomplished through teachers and university faculty collaborating to develop preservice curriculum, coteach university courses, and mentor preservice teachers (p. 51).

Securing the most empirical support as a change in practice, the mentoring role has been expanded and redefined (Berry & Catoe, 1994; Boles & Troen, 1994; Grossman, 1994; Lemlech et al., 1994; Morris & Nunnery, 1993; Nevins, 1993; Stallings, 1991; Stanulis, 1995; Yopp, Guillaume, & Savage, 1993-1994). As teacher educators, classroom teachers develop their own practices through overseeing the development of student interns. Collaboration among university faculty, teachers, and interns also affords greater opportunity for conversation and deliberation about teaching. A tighter coupling of university and school is accomplished through "blurring boundaries" that traditionally have separated the two institutions (Gehrke et al., 1991).

An example of this blurring or overlapping of institutional boundaries is provided by Lemlech et al. (1994). Teachers in their study deliberated with other professionals and coplanned both the school curriculum and aspects of the preservice program. University professors provided teachers with information about various models of teaching; consequently, teachers were able to provide meaningful feedback to interns regarding their use of the models.

As decision makers, teachers screened prospective student interns, led seminars, and collaborated with university faculty to write instructional cases regarding classroom dilemmas interns experienced. These cases became the subject matter for a problem-solving clinic designed for interns and facilitated by both university faculty and teachers. This collaboration began to transform relationships between university faculty and teachers only when teachers recognized their capacity to effect change and make important decisions (Lemlech et al., 1994, p. 171). Structured collaborative inquiry, time for purposeful interactions, and acknowledgment of shared expertise among professionals in both school and university were conditions that promoted a cohesive and collegial partnership.

New roles for teachers as university instructors and guest lecturers have also been advanced. Teacher researchers Boles and Troen (1994) observe how college teaching prompted some colleagues to examine critically their own practices. Additional responsibilities for school faculty included screening student intern applicants, mentoring them, and writing their evaluations. One teacher identified the value of these experiences: "Being forced to discipline yourself, to express what it is you do and why you do it . . . informs your teaching, and I would argue leads to greater success in teaching" (Boles & Troen, 1994, p. 15).

To provide greater support and continuity of experience for interns, one PDS extended the mentoring role over 2 years. Stanulis (1995) conducted case studies of elementary teachers who served as mentors during this period and concluded that sustained interactions between university and school-based personnel, based on shared responsibility and mutual respect, were successful in achieving congruence between both groups' understanding of teaching and learning and theory and practice. These common understandings were also communicated to novice teachers. The establishment of shared goals, collaboration, and the creation of new roles served to bridge the cultures of university and school.

Teachers as Political Activists

The advocacy literature is replete with calls for equity and social justice in schools and in the greater society. Teachers as "practical intellectuals" would engage in political activism in their communities to further the goals of social justice and greater equality (Holmes Group, 1990, p. 27). Their responsibilities include establishing connections between the family's culture and the academic culture of the school.

A comparison between the equity goals outlined in the advocacy literature and the actual achievement of PDSs indicates a large gap between realities and expectations yet to be fulfilled. The only evidence that this mandate is being addressed is provided through an anecdotal report of teachers within a PDS who jointly decided to examine how subordinate groups of students were silenced in their school, though at the time of publication they had not begun this research (Nihlen, 1992).

Although this study provides one of the only documented examples of teachers engaged in critical reflection regarding inequitable school practices, it is important to note that some PDSs have been created in urban centers with the explicit intent of exposing interns to "schools in transition"—schools with difficult problems (high student attrition, little community involvement, high teacher turnover, minimal resources). Committed to working in these sites, university and school personnel seek to challenge teacher stereotypes regarding children's learning and to examine issues of equity and diversity (Jett-Simpson et al., 1992; Lemlech & Hertzog-Foliart, 1993; Pasch & Pugach, 1990; Stallings, 1991; Yopp et al., 1993-1994).

Professional Development for Administrators and University Faculty

Although detailed information regarding professional development opportunities for administrators and university faculty within the PDS is lacking, growth opportunities that have been documented show promise. For example, Schack (Schack & Overturf, 1994), a professor at the University of Louisville who collaborated with four middle school teachers and a group of preservice students on a professional development team, stated that her "personal and professional growth was enhanced by the reality check of being in the classroom on a regular basis, participating in the intersection of theory and practice" (p. 11). Moreover, she was able to provide a "real-world connection" for her university students.

In another study, University of Washington faculty reported changing their college course curriculum to make subjects more integrated and coordinated as a result of their experiences in the PDS (Grossman, 1994). New roles for university faculty were also created including a "professor-in-residence" who served as a resource for teachers through observing in classrooms, developing action research projects, and providing guidance and support (Berry & Catoe, 1994).

It is clear that the work of principals is also critical to the establishment of a successfully functioning partnership. Lewis (1992) identified three school factors pertaining to the principal's role—the nature of school leadership and vision, schoolwide decision-making processes, and staff development—that are critical to the success of a PDS. After evaluating seven schools seeking to become PDSs, the researcher concluded that four sites were not appropriate due to the principals' leadership styles. At one site, for example, the principal could not allow teachers to make decisions about their development and tightly managed their work. At another, the principal assigned a teacher to coordinate the "project" thereby signaling a lack of commitment, which ultimately prevented the development of the partnership (Lewis, 1992, p. 21). Putnam (1992, p. 8) drew similar conclusions after a 3-year participant observation study, claiming that those principals who perceive teachers as initiators of action and professionals who can lead and make decisions may be more inclined to create contexts marked by incentives and rewards for personal initiative, innovation, and growth.

Although these studies provide insight, more information regarding the professional development of both school administrators and university faculty is needed. At present, we are not able to determine if the mandate issued by The Holmes Group for the continuous learning of all adults within the PDS is being met.

Facilitating Factors and Obstacles

The development of collaborative relationships between two culturally distinct institutions is extremely challenging, and continuous research and assessment provide needed direction. In this closing section, we examine PDS research for factors that appear to support lasting reform and obstacles that must be addressed if these reforms are to survive.

Participation Structures

What is known of those teachers in PDSs who are not engaged in professional development initiatives? Most initiatives are voluntary, and research has focused only on engaged participants (Boles & Troen, 1994; Boyd, 1994; Lemlech et al., 1994; Neufeld & Freeman, 1993; Nihlen, 1992; Putnam, 1992; Rushcamp & Roehler, 1992; Stallings, 1991). In cases of whole-school participation, selection processes often permitted uninterested teachers to transfer to other schools. In many schools, a small core of interested teachers participated. In others, teachers determined their level of involvement or chose to withdraw later.

Studies provide evidence that reforms are more apt to take hold when all teachers in a school are involved. Finding that their individual problems are shared by others, teachers are more willing to engage in collaborative ventures (Barksdale-Ladd, 1994). For example, within a PDS established between the Milwaukee Public Schools and the University of Wisconsin Center for Teacher Education (Jett-Simpson et al., 1992), teachers found it easier to change their literacy instruction from a skills-based approach to a child-centered approach because the initiative created its own momentum. Morale steadily improved for both teachers and students, and even marginally invested teachers made changes to their program.

Whole-school involvement also provides a context for examining broader issues such as how the school addresses the needs of diverse learners, and which structures further equity and the creation of a democratic learning community. In contrast, when PDS initiatives are initiated with small, voluntary groups of teachers who reflect on isolated aspects of their practice, there is a danger that needed schoolwide structural reform will be ignored. Zeichner (1992) elaborates on this concern:

> [An] emphasis on focusing teachers' reflections inwardly at their own teaching and/or on their students, to the neglect of any consideration of the social conditions of schooling that influence teachers' work within the classroom . . . makes it less likely that teachers will be able to confront and transform those structural aspects of their work that hinder the accomplishment of their educational mission. (p. 8)

On the other hand, whole-school involvement may support a broadening of this focus and make it more likely that teachers can develop a unified and powerful voice in pressing for needed structural changes. Engaging the entire faculty also enables a principal to dedicate staff meetings and professional development sessions to PDS initiatives, and within these sessions participants have the opportunity to collaborate and develop shared goals and a common language for talking about them (Jett-Simpson et al., 1992).

Fostering Collaboration

There is little uniformity among PDSs regarding the processes that are used to support professional development for teachers. Although school and university faculties jointly developed reforms in the PDS established between the Milwaukee Public Schools and the University of Wisconsin (Jett-Simpson et al., 1992), university faculty and school administrators direct many other professional development school initiatives (Berry & Catoe, 1994; Boyd, 1994; Jett-Simpson et al., 1992; Lemlech et al., 1994; Morris & Nunnery, 1993; Nihlen, 1992; Rushcamp & Roehler, 1992; Schack & Overturf, 1994; Stallings, 1991). Whether they present an agenda or strive to guide teachers to develop their own, university professors easily become identified as organizers and directors rather than colearners (Navarro, 1992, p. 11).

For example, Morris and Nunnery (1993) developed an initiative to empower teachers as mentors within the preservice education program; however, professional development occurred in a traditional inservice context. Experts provided teachers with 50 hours of "training" throughout the year. Teachers felt participation in the program enhanced their sensitivity to the problems and stresses experienced by interns, their willingness to share and work with peers, and their confidence as professional role models; however, 56% did not feel empowered as decision makers. Similarly, in another PDS (Barksdale-Ladd, 1994) university involvement was neither a major contributor to teachers' feelings of empowerment nor to their development of child-centered practices, in part because university personnel were perceived as "threatening" and domineering (p. 110).

In a PDS between Texas A&M University and an urban elementary school (Stallings, 1991), teachers were trained to lead student intern seminars and evaluate interns. University personnel observed and evaluated teachers, providing them with a profile of their own instructional behaviors. Findings suggested that teachers who supervised student teachers and attended weekly seminars significantly improved their own teaching skills. However, knowledge was transmitted from university professors to teachers rather than constructed with them, and university faculty, working from a position of higher authority, acted as teacher evaluators.

In contrast, some university personnel, even while they lead, are able to present themselves as colearners. In some cases, they gradually cede authority and responsibility for professional development to teachers. This transfer of authority may be critical to the promotion of changes that are truly transformational in nature, changes that support teacher leadership in a variety of capacities. Rushcamp and Roehler (1992), for example, describe how university professors sought to nurture "role shifts" among participants. Three teachers on the central planning team gradually became meeting facilitators as the university facilitator relinquished control (p. 21). In a separate study, a university professor (Boyd, 1994) worked with teachers to implement the National Council for Teachers of Mathematics math standards. Characterizing her role as one of facilitator and leader, she explained, "The professor must set the stage for that involve-ment . . . must facilitate the merging of theory and practice and the idea of teacher as learner and researcher" (p. 138). However, teachers perceived Boyd as a colearner because they were encouraged to assume greater responsibility for their own development.

Rewards and Incentives

The examples of professional development within the PDS outlined in this chapter highlight many new opportunities for teachers. As teachers engage in research, the education of interns, political reform efforts, and decision making, their isolation is replaced with collaboration, and their voices reach beyond the four walls of the classroom. These reforms are also instrumental in altering the perception that teachers aren't working unless they are with students (Putnam, 1992). However, working as members of site-based management teams, as student teacher supervisors, as family-school liaisons, as teacher researchers, or as university-school liaisons may detract from teachers' ability to fully perform their most critical function—educating their students. Apple (1986, p. 42) cautions that too many additional responsibilities may ultimately lead to teacher disempower-ment and a reduction in the quality of their work. Increasing teachers' responsibilities may force them to limit the time and effort they devote to any given area. One teacher, for example, acting as a PDS coordinator (Romerdahl, 1991), was forced to prioritize her commitments, explaining, "The [PDS] is not and never will be a top priority. My family is at the top, my students next, the various hats I wear at school . . . are next, then comes the [PDS]" (p. 7). Not surprisingly, then, some PDS initiatives have strug-gled to sustain teacher participation (Gehrke et al., 1991; Grossman, 1994; Lemlech et al., 1994).

Similarly, university faculty are not provided with rewards or incen-tives for PDS involvement. Professors risk fewer publications, heavier workloads, and lower status. Not surprisingly, most initiatives rely on a few committed faculty, who feel overwhelmed by the demands placed on their energy and time.

Still in its infancy, the PDS initiative faces many obstacles. Intensifica-tion of work demands, difficulties in leveling traditional hierarchical relationships, and involvement of small numbers of school and university faculties present critical challenges to the creation of a truly new institu-tion. Although it shows great promise, the PDS will be difficult to sustain unless these challenges are addressed.

References

Abdal-Haqq, I. (Comp.). (1993). *Resources on professional development schools: An annotated bibliography.* Washington, DC: ERIC Clearinghouse on Teacher Education and the American Association for Colleges of Teacher Education.

Apple, M. (1986). *Teachers and texts: A political economy of class and gender relations in education.* New York and London: Routledge.

Barksdale-Ladd, M. A. (1994). Teacher empowerment and literacy instruction in three professional development schools. *Journal of Teacher Education, 45,* 104-111.

Berry, B., & Catoe, S. (1994). Creating professional development schools: Policy and practice in South Carolina's PDS initiative. In L. Darling-Hammond (Ed.), *Professional development schools: Schools for developing a profession* (pp. 176-202). New York: Teachers College Press.

Boles, K., & Troen, V. (1994, April). *Teacher leadership in a professional development school.* Paper prepared for the American Educational Research Association Conference, New Orleans, LA.

Boyd, P. C. (1994). Professional school reform and public school renewal: Portrait of a partnership. *Journal of Teacher Education, 45,* 132-139.

Francis, R. W. (1992, October). *Issues in establishing rural professional development schools.* Paper presented at the annual Rural and Small Schools Conference, Manhattan, KS.

Gehrke, N., Young, D., & Sagmiller, K. (1991, April). *Critical analysis of the creation of a new culture: A professional development center for teachers.* Paper presented at the annual meeting of the American Educational Research Association, Chicago.

Gross, S. (Ed.). (1993). *Constructing teaching and research practice in elementary school mathematics.* East Lansing: Michigan State University, Center for the Learning and Teaching of Elementary Subjects, Institute for Research on Teaching. (ERIC Document Reproduction Service No. ED 364 405)

Grossman, P. L. (1994). In pursuit of a dual agenda: Creating a middle level professional development school. In L. Darling-Hammond (Ed.), *Professional development schools: Schools for developing a profession* (pp. 50-73). New York: Teachers College Press.

Holmes Group. (1990). *Tomorrow's schools: Principles for the design of professional development schools.* East Lansing, MI: Author.

Jett-Simpson, M., Pugach, M. C., & Whipp, J. (1992, April). *Portrait of an urban professional development school.* Paper presented at the annual meeting of the American Educational Research Association, San Francisco.

Lemlech, J. K., & Hertzog-Foliart, H. (1993). Linking school and university through collegial student teaching. *Teacher Education Quarterly, 20*(4), 19-27.

Lemlech, J. K., Hertzog-Foliart, H., & Hackl, A. (1994). The Los Angeles Professional Practice School: A study of mutual impact. In L. Darling-Hammond (Ed.), *Professional development schools: Schools for developing a profession* (pp. 156-175). New York: Teachers College Press.

Lewis, M. D. (1992, April). *Professional development schools: Conditions for readiness.* Paper presented at the annual meeting of the American Educational Research Association, San Francisco.

Miller, L., & Silvernail, D. (1994). Wells Junior High School: Evolution of a professional development school. In L. Darling-Hammond (Ed.), *Professional development schools: Schools for developing a profession* (pp. 28-49). New York: Teachers College Press.

Moore, K., & Hopkins, S. (1993). Professional development schools: Partnerships in teacher preparation. *Contemporary Education, 64*(4), 219-222.

Morris, V. G., & Nunnery, J. (1993, November). *Teacher empowerment in a professional development school collaborative: Pilot assessment* (Tech. Rep. No. 931101). Memphis, TN: Memphis State University, Center for Research in Educational Policy. (ERIC Document Reproduction Service No. ED 368 678)

Navarro, J. (1992). *Will teachers say what we want to hear? Dilemmas of teacher voice* (Report No. 92-5). East Lansing: Michigan State University, National Center for Research on Teaching Learning. (ERIC Document Reproduction Service No. ED 351 283)

Neufeld, J., & Freeman, D. (1993, February). *Teachers as teacher educators within a professional development school context.* Paper presented at the annual meeting of the American Association of Colleges for Teacher Education, San Diego, CA.

Nevins, R. J. (1993). *Classroom teachers as mentors: Their perspectives on helping novices learn to teach.* Unpublished doctoral dissertation, Michigan State University.

Nihlen, A. (1992, April). *Schools as centers for reflection and inquiry: Research for teacher empowerment.* Paper presented at the annual meeting of the American Educational Research Association, San Francisco.

Pasch, S. H., & Pugach, M. C. (1990). Collaborative planning for urban professional development schools. *Contemporary Education, 61*(3), 135-143.

Putnam, J. (1992). *Professional development schools: Emerging changes in educators and the professional community.* Michigan State University, East Lansing. (ERIC Document Reproduction Service No. ED 370-890)

Romerdahl, N. S. (1991, April). *Shared leadership in a professional development center.* Paper presented at the annual meeting of the American Educational Research Association, Chicago. (ERIC Document Reproduction Service No. ED 337 420)

Rosaen, C. L., & Lindquist, B. (1992, November). *Collaborative teaching and research: Asking "What does it mean?"* (Series No. 73). East Lansing: Michigan State University, Center for the Learning and Teaching of Elementary Subjects, Institute for Research on Teaching.

Rushcamp, S., & Roehler, L. R. (1992). Characteristics supporting change in a professional development school. *Journal of Teacher Education, 43,* 19-27.

Schack, G., & Overturf, B. (1994, April). *Professional development teams: Stepping stone to professional development schools.* Paper presented at the annual meeting of the American Educational Research Association, New Orleans, LA.

Snyder, J. (1994). Perils and potentials: A tale of two professional development schools. In L. Darling-Hammond (Ed.), *Professional development schools: Schools for developing a profession* (pp. 98-125). New York: Teachers College Press.

Stallings, J. (1991, April). *Connecting preservice teacher education and inservice professional development: A professional development school.* Paper presented at the annual meeting of the American Educational Research Association, Chicago.

Stanulis, R. N. (1995). Classroom teachers as mentors: Possibilities for participation in a professional development school context. *Teaching and Teacher Education, 11,* 331-344.

Whitford, B. L. (1994). Permission, persistence, and resistance: Linking high school restructuring with teacher education reform. In L. Darling-Hammond (Ed.), *Professional development schools: Schools for developing a profession* (pp. 74-97). New York: Teachers College Press.

Yopp, H., Guillaume, A., & Savage, T. (1993-1994). Collaboration at the grass roots: Implementing the professional development school concept. *Action in Teacher Education, 15*(4), 29-35.

Zeichner, K. (1992). *Connecting genuine teacher development to the struggle for social justice* (Issue Paper No. 92-1). East Lansing: Michigan State University, National Center for Research on Teacher Learning.

5 Collegial Support Teams

Peer Supervision and Professional Growth

Margaret J. Johnson

Lucy Brown

Margaret J. Johnson is Assistant Professor of Elementary Education at Texas Tech University in Lubbock, Texas. She has conducted research on institutional development through democratic restructuring. Recent publications include an article, "When Shared Decision Making Works," which appeared in the fall 1996 issue of *American Educational Research Journal.*

Lucy Brown is Principal of Ramirez Elementary School in Lubbock, Texas. She has been active in school-university partnerships and has done presentations on professional development schools at Holmes Group conferences (regional and national) and at the annual conference of the Association for Supervision and Curriculum Development.

ABSTRACT

Peer supervision, because it is a collaborative activity embedded in the everyday lives of teachers, has been touted as a promising means to building teachers' professional capacity. In this study, teachers in a large elementary school were organized into collegial support teams (CSTs) to supervise their teaching performance and promote their professional growth.

Results of the study indicate that the CST process fostered collegiality and experimentation. Specifically, the process created for the teachers a "safe zone" in which they could admit shortcomings and work to improve their practice. The organization of the teams as schools within the school is described and the support needed for the project's success is discussed.

Reforms that invest time in teacher learning and give teachers greater autonomy are our best hope for improving America's schools.

Linda Darling-Hammond (1996, p. 4)

School improvement efforts in the past decade have been moving away from the implementation of specific innovations and toward approaches that seek to improve education day to day (Joyce & Calhoun, 1995). Peer supervision, because it is a collaborative exercise embedded in the daily life of a school, holds promise as a means to educational improvement. Educators have long argued that collegiality is a key to building the capacity of teachers and of institutions (e.g., see Little, 1990). The shift toward more collaborative supervisory practices has the potential of reducing the isolation of traditional teaching and fostering a school culture conducive to teacher learning (see Darling-Hammond, 1990; Lieberman, 1990).

Theoretical Framework

Traditional supervisory practices have been found to thwart teacher collegiality and intensify the dominant-submissive relationship between teachers and principal (Haefele, 1992). Although teacher supervision is intended to enhance teachers' professional growth, it has had—too often— quite a contrary effect. Krovetz and Cohick (1993) described traditional teacher supervision as an "onerous and demoralizing" process (p. 331) that serves to keep teachers isolated from one another and to inhibit innovative practices.

The emphasis in traditional supervision is on the behavior exhibited by a teacher during a particular and limited observation period. Phillips and Glickman (1991) maintained, however, that skillful teaching is cognitive in nature and that professional growth is ongoing and developmental.

An evaluation system more conducive to cognitive growth and developmental change is one that promotes collegiality and involves teachers working in professional support teams (see Krovetz & Cohick, 1993). There is growing evidence that collegial supervision leads to professional growth. For example, in Nolan and Hillkirk's (1991) study of veteran teachers, the authors found that the opportunity to discuss rationales for professional decisions with colleagues had multiple, positive effects on teachers. Arrendondo, Brody, Zimmerman, and Moffett (1995) reported on what they called "a growing trend" of districts experimenting with supervision as group collaboration (p. 77). They found evidence that group supervision can lead to schools becoming more collaborative and reflective institutions.

Peer coaching is often an integral part of peer supervision. In the 1980s, Joyce and Showers (1980) advocated peer coaching as a way to implement specific educational innovations. Recently, they have come to think of peer coaching as a way to foster teacher improvement on a continuous basis (see Showers & Joyce, 1996). They argued that the coaching must center on curriculum and instruction and that the specific focus should emerge from the teachers' own teaching contexts.

Arnold (1995) noted that the principles underlying the creation of environments conducive to learning in children also underlie the creation of learning environments conducive to adult learning. Brooks and Brooks (1993), in their description of a constructivist classroom, asserted that learners only know the knowledge they construct themselves, that there is great learning potential in explaining something to others, and that learning takes place within a social context. Collegial support teams engaging in peer supervision can create just such a learning situation for teachers.

Background to the Study

The elementary school that served as the site of this study is located in a predominantly low-socioeconomic area of a midsized city in the Southwest. Approximately 95% of the 700 children attending the school receive free or reduced-price lunches. The school campus lies just outside the boundaries of a large university, and, since the fall of 1992, the school has had a professional development school (PDS) partnership with the university. As a PDS, the school has engaged in a number of programs to improve the professional growth of its teachers and the achievement of its students.

For 3 years, the school's 42 faculty members have been implementing a collegial support team (CST) project as an alternative to the state appraisal system (an observation instrument based on the elements of the lesson cycle). All teachers who have taught 3 years or more may use the CST as their only form of teacher evaluation. Novice teachers must still be appraised using the state-approved instrument but are also placed on CSTs to foster their professional development.

Teachers are grouped in CSTs of seven teachers across grade levels, kindergarten through sixth grade. Children move through the grades in cohort groups with the teachers in a particular CST, forming five small schools within the school. Subject specialist teachers are grouped in separate teams. Within each team, the teachers choose partners with whom they engage in a peer supervision sequence that includes a previsit conference, a classroom visit, and a postvisit conference (see Ackland, 1991). They are encouraged to visit other classrooms as well and frequently do so.

Teachers meet in their CSTs every week to discuss professional concerns. These include practical matters such as scheduling classroom visits and educational issues such as curriculum alignment. All teachers prepare professional portfolios, which they share with the principal and with the members of their CST. Teachers videotape their teaching and videotape conferences with their partners. They select clips of conferences and lessons to include in their portfolios. At the beginning of the year, all teachers prepare a contract explaining their professional goals for that year. The contract is shared with and signed by all members of the teacher's CST. At the end of the year, all teachers write a reflective essay on their professional growth. This is also shared with the other members of the CST. Other procedures (the number of visits, length of visits, emphases on improvement efforts) are decided by the individual CSTs.

Objectives

In this study, the researchers focused on the impact of the CST experience on the teachers' professional development. Little (1982) found that norms of collegiality and experimentation characterize successful schools. We sought to explore ways in which the CSTs were encouraging collegiality and experimentation. The teachers were asked the following questions in a CST survey:

1. Did the CSTs foster collegiality? If so, how so?

2. Did participation in a CST encourage experimentation? If so, how so?
3. How did the CST experience aid in personal, professional development?
4. What impact did the vertical alignment of the five CST teams of classroom teachers have on the effectiveness of the project?

Method and Data Sources

Data for this qualitative study were obtained from several different sources. All 42 teachers completed the open-ended survey form. We also read the reflective essays written by all teachers at the end of the school year (beginning with the second year of the project) describing their professional growth. In-depth interviews were conducted with 10 teachers selected to represent a variety of years of service and grade-level/subject assignments. All interviews lasted at least 30 minutes, were taped, and the tapes were transcribed. Interviews were conducted after collecting the surveys and also served to check the survey data.

Data were analyzed using the constant comparative method of content analysis (Glaser & Strauss, 1967; Strauss, 1987). Themes and patterns in the data were identified, clarified, and verified (see Guba, 1981). Issues of reliability and validity were addressed using the methods described by Goetz and LeCompte (1984).

Results

All teachers reported that the CST process fostered collegiality. Their comments on their CST experiences were overwhelmingly positive. We found there were several factors that contributed to teachers' enthusiasm. The most frequently mentioned factor was the opportunity the CSTs afforded for improving teaching without reprisals for admitting weaknesses. Teachers also told us that visiting each others' classrooms provided them with a rich, professional resource. They reported an increase in experimentation informed by their talk with their colleagues. As the children progressed in cohort groups through the grades, they were assigned to teachers in the same CST. All teachers began to think of all children taught by CST colleagues as "theirs." Teachers expressed a sense of responsibility for the professional development of their peers. Although they acknowledged the time, effort, and training required for CST success, they reported—to a person—their support for the process and their desire for it to continue.

Creation of a Safe Zone for Professional Growth

Lortie (1975) claimed that the culture of schools does not permit teachers to talk about classroom failure, or even to ask questions in a way that might be construed as asking for help. Teachers in this study noted that the CST process allowed them to invite help from peers without worry about adverse judgments. One teacher described the difference between CST appraisal and the state system as "more freedom, less worrying about failure." Another teacher said that the CST process

> allows me much discretion as to the areas I'd like to strengthen. Therefore, I am truly growing with no fear of being labeled or singled out as the "teacher who is having problems." I am aware of problem spheres and I work to correct these with the aid of my colleagues.

And another teacher spoke about the "positive interaction" of team members. "In both teams I have been a member of," she noted, "the team has supported any targeted area a member wants/needs by observing and helpfully suggesting new approaches."

The perceived need for safety was mentioned by two thirds of the teachers. In the past, they admitted, they had been reluctant to confess weaknesses. "Now," one wrote, "I can work on my weaknesses without being intimidated." Observing one another also helped teachers see that their problems were not unique. "I no longer feel that I'm the only teacher with trouble areas." A 25-year veteran teacher wrote: "We get to learn that many of the problems we are trying to improve on also are shared by the colleagues we are trying to help! Therefore, together, we attempt to come up with great solutions."

Under the state appraisal system, a third-grade teacher reported that she would never have said to an administrator, " 'I'm having a hard time with questioning. Would you come in and help me with that?' You wouldn't admit it. With your CST members, you're honest. You ask for help when you need it." A 10-year veteran teacher said that when she had been observed by administrators in the past, she wanted everything to be "absolutely perfect. And things are not like that. With other teachers, I can say, this is my weakness, and I can focus on specific areas of improvement and not be worrying all the while."

A first-year teacher, who, by state regulation, was being appraised using the state-approved observation instrument, reported the benefits of being a novice who is part of a CST:

> It takes a lot of the pressure of "one visit" off. When the principal comes in to observe, it's OK. I'm used to having people watch me teach. Being in a CST gives me, my colleagues, and my principal a more accurate picture of what is happening in the classroom.

Value of Visiting Other People's Classes

The school's principal noted the benefits she had gained from observing teachers under the old appraisal system. "I learned so much from visiting classrooms. It made me realize how important it could be for teachers to visit each other." One teacher claimed that in the past teachers had rarely set foot in each other's classrooms. "I learn from looking at the teaching environment," she said. "I find that people on my team set up teaching bulletin boards and centers that let me see how the classroom environment can teach."

Another teacher reported that some of the teachers on her team had been taking graduate courses from the nearby university as part of the school's PDS partnership. "They are trying out different approaches, especially in literacy development. Now, even though the grade levels are different, I am learning things I can adapt to my situation." In the past, one teacher said, "We would sometimes tell about what we are doing in our classes. Sometimes. Now, we can *see* other teachers' teaching methods." A third-year teacher said that it had been beneficial for her

> to see these veteran teachers and get ideas from them. And, in turn, I'm able to share some new strategies, so I've been able to help them, too. Sometimes it's good to have fresh blood. With the CSTs, we can all learn from each other.

Showers and Joyce (1996) noted that many people assume that the heart of peer coaching comes from teachers offering advice after an observation. They claimed, however, that the one being observed is often the "coach" and the one doing the observing is the "coached." Darling-

Hammond (1996) asserted that when teachers work together, the wisdom acquired by excellent teachers becomes accessible to others. The teachers in this study reported benefits from observing, being observed, and the conversations that preceded and followed the observation periods. Like Arrendondo and her colleagues (Arrendondo et al., 1995), they found that peer observation leads to two-way growth.

An Increase in Experimentation

Little (1982, 1990) identified norms of experimentation as characteristic of successful schools. Arnold (1995) studied teacher dialogue and suggested that creating opportunities for professional discourse leads to greater experimentation among teachers.

In this study, teachers reported that many of them had experimented with their teaching in the past. With the advent of CSTs, however, they noted an increase in experimentation based on information and a rationale. They stated that in the past they had tried new things at the suggestion of colleagues or presenters at inservice sessions. The need to justify practices to peers, however, encouraged teachers to seek reasons for using new strategies or materials. One second-year teacher wrote that being in a CST "makes me think about my teaching because other teachers notice things that I might not. When I explain what I am doing, I give it more thought." Another teacher said that she had always experimented, "but now I do it with input from my peers."

A veteran teacher explained how restricted she had felt by the state appraisal system observation instrument and how the format of the instrument had driven her instruction. "I no longer feel it is important to incorporate the entire lesson cycle for every lesson. Parts of the cycle are just different for discovery learning, critical and creative thinking." She found that the CSTs gave her room for trying out innovative practices that would not have fit in the lesson cycle format.

A 25-year veteran teacher wrote that being a member of a CST "allows us as teachers to become more creative and bolder at trying new things/ objectives with our students. Allowing someone to coach us and encourage us really motivates us to become better at what we are doing." A fifth-grade teacher who had taught for 10 years said that she had always been innovative. "I am always trying new ways. This year, for example, I have really gotten into using computers in the classroom. But now, I can get feedback and help when I need it."

Benefits of Forming a
Small School Within a School

A number of educators have recently touted the benefits of the small school (see Boyer, 1995; Sergiovanni, 1995). Large schools can gain some of those benefits through structures that personalize teaching. Darling-Hammond (1996) claimed that when schools contrive ways to create personalized units within large schools, student achievement improves.

In this study, the teachers were organized into CSTs composed of groups of teachers who came to know each other and the children served by teachers in the CST very well. In the past, teachers had mainly exchanged ideas only with other teachers at their grade level. Although grade-level connections continued with the start of the CST process, placing teachers in groups across grade levels served to break up old conversational patterns and create new patterns of who talked to whom.

Teachers wrote about the value of articulating curriculum through the grade levels through vertical planning. "It has been very helpful to see what is being taught and what strategies are being used in the grades above and below." One teacher noted how surprised she was that she had so much in common with teachers at other grade levels. Interactions between classroom teachers working at different grade levels and among specialists working with different subject areas helped foster a greater appreciation for the work of others.

Teachers reported working across grade levels in buddy-pairing projects with colleagues on their team. They also reported an increase in collaborative planning and curriculum development work. The teachers were placed in their CSTs according to the cohort of students they taught. Children stay together as a group and, as they progress through the grades, move from one teacher to another in the same CST. As teachers observed children in the grade level below them, they were watching their future students. As they observed students in the grade levels above, they saw familiar faces. One third-grade teacher said that she felt the CST process

helps me get a better idea of where my kids are headed, what preparation they need. I get to know the kids that I will have next year. They know me a little bit and they feel comfortable about going into third grade. I visited the fourth-grade class of the kiddos I had last year and that was really neat because I could see how much they've grown.

A fifth-grade teacher spoke at length about the value she saw in vertically aligning the CSTs:

> We work closely with each other and we think of the children in the team's classes as our children because they *are* our children. You have a stake in the process. When I have concerns about children I can talk to teachers who had them in previous years. It is as though we have set up a plan for each child. They know what is coming. It is more personalized. We get to know the kids and we get to know their families.

The school has a total of about 700 students. Placing the teachers and their students in teams makes for smaller, more personal units even within a large elementary school.

Teachers Beginning to Take Responsibility for the Professional Development of Peers

Brooks and Brooks (1993) emphasized the importance of the social aspects of learning. Teachers in this study wrote personal growth plans at the beginning of the year, which were then read and signed by all members of their CSTs. At the end of the school year, all teachers compiled a portfolio of artifacts documenting their growth and wrote a reflective essay. These were shared with the other members of the team and with the principal.

Teachers noted that the CSTs created a nurturing atmosphere. One teacher observed that her "fellow CST members know what I am doing and are always encouraging and helpful." A veteran teacher said that she felt a responsibility when being observed by other teachers to exhibit good practice. "Being a member of a CST, I am encouraged to try to do my best as a model." Other veteran teachers spoke about the talk that takes place during the CST meetings. At the time of her interview, the teacher reported that much of the talk centered on the concerns of first- and second-year teachers. "They know they still have a lot of learning to do, that they are at an early stage, and now they are not afraid to ask." She observed that more-experienced teachers "naturally" take on a mentoring role within the CST.

Need for Collegial Support

This was not only a new project but a new concept, and teachers and administrators needed support in their efforts. The PDS relationship with a nearby college of education enabled the school's faculty to receive training in peer coaching, group dynamics, and collegial supervision from a university faculty member. Also, the principal engaged the services of a private consultant to provide additional training sessions.

Teachers commented on the increase in their workload with the CST process. Although they were very positive about their participation in CSTs, they observed that the process takes time. Arnold (1995) and Darling-Hammond (1996) argued that time must be found during the school day for meetings. This is not so at the school. Weekly CST meetings are held after school. Assembling portfolios, writing reflections, and pre- and postconferences also are often relegated to after-school hours.

"It is time-consuming but worthwhile" was a typical teacher comment. "Anyone who is thinking about using CSTs," a second-year teacher noted, "should be ready to do extra work because it is a lot of work. This is not something that happens twice a year; this is something that happens all year long."

Sahakian and Stockton (1996) observed that teachers' fears of being observed by peers often creates an emotional obstacle to peer observations. Teachers in this study noted that engaging in peer supervision is not something teachers automatically know how to do. "When we began," one teacher said, "it was such a new process, we were all a little concerned about how it would actually work out." The trainers helped the teachers understand the principles underlying peer supervision such as an emphasis on continual improvement and the need for building a supportive environment. They also provided some very practical suggestions. "We learned how to be positive," one teacher said, "how to sit together so that we are sitting side-by-side. How to listen to the concerns of the person you observe. How to feed back what you saw, simply tell them what you observed."

The individual CSTs have considerable freedom in deciding how and when they will conduct their meetings, what they will discuss, and how they will schedule their peer visits. If conflicts and problems arise, they are handled by the CST itself. Teachers mentioned, however, the need for ongoing support. "We need to continue having training on peer coaching, trust building, and problem solving or finding solutions to road blocks as they surface."

The process was supported from its inception by the school's administration. The principal applied for the necessary waivers and persuasively petitioned state authorities to allow the school to initiate alternative teacher assessment. She arranged for the inservice training and participated actively in the sessions to become educated herself, along with the faculty, in peer supervision practices. She worked with the faculty to plan the overall shape the CSTs would take.

Discussion

There is little doubt from their written comments and remarks during interviews that the teachers at the school perceived great value in their participation in their CSTs. All of them—from the first-year novice to the 25-year veteran—expressed the desire to improve their practice and noted that the CST process helped them do so. Those who had been evaluated using the state appraisal system recognized its inhibiting effect on their professional growth. They used words and terms such as "safe," "free-dom," and, more frequently, "comfortable" to describe the CST process when comparing it with the previous system. The CST process allowed for learning from mistakes and seeking solutions to problems without fear of recrimination. Whereas their previous system had encouraged teachers to hide their weaknesses, the current system encourages them to improve weak areas.

In all themes surfaced by the surveys, reflections, and interviews, collegiality played a key role. The CST process enabled teachers to visit each others' classrooms and provided a forum for professional conversations and collaborative planning. The safe zone teachers described was a shared zone, a place where, through interactions with peers, they could experiment and make informed attempts at professional improvement.

The CST process has been supported by the school's PDS relationship with a nearby college of education. The school's PDS status aided its waiver request to the state education agency to implement CSTs. A member of the college faculty provided training in peer supervision and was available to help the faculty as they learned to develop the trust levels necessary for the creation of that safe zone cited by many of the teachers. The school's principal was instrumental in instituting the CSTs and offered continual support and encouragement.

Implications

Any number of educators have urged teachers to unbolt the classroom door (e.g. Darling-Hammond, 1990; Lieberman, 1990) and engage in collaborative professional activities. For schools to reform and improve, teachers must—individually and collectively—build their professional capacity. There is strong evidence from educational research that this is facilitated through collegial interaction (see Donaldson, 1993; Little, 1990). The results of this study suggest that peer supervision in collegial support teams offers a promising means to promote collegial professional development. Darling-Hammond (1996) asserted recently that the possibilities for rethinking the responsibilities of teachers are probably greater now than they have ever been in the past. Evidence from this study indicates that when teacher responsibilities are expanded to include peer supervision, the process can foster collaboration, facilitate experimentation, and promote professional discourse. When teachers are grouped in collegial teams around cohorts of children, the process can also lead to a more personalized organization of a large school.

The project described here was in its third year. Participants had had time to receive training, gain confidence, and become comfortable with the process. Teachers and administrators reported great satisfaction with their experiences, but cautioned that it had taken them time to realize the benefits their CSTs could bring. Results suggest that collegial supervision—given time and support—may indeed foster personal and institutional growth.

References

Ackland, R. (1991). A review of the peer coaching literature. *Journal of Staff Development, 12*(1), 22-27.

Arnold, G. C. S. (1995). Teacher dialogues: A constructivist model of staff development. *Journal of Staff Development, 16*(4), 34-37.

Arrendondo, D. E., Brody, J. L., Zimmerman, D. P., & Moffett, C. A. (1995). Pushing the envelope in supervision. *Educational Leadership, 53*(3), 74-78.

Boyer, E. (1995). *The basic school: Community for learning.* Princeton, NJ: Carnegie Foundation.

Brooks, J. G., & Brooks, M. G. (1993). *The case for constructivist classrooms.* Alexandria, VA: Association for Supervision and Curriculum Development.

Darling-Hammond, L. (1990). Teacher professionalism: Why and how? In A. Lieberman (Ed.), *Schools as collaborative cultures: Creating the future now* (pp. 25-50). New York: Falmer.

Darling-Hammond, L. (1996). The quiet revolution: Rethinking teacher development. *Educational Leadership, 53*(6), 4-11.

Donaldson, G. A. (1993). Working smarter together. *Educational Leadership, 50,* 12-16.

Glaser, B., & Strauss, A. L. (1967). *The discovery of grounded theory: Strategies for qualitative research.* New York: Aldine.

Goetz, J. P., & LeCompte, M. D. (1984). *Ethnography and qualitative design in educational research.* Orlando, FL: Academic Press.

Guba, E. G. (1981). Criteria for assessing the trustworthiness of naturalistic inquiry. *Educational Communications and Technology Journal, 29*(2), 75-91.

Haefele, D. L. (1992). Evaluating teachers: An alternative model. *Journal of Personnel Evaluation in Education, 5,* 335-345.

Joyce, B., & Calhoun, E. (1995). School renewal: An inquiry, not a formula. *Educational Leadership, 52*(7), 51-55.

Joyce, B., & Showers, B. (1980). Improving inservice training: The message of research. *Educational Leadership, 37,* 163-172.

Krovetz, M., & Cohick, D. (1993). Professional collegiality can lead to school change. *Phi Delta Kappan, 75,* 331-333.

Lieberman, A. (1990). Navigating the four C's: Building a bridge over troubled waters. *Phi Delta Kappan, 71,* 531-533.

Little, J. W. (1982). Norms of collegiality and experimentation: Workplace conditions of school success. *American Educational Research Journal, 19,* 325-340.

Little, J. W. (1990). Teachers as colleagues. In A. Lieberman (Ed.), *Schools as collaborative cultures: Creating the future now* (pp. 165-194). New York: Falmer.

Lortie, D. (1975). *Schoolteacher.* Chicago: University of Chicago Press.

Nolan, J. F., & Hillkirk, K. (1991). The effects of a reflective coaching project on veteran teachers. *Journal of Curriculum and Supervision, 7,* 62-76.

Phillips, M. D., & Glickman, C. D. (1991). Peer coaching: Developmental approach to enhancing teacher thinking. *Journal of Staff Development, 12*(2), 20-25.

Sahakian, P., & Stockton, J. (1996). Opening doors: Teacher-guided observation. *Educational Leadership, 53*(6), 34-37.

Sergiovanni, T. (1995). Small schools, great exceptions. *Educational Leadership, 53*(3), 48-52.

Showers, B., & Joyce, B. (1996). The evolution of peer coaching. *Educational Leadership, 53*(6), 12-16.

Strauss, A. L. (1987). *Qualitative analysis for social scientists.* New York: Cambridge University Press.

6 Collaborative Action Research for Local School Improvement

Dennis C. Zuelke

Teresa M. Nichols

Dennis C. Zuelke is Associate Professor of Educational Administration in the College of Education and Professional Studies, Jacksonville State University, Jacksonville, Alabama. His current research interests include school climate studies involving perceptual survey research within local school communities. His latest book, *Educational Private Practice*, was published in 1996.

Teresa M. Nichols is Principal of Montevallo Elementary School, Montevallo, Alabama. She was formerly Associate Professor and Director of Clinical Experiences in the College of Education, Jacksonville State University, Jacksonville, Alabama. Her interests are primarily in the areas of teacher professional development and preservice teacher education.

ABSTRACT

This is really a story of two professors' efforts over 3 years to assist a high school to do action research and, more important, follow up with plans and action. An adaptation of Richard Sagor's model of collaborative action research was used to guide the project. Action research results indicated differing perceptions among teachers, students, and parents regarding the climate of the school for students. Teacher and student focus groups helped determine 14 improvement areas, some of which became targets for action planning for school improvement. Despite the efforts of the professors, the high school did not follow through on most of the action plans for school improvement based on the outcomes of the research. The professors learned that once control of a research project shifts to the school's staff, use of the findings is determined by that staff regardless of how the professors interpreted those findings. However, the five initial objectives of this collaborative action research were met.

The research and follow-up presented here were guided by the school improvement literature and generally followed the model for collaborative action research outlined by Sagor (1993). The project responded to calls for collaborative efforts between schools and colleges (Calhoun, 1993; Herrick, 1992; Jacullo-Noto, 1992; Knight, Wiseman, & Smith, 1992).

The Problem and Research Procedures

This research project was an effort to respond to the identified needs at a small-city high school in the school's efforts to improve relations among parents, teachers, and about 750 students in Grades 7-12. Two educational administration professors worked collaboratively with the high school principal, assistant principal, and two counselors in an action research project that consisted of developing, administering, and analyzing data from perception survey instruments that were anticipated to provide recommendations for action plans for school improvement. The project's objectives were to

1. Involve the administration, faculty, parents, and students of an area school in the process of action research through a collaborative effort with university professors.
2. Determine faculty, parent, and student perceptions of climate for students in advance and standard diploma programs.
3. Determine the faculty perceptions of school climate for emotionally conflicted students.
4. Determine faculty and parent perceptions of the educational needs of seventh- and eighth-grade students.
5. Assist school administrators to become more confident in designing, implementing, interpreting, and reporting action research.

A five-step action research process guided the project as follows: (a) problem formulation, (b) data collection through survey instruments, (c) data analysis and interpretation, (d) reporting the findings, and (e) action planning for school improvement.

The problem formulation step involved brainstorming sessions in the summer and early fall of 1993 with the principal, assistant principal, and counselors to address problems they have identified through a performance-based accreditation procedure mandated by the state department of education. This step indicated that a threefold problem should be investigated: (a) school climate for students in advance and standard diploma programs, (b) school climate for emotionally conflicted students, and (c) unmet educational needs of seventh- and eighth-grade students in the school.

Sagor (1993) argued that "analytic discourse" should occur during the problem formulation step along with "reflective interviewing" among the faculty in a school. The sharing of issues within a specified time frame and set of rules did not occur among the faculty. Only the four personnel (principal, assistant principal, and two counselors) were effectively involved with the professors in a sharing of issues during the problem formulation stage. Also, faculty members interviewing each other, as partners, within a specified time frame and set of guidelines on issues of concern to them did not occur. Instead, a form of analytic discourse occurred after the survey instruments had been administered, data compiled, and data analyzed by the two professors. The four key staff members were frequently involved in discussion of the findings with the professors. Later, discussions of the findings occurred among the school's faculty in small focus groups led by a teacher and student focus groups led by the professors. In these focus groups, a form of reflective interviewing occurred as questions were addressed concerning a selected number of findings derived from the analysis of the survey data.

The absence of direct faculty involvement in the formulation of the problem step may well be related to the way the faculty and, ultimately, the principal followed up on the findings and subsequent discussions toward action plans and interventions. Further discussion in this chapter reveals what actually happened in the follow-up stage of this collaborative action research project.

The data collection involved faculty, parent, and student perceptions through survey instruments designed by the university professors after several consultations with the school's administrators and counselors. Four perceptual response instruments were developed: two for two parent groups, one for teachers, and one for students in Grades 9-12. The instruments were piloted in a neighboring high school in November 1993. The teacher instrument was administered by the researchers during an after-school meeting in the high school library in mid-January 1994. The next morning, homeroom teachers administered the student instrument to the students during the homeroom period. Parent instruments were mailed to the households of students in Grades 7 and 8 and 9-12 at the same time.

Sagor (1993) recommended "triangulation" for data collection involving more than one source of information. Here the four key school personnel and the two professors stayed closer to the guidelines for action research enunciated by Sagor. There were three sources of perceptual information: teachers, students, and parents. Viewing what transpired in another way, the three sources could be (a) perceptions, (b) faculty focus group discussions, and (c) student focus group interviews.

The data analysis and interpretation step included the application of descriptive statistics, mainly measures of central tendency, and a one-way analysis of variance. The last two steps, reporting and action planning, are discussed throughout the remainder of this chapter.

Data Analysis and Findings

The high school had two academic levels for students: advance diploma and standard diploma. Generally, advance diploma students took more rigorous courses, including advanced placement or honors courses, and standard diploma students took less rigorous courses and were often found in the vocational education curriculum. Yet both diploma-level students could be in the same courses, subject to the same performance standards and eligible for "honors" student designation by achieving an 85% average in coursework. Of the 378 Grade 9-12 students who completed the perceptual questionnaire, 65% were advance diploma and 35% standard diploma. The number of students completing the questionnaire was 89% of the entire Grade 9-12 student body. Seventh- and eighth-grade students did not complete a questionnaire. Human subjects research restrictions would have required additional assurances paperwork for younger participants.

Parent characteristics indicated that mothers were most likely to complete the perceptual questionnaire. For the 18-question seventh- and eighth-grade parent questionnaire, mothers completed 80% of the questionnaires, and fathers completed 20%. For the 32-question Grade 9-12 parent questionnaire, mothers completed 77% of the questionnaires and fathers, 20%. About 69% of the Grade 9-12 parent respondents were parents of advance diploma students, 20% identified themselves as parents of standard diploma students, and 11% did not designate either diploma. A total of 265 parents returned completed questionnaires. Of this number, 157 were parents of students in Grades 9 through 12 and 108 were parents of students in Grades 7 and 8.

Of the 43 teacher respondents, 27 were women (63%) and 16 were men (37%). They completed three perceptual questionnaires: a 27-question instrument on advance and standard diploma students, the 18-question seventh- and eighth-grade questionnaire, and a 21-question instrument on emotionally conflicted and disruptive students. Approximately 56% currently taught seventh and eighth graders, and 44% did not. Of the latter group, 16% or seven teachers indicated they had never taught seventh and eighth graders. All but five of the teachers were regular education. Only 28% or 12 teachers had 10 or fewer years of teaching experience, 37% had 11 to 20 years, and 35% had 21 years or more. Just three teachers on the entire staff had 3 or fewer years of experience.

The hundreds of descriptive findings tended to show that teachers' perceptions differed, sometimes substantially, with those of students and parents. Hence, the school's climate was implicated by the many discrepancies. The analysis of variance (ANOVA) findings further substantiated the differing perceptions among respondent groups. There were more than 100 significant differences in the means of the respondent groups out of nearly 650 ANOVA analyses.

The ANOVA findings rather clearly indicated that teachers had more unanimity in their perceptions of school climate and program variables than students or parents. With fewer significant differences than the other groups, teachers reflected more stable, less volatile perceptions of the high school that perhaps appropriately fitted an aging, highly experienced teaching staff that had observed very little turnover in recent years.

By contrast, the ANOVA findings also indicated that parents and students had more disagreement among themselves concerning their perceptions of different categories of students, teachers, and the teaching-learning climate in the school. The differences here suggested that these respondent groups reflected less stable, therefore changing, and more heterogeneous views of what the high school should be doing on behalf of the students in attendance there.

The host of student and parent written comments on the questionnaires reflected much ambivalence over the issues presented in the questionnaires. Some pointed remarks challenged the teachers and the school to be more responsive to student needs in curriculum as well as attitudes toward students and in teaching techniques. There appeared to be fewer concerns here over disruptive or unmotivated students and unsupportive parents compared to the teachers' questionnaire responses.

Discussion of the Follow-Up to the Research Findings

In Sagor's (1993) model, it is crucial that action researchers find as many ways as possible to report the findings from the analysis of the research data. Led by the two educational administration professors, the findings or results were reported in several ways. First, there were ongoing meetings with the four key personnel in the school as additional data analyses occurred over time. Tables of descriptive and ANOVA statistics along with summaries were presented and discussed with these personnel. Furthermore, the tables and summaries were reviewed with eight teacher focus group leaders and to a lesser extent with students in their focus groups. Also, the professors provided to the school's faculty a synthesis of teacher and student thoughts and ideas derived from the interaction that occurred in the focus groups. The synthesis report identified 14 concerns with suggested "action" for each of the concerns.

On October 10, 1994, the teachers used an inservice day to discuss the implications of the descriptive and inferential statistical findings in small groups.

Eight small focus groups had from four to six participants and met in separate rooms throughout the school for at least 1 hour during the morning. At the conclusion of their meetings, the focus group leaders turned in the worksheets to the professors and principal. Over the noon hour, the small focus group meetings results were compiled, edited, and grouped by the professors and principal (with the superintendent looking on).

After lunch, the entire staff met in the school's library with the professors, principal, and assistant principal to hear and discuss the results of the small focus group meetings. Some 35 suggestions for improving teacher-student-parent communications and relationships were reported back to the staff. The principal and assistant principal commented on how informative the research had been for their practice as administrators and that they obtained further insights on faculty thinking regarding school climate improvement issues. One of the professors concluded the inservice activity by congratulating the staff on using perceptual survey research findings to help them determine ways their teaching and, ultimately, the school could continue to improve.

Slowness of Effort in Action Planning

A most critical point in a collaborative action research project is the action to be taken as a result of the research findings and conclusions. That point was reached after the October 10 inservice day. In addition to the issues of differing purposes among the collaborators and the shift of project ownership to the school's staff, the enthusiasm to keep moving ahead was likely to wane for one or both parties to the collaboration (Bickel & Hattrup, 1995; Calhoun, 1994; Cohen & Manion, 1994).

The professors perceived that any planning for action by the school's staff in light of the concerns identified during the October inservice day had not taken place in the succeeding weeks. Whereas several reasons may have contributed to the apparent lethargy, the essential one appeared to be the lack of ownership by the staff, students, and parents in the project. The school's administrators or counselors had not pursued any action of their own or asked the staff to take hold of the project and plan for action.

Energizing the Action Effort, Involving Students

In late November, the professors contacted the school's principal and suggested that a meeting occur between the professors and the eight faculty focus group leaders to identify those teacher and student survey questions that analysis showed were concerns and, also, were of interest to the teachers. The professors indicated that the questions should then be presented to small student focus groups composed of 11th- and 12th-grade advance and standard diploma students for discussion and their suggestions. The two professors offered to chair the student focus groups to encourage openness and discussion by the students. The principal agreed, and a meeting was arranged in early December between the professors and the faculty focus group leaders.

The professors asked the faculty focus group leaders to each submit four or five questions that they thought were important for the students to address based on the analytical findings for these questions. The leaders agreed to submit the questions to the principal in a week's time. The principal then sent the questions to the professors. On receipt of the questions from the principal, the professors collated and compared the questions. The result was the identification of eight questions the professors would discuss with the students.

In early January, the professors contacted the principal to inform him of the recommended questions for the small student focus groups. The principal and professors then finalized the dates and times for the student focus groups to meet before the end of the month. The professors met with four student focus groups, two advance and two standard diploma, composed of 8 to 10 counselor- and administrator-selected students. The 1-hour meetings occurred virtually on the anniversary of the completion of the survey questionnaire by the school's students.

Jumping-Off Point for Action Planning: The Issues Report

The professors analyzed the students' responses to the questions. Then they prepared a report titled "A Synthesis of Teacher and Student Perceptions at JHS From Focus Group Interaction During 1994-95" that they shared with the administrators and counselors in February 1995.

In early March 1995, the professors met with the school's staff during a faculty meeting to share highlights of the report. The issues/concerns and suggestions/recommendations were quickly presented during the meeting by the professors. Each school staff member got a copy of the report to read more carefully later. The principal reiterated to the staff his support for the action research project and stated that the report was what he really wanted out of the project (the numerous quantitative analyses did not mean as much to him).

The Action Planning Timeline Spreadsheet

As the 1994-1995 school year drew to a close, the school's staff had not yet responded to the report with any action plans. Therefore, the professors developed a spreadsheet that had a column for the issues, a resources needed column, and a third column for the activities to be undertaken to address the issues. Following the three columns was a timeline divided into months beginning with August 1995 and ending with July 1997. The issues to be addressed were to be fitted into the timeline over a 2-year period.

The professors contacted the school's principal in late April 1995 and asked that a meeting with the teacher focus group leaders be arranged as soon as possible to discuss the spreadsheet. The principal agreed and he, the focus group leaders, and the professors met at the school in early May. At that time, with the principal's strong urging, the focus group leaders agreed to address the issues by prioritizing them in terms of immediate action and longer-term action. They agreed to use the spreadsheet as presented by the professors. Furthermore, they agreed to respond with an initial action plan within 10 days. Finally, it appeared, the school's staff was about to take ownership of the action research project nearly 2 years after it was conceived in the summer of 1993.

When the principal and focus group leaders met again, they did so without the two professors (for the first time). They agreed on an action plan that would begin in August when the school's staff returned for the 1995-1996 school year.

The longest-range action step planned involved the continuing study of block scheduling with implementation projected for the fall of 1996. In their report, the professors suggested that block scheduling could help in ameliorating a number of the issues. These issues included teacher expectations for students, adult respect for students, updating teaching techniques, helping and encouraging students, classroom disruptions, and discipline.

The School's 10-Year Self-Study

One of the more immediate uses of this collaborative action research effort was the incorporation of selected findings in the high school's 10-year self-study in October 1995. The self-study was in preparation for the visiting committee of the Southern Association of Colleges and Schools (SACS). Reference was made to perceptual climate research in several places in the self-study report, such as in the Evaluation and Research subsection of Section 9: School Staff and Administration.

The Section 9 committee was chaired by the high school's principal, and six teachers were on the committee. This group reported in writing that the results of a "perception survey" were reviewed with the school's faculty during 2 inservice days and "follow-up activities will be initiated to bring about improvement in the areas noted."

The most use of the collaborative action research occurred in the School Climate subsection of Section 2: School and Community. Here the committee composed of the assistant principal and nine teachers explained the procedures involved in administering a "student opinion survey" one day in January 1994. This committee broadly concluded that the "perception of the students is that the climate is favorable to the learning process" and overgeneralized that students were "pleased with their teachers, the curriculum, and extracurricular activities offered" in the school. In answer to the question concerning the significant findings of the survey, five well-selected positive conclusions were stated. Implications were that "students are pleased with the curriculum offered and the way their teachers work with them" and students surmise that the school "offers a quality education for all students."

Equally glowing were the discussions for faculty and community perceptions. The committee concluded that "there were no significant differences in perceptions between students, teachers and community [parents]." In the end, the committee hedged somewhat by writing that parents who responded (about 34%) thought the school was doing an acceptable job and that a "majority" of the students believed the school provided "a proper learning environment with a good curriculum." Finally, a "majority" of teachers "enjoyed their profession and their students."

The Professors' Diminished Role

The professors have not been asked to do any more on the action research project. By the fall of 1995, the professors had determined that the school's staff should take responsibility (and ownership) of the project after nearly 2 years of nurturing and gradual shifting of control away from the professors. Bickel and Hattrup (1995) contended that both parties in a teacher-researcher collaboration need to be committed to the partnership. Aside from the principal, it was not always certain in this case that such dual commitment existed. Bickel and Hattrup further argued that "meaningful collaboration" took time to unfold. Because collaboration tends to wane after the initial novelty of and excitement about the partnership, sustaining the collaboration after it has operated for a while is difficult for both parties. Other problems and projects get in the way over time, and any particular collaboration becomes less of a priority. The two professors in this reported collaborative action research project can attest to the difficulty.

In Sagor's (1993) model, the role of the teacher in action research is featured. The role of consultants or experts is to be minimized. That role Sagor called the "critical friend." Sagor warned school personnel against falling prey to the dominance of the critical friend in the action research process. He issued nine guidelines for critical friend involvement, and eight of the guidelines identified responsibilities of the critical friend; only one discussed responsibilities of the school personnel (p. 47). Based on their actual experience, the professors would ask Sagor to revise those guidelines to place more responsibility for the integrity of the collaborative action research process on the shoulders of school personnel.

A Setback for the Principal

The school's principal suffered a setback to his restructuring hopes when most of the faculty declined further consideration of block scheduling at the end of November 1995. He said about 75% of the teachers were against implementing block scheduling. Also, the principal claimed there were too many distractions, including the planning to build a new high school on a different site, to pursue much, if any, of the short- or long-range activities derived from the collaborative action research project. The principal had been surprised by the faculty's response to block scheduling especially because the current six-period day had to be changed to accommodate new state-mandated subject completion standards. The professors perceived a disappointed principal who was not willing or able to push forward on projects or activities related to the collaborative action research project. As Sagor (1991) concluded, "As powerful a tool as collaborative inquiry appears to be, it will not transform the school in the absence of leadership [and] collegial respect" (p. 10).

The professors made one last attempt to determine if the principal and faculty were going to follow up with the staff development implications of the research project's results. During a meeting with one of the professors in March 1996, the principal said he would survey teachers in regard to topic choices for ongoing staff development for using time in longer class periods or blocks. It was understood that any ongoing staff development would be coordinated or provided by College of Education staff at the professors' university. The outcome of the survey was not shared with the professors.

The professors' concerns over flagging enthusiasm, warned about in the literature, appeared to be real. The principal had been out in front of the teachers in advocating the project and promoting the results. Apparent from the start, the principal was the driving force and not the teachers. In Bickel and Hattrup's (1995) terms, "meaningful collaboration" had been attempted, but, in the end, did not fully unfold.

Conclusion

Reported here was a school-university collaborative action research effort augmented and facilitated by two educational administration professors. The university's services, in this case, were used to assist a school's staff members to do what they thought was important. Instead of a school, its staff, and students making themselves available for a university-inspired (-owned) research project, university professors and resources were used to help a school do its own research and take action to improve itself in accordance with its needs and priorities. This newfound role for a university, especially its College of Education, despite the difficulty, has the potential to make a university and its professors more relevant and useful partners to schools interested in improving climate, curriculum, instruction, and communications with parents and students.

The high school's self-study report showed, however, that university professors may need to be wary of how they and their work in schools may be manipulated when control shifts to the local school's staff. In retrospect, the school's administration and staff got what they wanted out of the collaborative action research project. They obtained the data they needed, and their interpretations of it, for their 10-year regional accreditation review. Further sustained follow-up was not a priority for them. Although the principal may have desired more from the research project, he did not push to make more happen in the absence of teacher initiatives.

Perhaps the outcome here was as it should be. Yet the professors expected more from both the principal and teachers. Should the professors have insisted on visible teacher involvement during the problem formulation step of this project? Should they have done what, in fact, they did do, let the principal involve only a few others (assistant principal and two guidance counselors) and no teachers? As Bickel and Hattrup (1995) indicated, the parties to a collaboration must be committed, and that commitment is not easy to sustain over time. The literature, as cited at the beginning of this article, argued for a stronger decision-making role for schools in the collaborative relationship. The initial objectives of this collaborative action research project were met. Despite the shortcomings, the professors and the school's personnel accomplished a research project not commonly done in public schools, especially high schools, in this country.

References

Bickel, W. E., & Hattrup, R. A. (1995). Teachers and researchers in collaboration: Reflections on the process. *American Educational Research Journal, 32*(1), 35-62.

Calhoun, E. F. (1993). Action research: Three approaches. *Educational Leadership,* 51(2), 62-69.

Calhoun, E. F. (1994). *How to use action research in the self-renewing school.* Alexandria, VA: Association for Supervision and Curriculum Development.

Cohen, L., & Manion, L. (1994). *Research methods in education* (4th ed.). New York: Routledge.

Herrick, M. J. (1992). Research by the teacher and for the teacher: An action research model linking schools and universities. *Action in Teacher Education,* 14(3), 47-54.

Jacullo-Noto, J. (1992). An urban school/liberal arts college partnership for teacher development. *Journal of Teacher Education, 43,* 278-281.

Knight, S. L., Wiseman, D., & Smith, C. W. (1992). The reflectivity-activity dilemma in school-university partnerships. *Journal of Teacher Education, 43,* 269-277.

Sagor, R. (1991). What Project LEARN reveals about collaborative action research. *Educational Leadership, 48*(6), 6-10.

Sagor, R. (1993). *How to conduct collaborative action research.* Alexandria, VA: Association for Supervision and Curriculum Development.

RECONCEPTUALIZATION OF ROLES IN THE SCHOOL-UNIVERSITY COLLABORATIVE: REFLECTIONS

Nancy Fichtman Dana

The theme that ties the three chapters in this division of the yearbook together is role reconceptualization by the major players in school-university collaborative projects—teachers, administrators, and teacher educators. Although this topic is not new and has been discussed by numerous scholars (see, e.g., Clift, Veal, Holland, Johnson, & McCarthy, 1995; Dana, 1992; Levine, 1992; Miller, 1992; Trubowitz, 1986), these chapters give us further insight into the promise, possibilities, problems, and pitfalls of role reconceptualization within the school-university collaborative.

Promise and Possibilities:
Building Cultures of Collegiality and Collaboration

The Frankes, Valli, and Cooper chapter indicates that when teachers' roles are expanded to include teacher as decision maker and teacher educator, status boundaries between schools and universities diminish and a new culture emerges that is characterized by trust, shared goals, and collaboration. Similarly, when the teachers in Johnson and Brown's study expanded their roles to include peer supervisor and coach, a culture of collegiality emerged in the school.

The Johnson and Brown chapter is valuable in offering the successful story of teachers creating a collegial climate. We are reminded in this study of the importance of collegiality versus congeniality, a distinction made by Barth (1990). Congeniality suggests that people get along in schools, talk in the teachers' room about plans for the weekend, and perhaps engage in ritual celebrations such as baking birthday cakes for each other. Although congeniality is important and characterizes the culture in many elementary schools, it is not collegiality. Collegiality is described by Little (1981) as the presence of four behaviors: Adults in the school (a) talk about practice, (b) observe each other engaged in the practice of teaching and administration, (c) engage in work on curriculum, and (d) teach each other what they know about teaching and learning. Through peer coaching and the reorganization and restructuring of an elementary school into collegial support teams, the teachers in the Johnson and Brown study experienced collegiality. This study gives educators hope in that even in an extremely large elementary school, a culture of collegiality is not only possible, but can thrive!

The Zuelke and Nichols chapter describes an attempt to change the culture of a senior high through a collaborative action research project designed to examine the climate of the school for advance and standard diploma program students, emotionally conflicted students, and seventh- and eighth-grade students. Although much of the pertinent information that was gathered through survey instruments sent to parents, teachers, and students was not acted on, the project was valuable in that it led to the development and distribution of a parent newsletter. Perhaps the greatest promise in this piece, however, is that the key players in this action research project were two administrators at the school—the principal and assistant principal. Although much has been written about the teacher as researcher movement (e.g., Carr & Kemmis, 1986; Cochran-Smith & Lytle, 1993; Kincheloe, 1991), there has been far less written on principals as researchers. This chapter is useful in offering an example of university researchers and principals engaging in collaborative efforts at educational reform. It adds to the work of others who have begun such efforts (e.g., Dana & Pitts, 1993; David, 1991; Dolbec, 1996; Foster, 1991; Gee, Hollis, Maddox, Mickler, & Gettys, 1991; Moller, 1996; Murphy, 1991).

Problems and Pitfalls:
Role Compartmentalization and Work Intensification

Frankes et al. conclude that the teachers' roles of researcher and political activist are still in an early stage of development at the professional development school (PDS) site. Yet these roles are key to actualizing simultaneous reform in public school education and teacher education. Whereas the compartmentalization of teacher roles as classroom teacher, decision maker, teacher educator, teacher researcher, and political activist helps us understand role reconceptualization, this reduction of roles is also problematic. For these roles are not discrete entities unrelated to each other, and there is a danger in thinking of them as such. When looked at individually, Frankes et al. concluded that the teacher as teacher educator role and the teacher as decision-maker role have developed to a much greater extent than the teacher as researcher role or the teacher as political activist role in PDS sites. Yet any one of these roles is limited in the extent it can develop in the absence of development in the others. For example, although such behaviors as team-teaching university courses and supervising interns are important in characterizing the teacher as teacher educator, one must question what practices teachers are teaching in these courses and how they are shaping their supervisory roles if they are not engaged in their own inquiry or think of research as a part of the work that teachers do.

The roles of teacher researcher and teacher as political activist are also tightly linked. In action research, teachers are engaged in a process where they ask serious questions about what is taught, how it is taught, and what should constitute the larger goals of education (Carr & Kemmis, 1986). The basic premise of teacher research, coupled with a societal image of teachers that according to Kincheloe (1991) is not characterized by "individuals engaged in reflection, research, sharing their work with others, constructing their workplace, producing curriculum materials, and publishing their research for teachers and community members in general" (p. 24), inescapably embeds the political role of promoting critical self-reflection in the society into the teacher as researcher role.

By looking at teacher roles as discrete entities unrelated to each other, we risk adding to the work that teachers do rather than reconceptualizing and redefining their work. When this occurs, an inescapable pitfall is the intensification of teacher work. Rather than the nature of teacher work being transformed and becoming different in a PDS or other school-university collaborative project, it simply becomes more. This pitfall is exemplified in all three chapters, articulated most explicitly in general terms by Frankes et al., who conclude:

> [Teachers] working as members of site-based management teams, as student teacher supervisors, as family-school liaisons, as teacher researchers, or as university-school liaisons may detract from teachers' ability to fully perform their most critical function—educating their students. . . . Too many additional responsibilities may ultimately lead to teacher disempowerment and a reduction in the quality of their work. Increasing teachers' responsibilities may force them to limit the time and effort they devote to any given area. (p. 80)

Teachers in the Johnson and Brown study commented on the increase in their workload with the collegial support team (CST) process. Also noteworthy in this study is that no time was given to the teachers during the school day to hold CST meetings, assemble portfolios, write reflections, and hold pre- and postconferences. The lack of restructuring of time symbolically represents role add-on versus role reconceptualization. In this study, it is acceptable for teachers to take charge of their own professional development by supervising each other, but only if the time needed to engage in meaningful professional development does not interfere with the traditional role of the teacher during the school day. The teachers in the Johnson and Brown study risk experiencing the burnout and disempowerment described by Frankes et al.

Although termed an action research project, teachers were not the central feature in the work described by Zuelke and Nichols, and this research project had little impact on their role reconceptualization. Rather than being teacher researchers, they were participants in an administrator research project. As discussed earlier, it is promising that this chapter reports a collaborative action research project initiated by principals. However, it is problematic that the teachers were expected to complete the "action" component of administrator research. It should not be a surprise that the teachers did not implement the plans resulting from this study, because they were not involved in the design and conceptualization of the project from the beginning. Rather, they played role of research subject (by filling out the questionnaire) and discussion leader or participant (through discussing the results of the questionnaire). Likely, these roles did little to transform the work of the teachers. Rather, the teachers were involved in extra work with the ultimate purpose of developing a self-study report in preparation for the visiting committee of the Southern Association of Colleges and Schools. Zuelke and Nichols inquire at the close of their chapter, "Should the professors have insisted on visible teacher involvement during the problem formulation step of this project?" Perhaps the larger question this chapter raises is, "Can professors (or anyone) insist on involvement in an action research project?" If teacher participation in action research is "insisted on" or mandated, action research risks becoming another imposition on teachers rather than an opportunity for teachers to take charge of their professional development and improve education.

A parallel tension between teacher role reconceptualization versus teacher role add-on is experienced by university-based teacher educators. Frankes et al. discuss how teacher educators involved in PDS work risk fewer publications, heavier workloads, and lower status within the university. Zuelke and Nichols hint of this frustration when they discuss the length of time invested for their action research project: "Finally, it appeared, the school's staff was about to take ownership of the action research project nearly 2 years after it was conceived in the summer of 1993" (p. 106). The two professors in this study invested a significant portion of their time, and although they met the original goals of their project, the high school did not follow through on most of the action plans for school improvement based on the outcomes of the research. Because the traditional measures of success for a university faculty member are connected to teaching, research, and service, a question is raised as to the extent this 3-year effort yields "evidence" in these areas that can be used to secure promotion, tenure, and merit increases. In this case, a 3-year effort had limited impact on the school site, with great professional cost to the university professors in terms of personal investment and time.

Additionally, unless the work of university professors is reconceptualized, they risk being used by schools for the schools' own purposes, quite similar to the way university researchers have been accused of using practitioners only as research subjects in the past. Barth (1990) writes,

> The researcher who does not convey findings to the adults in the school risks joining the tainted cadre of outsiders who take advantage of schools for their own professional purposes and run, leaving behind little benefit to the school in return for the precious energies that practitioners have invested in the study. (p. 87)

The professors in the Zuelke and Nichols study were taken advantage of by the school administration, who used selected elements of the research data as propaganda to make the school look good to a visiting committee and other readers of the self-study and excluded vital data about percep-tual differences between students and teachers, teachers and parents, and between students themselves. It seems that once the selected data were used to paint a glowing report of the high school, interest waned in the action research project and in making any meaningful change based on the data collected. Actions such as these that are taken by schools in a collaborative project not only limit the benefit of collaboration to schools but are likely to sour university professors who have invested precious time and energies into a study. Although much has been written about the need for university personnel to gain the trust of practitioners and under-stand their culture, the reverse must also occur. School practitioners must understand the world of the university and the lives of teacher educators. Each must help and support the other to effect meaningful and needed change in both institutions.

Summary and Conclusions

Much has been written in the past decade regarding the importance of school-university collaboration and the role of collaboration in school and teacher education reform (e.g., Levine, 1992). One factor remains constant: To develop and sustain a meaningful school university partner-ship takes a great deal of time and effort. According to Sirotnik and Goodlad (1988), "For a school-university partnership to effect major edu-cational reconstructions in a relatively short time frame, say five years, would be miraculous" (p. 188).

The work reported in this section of the yearbook further reminds us of the time and energy expended by teachers, administrators, and teacher educators as they work to redefine and reconceptualize their traditional roles while experiencing cultural and institutional pressure to hang onto outlived professional identities. Hanging onto outlived identities limits development of new identities and leads to work intensification for all members in a school-university collaborative. We must continue to document the stories of school-university collabora-tive efforts as well as the struggles of the participants that are inherent in attempting large-scale reform and change in education. In so doing, we reconceptualize career-long professional development and change as well.

References

Barth, R. S. (1990). *Improving schools from within: Teachers, parents, and principals can make a difference.* San Francisco: Jossey-Bass.

Carr, W., & Kemmis, S. (1986). *Becoming critical: Education, knowledge and action research.* New York: Doubleday.

Clift, R. T., Veal, M. L., Holland, P., Johnson, M., & McCarthy, J. (1995). *Collaborative leadership and shared decision making: Teachers, principals, and university professors.* New York: Teachers College Press.

Cochran-Smith, M., & Lytle, S. L. (1993). *Inside outside: Teacher research and knowledge.* New York: Teachers College Press.

Dana, N. F. (1992, November). *Discovering researcher subjectivities, perceptions and biases: A critical examination of myths, metaphors, and meanings inherent in university-school collaborative action research projects.* Paper presented at the 18th annual meeting of the Research on Women in Education Conference, University Park, PA. (ERIC Document Reproduction Service No. ED 352 342)

Dana, N. F., & Pitts, J. H. (1993). The use of metaphor and reflective coaching in the exploration of principal thinking: A case study of principal change. *Educational Administration Quarterly, 29,* 323-338.

David, J. L. (1991). What it takes to restructure education. *Educational Leadership, 48*(8), 11-15.

Dolbec, A. (1996, April). *Collaborative inquiry with school principals to implement a continuous learning culture.* Paper presented at the annual meeting of the American Educational Research Association, New York. (ERIC Document Reproduction Service No. ED 396 450)

Foster, A. G. (1991). When teachers initiate restructuring. *Educational Leadership, 48*(8), 27-31.

Gee, M. J., Hollis, K., Maddox, B., Mickler, M. J., & Gettys, C. M. (1991, April). *One school's restructuring for school change: Contributions of the teachers, the principal, and the university teachers/researchers.* Paper presented at the annual meeting of the American Educational Research Association, Chicago.

Kincheloe, J. (1991). *Teachers as researchers: Qualitative inquiry as a path to empowerment.* New York: Falmer.

Levine, M. (1992). *Professional practice schools: Linking teacher education and school reform.* New York: Teachers College Press.

Little, J. W. (1981). *School success and staff development in urban desegregated schools: A summary of recently completed research.* Boulder, CO: Center for Action Research.

Miller, J. L. (1992). Exploring power and authority issues in a collaborative action research project. *Theory Into Practice, 31*(2), 165-172.

Moller, J. (1996, April). *Educating reflective principals in a context of restructuring.* Paper presented at the annual meeting of the American Educational Research Association, New York. (ERIC Document Reproduction Service No. ED 399 245)

Murphy, C. U. (1991). Lessons from a journey into change. *Educational Leadership, 48*(9), 63-67.

Sirotnik, K. A., & Goodlad, J. I. (1988). *School-university partnerships in action: Concepts, cases, and concerns*. New York: Teachers College Press.

Trubowitz, S. (1986). Stages in the development of school-college collaboration. *Education Leadership, 43*(5), 28-32.

DIVISION III

WHAT WE KNOW ABOUT THE RELATIONSHIP OF PROFESSIONAL TEACHER DEVELOPMENT AND CHANGE TO STAFF DEVELOPMENT, SCHOOL RESTRUCTURING, AND TEACHER BELIEFS: OVERVIEW AND FRAMEWORK

Elaine Jarchow

Elaine Jarchow is Dean of the College of Education at Texas Tech University. She is also Professor of Curriculum and Instruction. Her research interests include international education, curriculum development in emerging democracies, and teacher education. She serves on the AACTE Board of Directors and the ATE Commission on International Affairs.

When teacher preparation entities have completed their work, a teacher's lifelong professional development begins. We all know of models that do not work and of some that do. For example, staff development models that merely present teachers with an exciting, motivational speaker at the monthly inservice session do not work. However, career-long, enhancement programs that allow for professional growth, teacher input, change through reflection, and exposure to best practices have every chance for success.

In 1985, the Association of Teacher Educators (ATE) published *Developing Career Ladders in Teaching*. Some of the ideas expressed in the publication are still relevant today. For example, the authors note that a career ladder must be based on such assumptions as improving the teaching-learning process; rewarding outstanding teachers, providing time for reflection, strengthening the school organization, and focusing on on-the-job staff development.

Grappling with the change process, the architects of career ladders must involve many stakeholders, strike a balance between change and stability, and recognize the notion of continuous involvement. Career ladders must have clearly defined purposes that provide direction, incentives, and effective staffing patterns (ATE, 1985).

The 1990 Association for Supervision and Curriculum Development yearbook, *Changing School Culture Through Staff Development* (Joyce, 1990), describes what the knowledge base tells us as well as what roles shareholders must take. The yearbook authors offer a number of insightful perspectives:

- Genuine restructuring must take place through the redevelopment of the institution's culture.
- Teachers themselves must be self-educated and empowered to change their own behavior.
- The psychological states of teachers affect whether they will be fully functioning learners.
- Principals must be learning facilitators.
- Collegial workplaces can yield outstanding staff development models.
- Pre-K–12 schools and universities must be connected as seamless webs (Joyce, 1990).

The Center on Organization and Restructuring of Schools at the University of Wisconsin–Madison offered the public a 1995 report, *Successful School Restructuring* (Newmann & Wehlage, 1995). At the heart of the work that resulted in the report was the goal to increase student learning. To accomplish this goal, the report called for external support, school organizational capacity, authentic pedagogy, and student learning.

The report's conclusions are relevant to understanding career-long professional development.

- Three general features characterize schools that are professional communities: "Teachers pursue a clear, shared purpose for all students' learning. Teachers engage in collaborative activity to achieve the purpose. Teachers take collective responsibility for student learning" (Newmann & Wehlage, 1995, p. 30).
- Relevant staff development topics such as "shared decision making, cooperative learning, reading instruction, and assessment by portfolio" can support school restructuring (p. 43).
- Staff development that is continuous and coordinated can challenge teachers to invent new ways of teaching, which ultimately lead to restructured schools.

Many believe that teachers can grow professionally in democratic schools. Michael Apple (Beane & Apple, 1995) characterizes these schools as engaging in (a) participation in issues of governance and policy making, (b) participation in communities of learning, (c) commitment to diversity, and (d) development of a curriculum of exploration (pp. 9-13).

The concerns of democratic schools are

a. The open flow of ideas, regardless of their popularity, that enables people to be as fully informed as possible
b. Faith in the individual and collective capacity of people to create possibilities for resolving problems
c. The use of critical reflection and analysis to evaluate ideas, problems, and policies
d. Concern for the welfare of others and "the common good"
e. Concern for the dignity and rights of individuals and minorities
f. An understanding that democracy is not so much an ideal to be pursued as an idealized set of values that we must live and that must guide our lives
g. The organization of social institutions to promote and extend the democratic way of life (Beane & Apple, 1995, pp. 6-7)

Jerry Patterson in *Leadership for Tomorrow's Schools* (1993) notes that the values that promote democratic schools are openness to participation, openness to diversity, openness to conflict, openness to reflection, and openness to mistakes.

The following values will characterize tomorrow's schools:

a. Our organization values employees actively participating in any discussion or decision affecting them.

b. Our organization values diversity in perspectives leading to a deeper understanding of organizational reality and an enriched knowledge base for decision making.

c. Our organization values employees resolving conflict in a healthy way that leads to stronger solutions for complex issues.

d. Our organization values employees reflecting on their own and other's thinking to achieve better organizational decisions.

e. Our organization values employees acknowledging mistakes and learning from them. (Patterson, 1993, pp. 5-12)

Questions that a school might ask itself are as follows:

To what extent does the district

a. Value commitment to the development of the individual within the district?

b. Value treating all individuals as significant stakeholders in the organization?

c. Value a "we" spirit and feeling of ownership in the organization?

d. Value empowering employees throughout the district to assist in achieving the mission of the school district?

e. Value equal access by all employees to support information and resources?

f. Value all employees as equally important members of the organization?

g. Believe that employees act in the best interest of students and the organization?

h. Value employees as having the expertise to make wise decisions?

i. Value investing in the development of employees?

j. Value placing decision making as close to the point of implementation as possible?

k. Value the opportunity for input in districtwide decisions?

l. Value decisions being made by those who are directly affected by them?

m. Value honesty in words and actions?

n. Value consistent, responsible pursuit of that for which we stand?

o. Value the unwavering commitment to ethical conduct?

p. Value differences in individual philosophy and practices?

q. Value differences in perspective?

r. Value schools and the children within them celebrating their distinct character?

s. Value students as inherently curious learners?

t. Value doing whatever it takes to achieve student success?

u. Value students being meaningfully engaged in work that has personal value to them? (Patterson, 1993, pp. 93-95)

The relationship of professional teacher development and change to staff development, school restructuring, and teacher beliefs is a complex one. We know that short-term answers to difficult problems do not work. We know about the characteristics of successful professional teacher development, but we often lack the means to connect these characteristics to meaningful career-long teacher education. Perhaps these next three chapters will move us forward and provide us with new ideas and a 21st-century focus.

Three Chapters

The thread that links the following three chapters is one of growth through reflection. Both beginning and mature teachers must grapple with a host of postmodern dilemmas and paradoxes.

In Chapter 7, Reitzug and O'Hair outline five struggles with which schools moving toward democratic practice must grapple. Describing the implications for career-long teacher education, they advocate a new mind-set. Kadel-Taras in Chapter 8 tackles the questions of when, why, and how high school teachers change their behavior. Her rich examples of teacher learning and teacher control weave an illustrative tapestry of change. Finally, in Chapter 9, Fleener and Fry describe the tensions between modernity and postmodernity and accompanying paradoxes. Using teacher critical reflection as a common theme, they outline a "solutions" model of adaptive teacher reflectivity.

References

Association of Teacher Educators. (1985). *Developing career ladders in teaching.* Reston, VA: Author.

Beane, J. A., & Apple, M. W. (1995). The case for democratic schools. In M. W. Apple & J. A. Beane (Eds.), *Democratic schools* (pp. 1-23). Alexandria, VA: Association for Supervision and Curriculum Development.

Joyce, B. (Ed.). (1990). *Changing school culture through staff development.* Alexandria, VA: Association for Supervision and Curriculum Development.

Newmann, F. M., & Wehlage, G. G. (1995). *Successful school restructuring.* Madison, WI: Center on Organization and Restructuring of Schools.

Patterson, J. (1993). *Leadership for tomorrow's schools.* Alexandria, VA: Association for Supervision and Curriculum Development.

7 Struggling With Democracy

Implications for Career-Long Teacher Education

Ulrich C. Reitzug

Mary John O'Hair

Ulrich C. Reitzug is Chair of the Department of Educational Leadership and Cultural Foundations at the University of North Carolina–Greensboro. His work focuses on leadership and school renewal. Recent publications have appeared in the *American Educational Research Journal* and the *Journal of Curriculum and Supervision*.

Mary John O'Hair is Associate Dean for Graduate Programs and Research at the University of Oklahoma. Her work centers around restructuring toward democratic schooling. She codirects the Oklahoma Networks for Excellence in Education (ONE) and was the founding editor of the Teacher Education Yearbook series.

ABSTRACT

Currently, there is renewed emphasis among theorists and practitioners on democratic schooling. Although frequently equated with school governance, democratic schooling extends beyond governance structures into all aspects of school and classroom practice. This chapter reports the results of a qualitative study that examined the struggles of schools engaged in striving to become more democratic. Three themes were identified that characterize the practices of these schools. Practices existed in tension with several types of struggles. The implications of practices and struggles for career-long teacher education are discussed.

There has been a significant resurgence of interest in recent years in the connection between schools and democracy. The emphasis has focused both on schooling for democracy and on schools as democracies.

The focus on schooling for democracy has emphasized reconnecting schools to their original purpose, that is, to prepare students for life in a democracy. Glickman (1993), for example, argues that "the basic goal of our schools is to prepare students to engage productively in a democracy" (p. xii). Similarly, Soder (1996) asserts that the "major purpose of schools is to teach the young their rights and responsibilities as citizens in a democracy" (p. xi). Relatedly, Goodman (1992) notes that schooling should "serve as a vehicle for critical democracy" (p. 1) and Beane and Apple (1995) term democracy a "half-forgotten idea that was to guide the purposes and programs of our public schools" (p. 2).

The focus on schools as democracies has been on creating schools that are organized, are governed, and practice as democracies. The discourse about schools as democracies has frequently concentrated on the governance of schools and specifically on increasing the participation of various stakeholders in school decision making through initiatives such as site-based management. Unfortunately, a focus exclusively on democratic governance overlooks significant aspects of schools as democracies that are played out in various aspects of school policy as well as in issues of daily practice. Dewey (1916), for example, argues that democracy includes a whole manner of "associated living" and occurs in "multiple realms of social life." According to Dewey's conception, democracy requires that (a) all stakeholders are represented in governance and the other realms of social life, (b) there is widespread inclusion and sharing of perspectives, and (c) the objective is the transformation of perspective and practice. Strike (1993) adds that in a democracy, discourse must be equitable with no individual or group dominating due to power differentials and that inquiry (rather than power) determines the strongest argument. Beane and Apple (1995) caution, however, that democratic practices do not always serve democratic ends. Specifically, they observe that "local populist politics" (p. 9) may result in practices such as "racial segregation and denial of access to all but the wealthy" (pp. 9-10). Democracy requires not only equity in discourse but also equity in practice.

Democracy, thus, has at its core notions of voice, inquiry, equity, and transformation. In an earlier work, we explored what this means for the practices of principals (see O'Hair & Reitzug, 1997). In this chapter, we focus on the struggles encountered by school communities as they attempt to restructure and reinvent practice as democracies. We conclude by reflecting on the relationship between the quest for democratic education and career-long teacher education.

Methodology

This study was conducted using qualitative research methodology.

Data Sources

Schools from which data were collected for this study were selected in a purposive manner. The objective was to select schools that were engaged in democratic restructuring. Teachers, principals, and members of the communities in which our research was conducted nominated schools they perceived to be engaged in restructuring toward democratic schooling.

From the nominated schools, 20 schools representing rural, urban, and suburban settings were included in the sample. Schools included 10 elementary schools, six middle schools, and four high schools. Schools were located in four states in the Northeast of the United States and two states in the Southwest.

Data Collection

Data were collected for this study via interviews with teachers, principals, parents, and school board members. Additionally, at seven schools observations were conducted. At each of the seven sites, we spent 2 to 3 days observing school proceedings and discussing school practices with the principal, teachers, staff, and parents. Field notes were taken throughout the site visits. Data were collected over a 2-year period. This report is based primarily on interview data from teachers.

Data Analysis

Data analysis involved a multiple-step process. In the first step, we analyzed the data as they were being collected, responding to the questions,

"How does this school function as a democracy?" This ongoing informal analysis guided subsequent interviews and observations. As we engaged in this informal analysis, it became evident that the schools were encountering many struggles as they attempted to become more democratic. Thus, we began asking a second question of the data, "What are the struggles this school is encountering as it attempts to practice as a democracy?" Subsequent to the data collection period, the same questions were again asked of the data, and data were coded as appropriate.

Establishing Trustworthiness

Trustworthiness was established in several ways. Three different forms of triangulation were used. Triangulation occurred through the use of different forms of data collection (i.e., interviews and observation), different data sources (i.e., principals, teachers, parents, and school board members), and different researchers engaged in interaction with the data (i.e., two university professors). Member checks were conducted after data were collected to ensure the accuracy of data collection and to clarify ambiguous areas. A second round of member checks was conducted after initial data analysis.

Results

Our earlier analysis found that three broad objectives characterized the efforts of the schools in this study to facilitate democratic practice. Specifically, these schools attempted to

- Expand the scope of involvement in school decision making and discourse
- Focus attention on connections between beliefs, practices, individuals, and communities
- Promote inquiry around core beliefs (see O'Hair & Reitzug, 1997, for further details)

The movement of schools toward more democratic practice was not, however, without struggle. Although teachers, principals, parents, and school board members spoke positively of the progress of their schools, their comments were also characterized by a significant amount of frustration.

Frustration was born out of the struggles in which they continually engaged. Struggles corresponded with the three objectives the schools were promoting in their movement toward more democratic practice. Specifically, struggles with time accompanied efforts aimed at expanding involvement in school decision making and discourse, struggles with communication accompanied efforts aimed at focusing attention on connections, and struggles of relevance accompanied efforts aimed at promoting inquiry around core beliefs. Subsequent sections will explore each of these struggles in greater detail.

Expanding Involvement

The Struggle to Find Time for Involvement in Decision Making and Discourse

Although many teachers expressed enthusiasm for democratic restructuring efforts and understood the value for practice of collaborative inquiry, discussion, and planning, they struggled with the time constraints school schedules and structures placed on legitimate collaboration. One teacher observed,

> The question of how do we encourage people to take on leadership roles and yet support them . . . has been an issue that's been around in this district very strongly since I've been here, which is 10 or 11 years. Whenever teachers get together and talk about their needs, time comes up. Time to take on more leadership roles, time to serve on these committees, time to talk to colleagues, time to reflect on our practice. And it's something that even though we've looked at restructuring we really haven't resolved or restructured towards.

Another teacher, in discussing a collaborative planning and teaching effort that occurred as part of a university course, noted,

> You know, it was 2 hours a day . . . but we were learning a lot of things . . . and we became a real powerful unit . . . the only thing about this is it's not real and could not happen in a school because there's absolutely no way that you can have that kind of planning time.

Not only did teachers understand the constraints of schedules and structures on the potential for their schools to be truly democratic and collaborative, they also realized the systemic nature of structural change that would be required to make truly democratic practice possible. One teacher argued,

> We need a new collaborative work culture. We must reduce teacher and staff isolation by restructuring work life, calendar (not just tinkering), to honor the importance of communication, collaboration, and thoughtful practice. We should create new models for instruction—no longer one teacher and 25 students. Create a structure where adults are working together, literally, and do not have to be brought together after the fact through meetings, etc.

The implication for school practice suggested by these sentiments is that restructuring efforts must temporarily be concerned with how schedules, calendars, teaching assignments, and other structural aspects of school organization affect the potential for teachers to learn and grow. Perhaps the latter comes first. That is, for schools to have sufficient time to collectively address teaching practice and the learning of their students, school structures need to be reviewed with a focus on creating teacher time for reflection, inquiry, discussion, and decision making. However, as Newmann and Wehlage (1995) point out, successful restructuring efforts must move beyond this and eventually focus on continually and explicitly linking structural considerations to their impact on increased student learning.

Focusing Attention on Connections

The Struggle to Communicate in a Manner
That Facilitates the Forging of Connections

Democratic restructuring efforts regularly focused on connecting beliefs and practices, connecting individuals with each other, and connecting the school to the community. The most significant struggle that schools encountered in these efforts was the struggle to communicate in a manner that facilitates the forging of connections.

One key aspect of the struggle to communicate had to do with communicating openly and respectfully, even in the face of dissenting opinions.

Teachers recognized the importance of dissenting viewpoints. One teacher noted,

> I don't think I'm getting honest information all the time. Some people are thinking certain things that they don't want [to disclose]. Because of the dynamics of the group, they won't really express their view. [They'll] shy away from conflict of any kind.

The lack of respect that sometimes occurs in articulating viewpoints and its consequences were also articulated as being problematic. One teacher observed, "I'd like to see a little more respect for each other and respect for each other's ideas . . . [to be able to] communicate without feeling put down or without feeling inadequate." Similarly, another teacher observed,

> I have heard teachers say that they would like to say something in a teachers' meeting but when five people are very vocal or angry . . . other people shut down. They are afraid to speak out against a person who has slammed her fist down on the table and said, "Goddamn it! We've done this 15 times and I'm sick and tired of this conversation." Teachers that are really trying to solve that problem sort of shrink and they don't deal with it.

For teachers to form collaborative connections with each other and with the community that result in continual alignment and realignment of beliefs and practices, open, honest, respectful, and conflictual discussion must be valued. That is, dissenting opinions should not be viewed as opposition or resistance but rather as opportunities to confront incongruencies such as those that might exist between beliefs and practices. Fullan (1993) argues that "problems are our friends" (p. 25) and "must be confronted for breakthroughs to occur" (p. 26). Yet in schools, in our efforts to keep the peace and not rock the boat, we frequently engage in a rush to consensus, internalizing our questions and uncertainties about beliefs and practices and, consequently, legitimating incongruencies by our silence.

Promoting Inquiry Around Core Beliefs

The Struggle for Information Adequacy

One aspect of the struggle to promote inquiry around core beliefs had to do with the adequacy of the information that teachers and others had in commencing the inquiry process. Information inadequacy can be characterized by either too little information or information overload. In the schools in our study, the latter appeared to be a more significant problem. One teacher noted how quickly a three-ring binder had been filled in which she filed memos, bulletins, and other forms of written information. Another teacher described how she dealt with the voluminous amounts of information she received.

> I think that we are given a lot of information to deal with . . . when you begin to estimate that every piece of paper needs to be glanced at, this is what happens. You glance [at the paper], you read the top line, you're not interested, it's IST, I'm not on it officially, boom, you file it or put it in the recycle bin. Because you just can't absorb—I think that's part of the problem. So is more going to help? I don't think so.

Although information overload was a more prevalent problem in the schools in our study, too little information is also problematic. If teachers and other members of the school community are to make informed decisions, information needs to be disseminated from school board members, superintendents, district office administrators, principals, and other traditional information gatekeepers to all those who are involved in making decisions. Failure to decentralize information may result in inefficient or ineffective communication, the inability to forge connections between beliefs and practices due to incomplete information, intentional or inadvertent perpetuation of the current hierarchical relationships that characterize many schools and districts (Reitzug & Cross, 1995), and the inability to forge connections between individuals or the school and the community due to the perpetuation of hierarchical relationships.

Perhaps the key recommendation for information gatekeepers with respect to information adequacy is that they should be cognizant of the distinctions between disseminating information and providing access to information and between needing-to-know and wanting-to-know information. Disseminating all available information to all individuals is likely to lead to information overload. Individual needs and desires for information will differ. Undoubtedly, many instances exist where individuals may not need to know certain information but may want to know information. Barring legal or ethical implications, individuals wanting to know information should be able to readily access the desired information (perhaps via technology). Similarly, for information that individuals need to know, the standard is higher. Rather than simply providing access to such information, information gatekeepers should ensure that need-to-know information is disseminated to all appropriate individuals.

The Struggle to Connect Discussions and Committee Work to Classroom Practice

A second aspect of the struggle to promote inquiry around core beliefs concerned connecting discussions and committee work to classroom practice. One teacher observed, "I think it [restructuring] affects the teachers but . . . the classroom as far as teaching and the learning environment—no, I don't think it affects that at all." Another teacher articulated this disjuncture by forcefully arguing,

> People feel like all I want to do is teach. . . . I'm sick of going to these transition meetings. . . . There is a kind of back-to-work attitude. I know there's all of these things going on, but I've got to concentrate on the classroom now.

Still another teacher noted,

> It's like you're "committeed" to death. You go to work and you do your job and then you go to a committee meeting, and meeting, meeting, meeting . . . so yeah, I would like to have the time to share [information about classroom practices] with other professionals in the building.

One teacher described it as a "question of how much can you give and does it distract from your teaching?" Still another teacher reflected, "I always get a sense from teachers that committee work is something that's apart and aside, is another piece of what they do. But that it's not an extension of [classroom work]. Like it's another folder, another pocket."

The concern of many of the teachers was less with the amount of time spent in meetings and discussion than with the connection between the discussions and their teaching practice. The teachers cited here seem to make a distinction between committee meetings and reflective, inquiring, classroom-focused practice. The issue may be one of either connection or relevance. That is, restructuring discussions may have a connection to teaching practice, but teachers may not be making this connection. The implication for school practice is that part of meetings be devoted to explicitly drawing out and articulating the connections of discussions for teaching practice. Alternatively, discussions may not always be relevant to classroom practice. In this case, the implication for schools is that meetings need to go beyond dealing with management issues and vested interests to dealing explicitly with issues of teaching and learning and by using a more inquiry-oriented process that links discussions to the school's core values and beliefs.

The Struggle to Follow Discourse With Action

A third aspect of the struggle to promote inquiry around core beliefs had to do with the distinction between communication and action. Many teachers spoke of the extensive communication that occurred in their schools but often cited a frustration with the failure of communication to lead to subsequent action. In some cases, inaction was due to a never-ending cycle of discussion that failed to moved beyond the talk stage. One teacher observed,

> A lot of us are beginning to feel that we've said these things over and over again. . . . Many, many committees go by on issues of how to build or reorganize . . . and those are very frustrating. To be part of it and then see it not go anywhere.

Another teacher noted,

> We have lots of committees in this district that people put tremendous amounts of energy into that go absolutely nowhere. And people will say afterwards, "What was that all about? We went through this process, we gave up evenings with our families. . . . Where does it go from here?" It just seems to fade and then another committee comes and then another.

In some instances, lack of follow-up action was due to decisions and recommendations being overruled by those higher in the hierarchy. One teacher noted,

> I feel a lot of cynicism . . . cynicism in the sense that we're being asked but we're not being listened to. And so we do a lot of committee work . . . we have task forces for this or that but what

does it do? . . . The edict comes down [and it's clear] that we weren't listened to.

Giroux (1992) has argued for the necessity of not simply engaging in a "language of critique" but also incorporating a "language of possibility" that identifies possible courses of action. Clearly, when discourse grounded in a school's core values and focused on developing practices congruent with those values is not followed by appropriate action, the belief-practice connection that democratic schools strive to attain is inhibited.

The implications for practice go beyond the obvious implication that discourse needs to be focused on possibility and be followed by action. Perhaps discourse does affect action more frequently than teachers realize. In some instances, these changes may be at the individual classroom level and thus totally invisible to all but the classroom teacher and perhaps a close collaborator. In other instances, the impact may be at a more organization-wide level, but changes may be minor and evolutionary and not easily evident to insiders whose closeness to daily events makes incremental changes invisible. Alternatively, the impact on practice may be more sudden and dramatic. Yet participants may not connect previous discourse and committee work with the change in practice. The implication for school leaders in any position is to explicitly determine what action should be taken as a result of discourse and committee work and to regularly publicly review what action has occurred as a result of the discourse community's efforts.

Implications of Democratic Struggle for Career-Long Teacher Education

The struggles of schools engaged in the quest for democratic schooling have significant implications for the continued education and development of teachers. Implications revolve around a new mind-set of teacher role and interaction required by democratic schools. The seeds of this new mind-set must be present in teachers as their schools attempt to become democratic. The mind-set, however, is developed to its full fruition by the process and struggles of striving for democratic ideals in the school community.

Central to the new mind-set of the democratic teacher is the notion of connectedness—connectedness to colleagues, connectedness to schoolwide practices, connectedness to the school's core values, and connectedness to the greater school and global community. By contrast, the old mind-set is one of isolation and separation—isolation from colleagues and separation from school events that are external to a teacher's classroom and from the community. Additionally, the old mind-set is focused on individualism, specifically with respect to the pursuit of individual (rather than shared) values. The democratic teacher mind-set requires being involved in all aspects of education in the school, not simply in the shared governance of the school. The role of democratic teachers is much larger than a political process. O'Hair, McLaughlin, and Reitzug (in press) describe the interconnectivity of democratic education as defined by the content of the academic curriculum, by the social curriculum that occurs in classrooms and the school, by grouping and inclusion practices, by the uses and misuses of testing, by the development and content of staff development, and by the nature of parent and student involvement. In short, the new mind-set of the democratic teacher is fostered by and enacted within the range of relationships that exist between and among the school community's members, the content of the curriculum, and the processes of instruction.

Shedding the old for the new is never without problem. Thus, as the schools in our study attempted to move toward democratic ideals they encountered numerous struggles. Struggles fostered teacher growth and movement toward a democratic teacher mind-set that incorporates ideals of inquiry, voice, equity, and transformation.

As noted, finding time was a struggle in our schools as they attempted to expand involvement in school discourse and inquiry. Via inquiry, teachers wrestle with data and perspectives that might otherwise remain invisible. Via inquiry, teachers struggle with which information is relevant and merits gathering and with which information is irrelevant and requires discarding (a second of the struggles our schools encountered). The result of inquiry in many instances is teacher growth resulting from a deeper understanding of personal and school practice.

Another struggle encountered by our schools was engaging in discourse characterized by legitimate voice. Legitimate voice involves communication that is open, honest, and respectful, but not conflict avoiding. Legitimate voice results in growth opportunities for teachers and other participating members of the school community. Growth opportunities occur as a result of individuals being able to hear and analyze varying perspectives on an issue, especially perspectives grounded in positional and cultural backgrounds different than the individual's own.

The struggle to communicate openly and honestly was also about equity. Overpowering and disrespectful communication leads to inequitable discourse (see Glickman, 1993). Such communication runs counter to the democratic ideal of equity. Data from this study and previous field-based research in which we have been involved (see, e.g., Reitzug & Cross, 1995) indicates that schools striving for democratic ideals are initially very concerned with equitable representation in school governance (i.e., for teachers, but not necessarily parents and others). They appear less concerned with critiquing subsequent discourse in terms of equity or with analyzing equity for students in school practices. Frequently, teachers and other educators homogenize educational practices, making decisions based on "what's good for students" without ever considering that practices good for some students may not be good for other students. Overt consideration of the differential effects of school practices and policies on students (particularly in terms of effects that are correlated with race, class, gender, disability, and sexual orientation) is one essential avenue for teacher growth that can be facilitated by the struggle to reach democratic ideals.

A fourth struggle with which the schools wrestled was in connecting discussions and committee work to classroom practice. Newmann and Wehlage (1995) argue that authentic pedagogy "requires students to think, to develop in-depth understanding, and to apply academic learning to important, realistic problems" (p. 3). Similarly, authenticity in discussions and committee work in democratic schools could be argued to require teachers to think, develop understanding, and to connect discussions to classroom practice. Frequently, committee work and discussions may be connected to classroom practice. However, teachers still operating partially from an old mind-set may not see the connection. Explicit questions and discussions that probe the presence and nature of the relationship between a committee's work/discussion and classroom implications can facilitate teacher growth through a broader understanding of the relationship between schoolwide practice and classroom practice.

The final struggle with which our schools wrestled was concerned with the relationship between communication and action. Foster (1989) argues that leadership must be critical, educative, ethical, and transformative. Critical, educative, and ethical components of leadership are embodied in the democratic ideals of voice, inquiry, and equity. However, to ensure that democratic discourse does not result in merely words without follow-up action, leadership that results in transformative action is often required. In a democratic school, leadership does not come simply from the principal or others in designated positions of authority, but may come from anyone in the school community. In some instances, leadership may come from the principal; in most instances, it should come from teachers, parents, students, or other members of the school community. As teachers facilitate the engagement of others in discourse, inquiry, and transformative action, they experience the personal growth that results from moving beyond leadership with students to leadership with students and adults.

Conclusion

Research suggests that the career-long professional development of teachers occurs as a result of the presence of widespread knowledge acquired by teachers through their daily involvement in "defining and shaping the problems of practice" (Lieberman, 1995, p. 592) and the necessity of teacher learning that is "sustained, ongoing, [and] intensive" (Darling-Hammond & McLaughlin, 1995, p. 597). Research has also found that schools in which teachers continue to learn embrace norms of collegiality and experimentation with professional discussion focused on teaching and its relationship to "the complexities of the classroom" (Little, 1982, p. 334) occurring throughout the school and day. Such schools function as learning communities characterized by collaboration; the deprivatization of practice; reflective dialogue; conversations that "hold practice, pedagogy and student learning under scrutiny"; a focus on student learning; and shared values (Kruse, Louis, & Bryk, 1995, p. 30). These images of professional growth are consistent with the ideals and struggles of schools engaged in the journey toward more democratic schooling. Schools in which significant teacher professional growth occurs, in essence, are democratic communities of inquiry.

In conclusion, for those who criticize democratic schooling as being incongruent with "the real world," we leave you with one final thought. Perhaps a new mind-set is required. Such a mind-set might hold that democratic schools are the real world. Contrastingly, the world of poverty, inequality, and injustice is the false world we have created by our neglect of democratic ideals in schools and in other arenas.[1]

Note

1. We are indebted to Robert McCarthy, former Acting Director of the Coalition of Essential Schools, for this thought.

References

Beane, J. A., & Apple, M. W. (1995). The case for democratic schools. In M. W. Apple & J. A. Beane (Eds.), *Democratic schools* (pp. 1-23). Alexandria, VA: Association for Supervision and Curriculum Development.

Darling-Hammond, L., & McLaughlin, M. W. (1995). Policies that support professional development in an era of reform. *Phi Delta Kappan 76*, 597-604.

Dewey, J. (1916). *Democracy and education*. New York: Free Press.

Foster, W. (1989). Toward a critical practice of leadership. In J. Smyth (Ed.), *Critical perspectives on educational leadership* (pp. 39-62). Philadelphia: Falmer.

Fullan, M. G. (1993). *Change forces*. New York: Teachers College Press.

Giroux, H. A. (1992). Educational leadership and the crisis of democratic culture. *Educational Researcher, 21*(4), 4-11.

Glickman, C. D. (1993). *Renewing America's schools: A guide for school-based action*. San Francisco: Jossey-Bass.

Goodman, J. (1992). *Elementary schooling for critical democracy*. Albany: State University of New York Press.

Kruse, S. D., Louis, K. S., & Bryk, A. S. (1995). An emerging framework for analyzing school-based professional community. In K. S. Louis & S. D. Kruse (Eds.), *Professionalism and community: Perspectives on reforming urban schools* (pp. 23-42). Thousand Oaks, CA: Corwin.

Lieberman, A. (1995). Practices that support teacher development: Transforming conceptions of professional learning. *Phi Delta Kappan, 76*, 591-596.

Little, J. W. (1982). Norms of collegiality and experimentation: Workplace conditions of school success. *American Educational Research Journal, 19*, 325-340.

Newmann, F. M., & Wehlage, G. G. (1995). *Successful school restructuring*. Madison, WI: Center on Organization and Restructuring of Schools.

O'Hair, M. J., McLaughlin, H. J., & Reitzug, U. C. (in press). *The foundations of democratic education*. Fort Worth, TX: Harcourt Brace.

O'Hair, M. J., & Reitzug, U. C. (1997). Restructuring schools for democracy: Principals' perspectives. *Journal of School Leadership, 7*, 266-286.

Reitzug, U. C., & Cross, B. E. (1995). Constraining and facilitating aspects of site-based management in urban schools. *International Journal of Educational Reform, 4*, 329-340.

Soder, R. (1996). Preface. In R. Soder (Ed.), *Democracy, education, and the schools* (pp. xi-xvi). San Francisco: Jossey-Bass.

Strike, K. A. (1993). Professionalism, democracy, and discursive communities. *American Educational Research Journal, 30*, 255-275.

◙

8 Teacher Centered for Teacher Change

Stephanie Kadel-Taras

Stephanie Kadel-Taras recently received her Ph.D. in cultural foundations of education from Syracuse University. Her research interests
include the change process in classrooms and schools and collaborative efforts among people and systems. She is currently working as a
writer in Ann Arbor, Michigan.

ABSTRACT

Using findings from qualitative research with teachers in one
urban, public high school, the author argues that teachers are
and need to be teacher centered to change their practices and
work toward improvement for the benefit of themselves and
their students. Teachers in this study recognized that to do their
best for students, they needed to center some of their energy
and efforts on their own interests and requirements as learners
and on their own needs for control, security, power, and a life
outside of school. This chapter describes how teachers in one
school acted on their own desires as learners and maintained
control in the classroom and control over self to change their
practices. It concludes that efforts to empower teachers as
change agents must recognize their needs and allow teachers
to articulate how they can best be supported in their work.

With school improvement and professional development taking prominence in educational policy and practice discussions, research on the
change process in schools and classrooms has been plentiful in recent
years. Although much has been learned about how schools as organiza-
tions respond to and work through changes, the experiences of individual

teachers with change, especially with changes that they undertake for their own purposes, is not well understood. Learning more about how teachers change their practices throughout their careers and grow and renew themselves as professionals is necessary for understanding how to improve the learning environment in schools for all who work there. In this chapter, I will report on a qualitative study in one public high school that looked at when, why, and how teachers change their practices.

Researching Teacher Change

This study adds to a body of research on educational reform that focuses on teachers' roles in the change process to improve teaching and learning. Most of this literature has focused on how teachers respond to changes proposed by outsiders (e.g., Chenoweth & Kushman, 1993; D. K. Cohen, 1991; Schofield, 1989) even when some of these studies have emphasized teachers' views of and experiences with change (e.g., Fullan, 1991; Stephens, Gaffney, Weinzierl, Shelton, & Clark, 1993; Wilson, 1988). Only recently have some researchers, many of them teachers themselves, begun to explore the change process as it is initiated and carried out in classrooms by teachers for their own purposes (e.g., Ball & Rundquist, 1993; R. M. Cohen, 1991; Louden, 1991; Wasley, 1990; Wideman, 1991; Wilson, Miller, & Yerkes, 1993; Wolk & Rodman, 1994).

The latter studies have presented teacher change as an ongoing search for better ways to teach and address students' needs and have valued the teacher's role as a learner. Such research recognizes that teachers do not just continue business as usual in their classrooms until someone comes along to tell them to change. Rather than merely receiving and implementing change, teachers themselves plan and design new approaches, facilitate one another's growth, seek new knowledge, and research what works. Approaches to educational improvement and school reform can be enhanced by exploring teacher change in its ongoing, spontaneous, problem-centered, teacher-directed forms. Research from this perspective has prompted new questions about teachers' understandings of their work, teacher empowerment, and the purpose of professional development (Cuban, 1990; Kahaney, 1993; Richardson, 1990, 1994a, 1994b; Rud & Oldendorf, 1992).

In seeking to understand more about teacher change, I studied nine teachers' voluntary, ongoing changes in instructional practice and the ways they made sense of what they were doing. My examination involved asking teachers to tell me about changes they were trying to make in their instruction and accepting their definitions of change in their practice. In using the qualifier *ongoing*, I am referring to my assumption that most teachers change all the time. I share Lieberman and Miller's (1991) notion of teaching practice as "craft" because it is concerned with "the making and remaking of an object until it satisfies the standards of its creator" (p. 95). I talked with teachers about the kinds of changes that they make all the time in response to the changing needs of students, new knowledge they have gained, and their own needs for growth and development as professionals.

The study took place at Davis High School[1]—a public high school—during the end of the 1993-1994 school year and throughout the 1994-1995 school year. Davis High is located in a residential neighborhood of a medium-sized Northeastern city and serves a diverse population of 1,100 students in Grades 9 through 12. These students come from the surrounding neighborhood that includes homes of middle-class professionals and a lower-income community of rented houses and apartments. About 45% of the students qualify for free or reduced lunches. During the year that I engaged in fieldwork at Davis High, the administration reported that 41% of the students were black, 39% were white, 3% were Asian, 2% were Hispanic, and 15% were "other," which included students of mixed ethnic background.

The teaching staff at Davis High is not as diverse. The faculty in 1994-1995 included 1 Asian, 9 black, and 71 white teachers. One teacher with whom I spoke believed that the faculty was made up of primarily older and more experienced teachers, and the school office staff estimated that 50% of the teachers would be eligible for retirement within 10 years. Only 10% of the faculty have been teaching fewer than 5 years.

I began my research at Davis High by asking various school staff members—including the staff development facilitator, the librarian, the principal, and two teachers who are on the School Improvement Committee—to identify teachers who were "doing new things." Consistent with a grounded theory approach to qualitative research, I used theoretical sampling to decide which of the teachers to include in the study (see Bogdan & Biklen, 1992; Glaser & Strauss, 1967). Nine teachers participated. Two were men (both white), and the rest were women (five white and two black). The sample included two English teachers and one teacher each in math, physics, chemistry, English as a second language (ESL), Spanish, and social studies. The ninth teacher, who had previously taught English at Davis, was currently working full-time as the school's staff development facilitator and did not have her own classroom. Two teachers had taught fewer than 5 years, four had taught between 10 and 20 years, and three had taught more than 20 years, but not all continuously; some had left teaching for a time to raise families and work other jobs.

I studied these teachers' work one at a time by observing several class periods over a week or two, talking with them after classes, and then interviewing them. Classroom visits allowed me to build rapport with the teachers before interviewing them in-depth and to get some idea of their styles and strengths, relationships with students, classroom challenges, and understandings of their work in daily practice. Each formal interview lasted between an hour and 90 minutes and took place in the teacher's classroom. DeVault's (1990) hope for interviewing is that "the researcher is actively involved with respondents, so that together they are constructing fuller answers to questions that cannot always be asked in simple, straightforward ways" (p. 100); I tried to create an atmosphere for this kind of discussion with the teachers. Following Strauss's (1987) suggestions for seeking "conceptual density" in one's interpretation, I analyzed data throughout the fieldwork by engaging in line-by-line coding of the field notes, writing reflective and speculative memos, and keeping an eye out for possible "core categories."

Teacher Centered for Teacher Change

I learned much from the teachers about the kinds of changes in practice that they undertake, why they make changes (to improve students' learning experiences, to seek excellence in their work, to avoid boredom), how teachers' understandings of their work influence their decisions about change, what challenges they face in trying to improve, and what support is and could be helpful to them as they change (see Kadel-Taras, 1996). The most intriguing findings for me, however, centered on teachers' behaviors, attitudes, and understandings of their work that affected when and how they changed their practices and how they benefited from the effort to change. Although their primary purpose for change, they told me, was to better address the learning needs of students, teachers also expected that this work would benefit themselves as professionals and individuals. In this way, teachers appear to be teacher centered as well as student centered in their professional activities and efforts to improve. As one teacher put it, "I like to get involved in things, and try to improve things, but as much as anything, I think I thought I could learn something from the process. So I could give something and get something." The data of this study revealed that certain teacher-centered behaviors and attitudes are important for facilitating teacher change and that to do their best for students, teachers need to center some of their energy and efforts on their own interests and requirements as learners and on their own needs for control, security, power, and a life outside of school.

Focusing on the benefits of being teacher centered does not preclude being student centered and being attentive to students' experiences, interests, ways of learning, abilities to teach one another, and interpretations. In fact, my findings point to the importance of teacher-centered behavior for such student-centered classrooms. The data suggest that teacher-centered teachers encourage student learning by being learners themselves. They need to feel in control of their lives and classrooms so that they can experiment with new practices such as allowing their students more control over learning experiences. Cohn and Kottkamp (1993) defend this position:

> For schools to be positive learning environments for students, they must be positive learning environments for teachers as well. Teachers who are not free to construct their own activities, inquire, engage in meaningful learning, take risks, make decisions, and assess their own competence will be unable to create those possibilities for students. Teachers who do not have self-esteem and a sense that they can control their own destinies will find it difficult to foster those beliefs in others. (p. 223)

Teacher Learning

Most of the teachers in my study recognized their own needs as learners. They were involved in various endeavors that led to better understandings of youths, teaching and the learning process, the teacher's subject of expertise, other content areas, and themselves. Their continual search for better ways to deal with the ongoing need for change (created by the ever-changing needs of students) led them to choose topics or instructional strategies for their classes that they wanted to study or explore. In this way, teacher learning and teacher change are mutually reinforcing: Teachers often learn by changing their practice, and when teachers act on their desire to learn, often they are led to change. For example, when I asked Fran Naylor (an English teacher) how she had come to believe in the importance of connecting literature to students' lives and diverse backgrounds, she seemed surprised by my question, as if the answer were obvious: "Because I'm a reader!"

Primarily, teachers in this study learned from changing their practice by choosing topics or projects for their classes that allowed them to study or experiment with something new. June Harding (a social studies teacher) teaches topics that she herself wants to study: "Some of what I do is because I have books on my bookshelf at home that I got through [a] bookstore, and I say, 'I always wanted to read this.'" Ella Paxton (a chemistry teacher) commented that she saw teaching as the only job where one can read, study, and "play with your toys," and do something different every year.

Teachers also attended to and talked about their own learning styles, and their approaches to learning clearly influenced their approaches to teaching their students. Lisa Monroe (a Spanish teacher) discussed her own need to be physically active while she challenged her mind, and she believed many students had the same need. Just as she admitted that she has "never appreciated a class" in which everyone is expected to be quiet and still—"I need to be doing something, or my head goes down on the desk and I fall asleep," she said—Lisa also worried about her own students being bored: "You gotta do something, or they put their heads down." Another connection between teacher learning and teacher change is that teachers who follow their own interests are more likely to be enthusiastic about their teaching and want to create equally stimulating opportunities for students. Gene Evans (who teaches physics) states this directly: "If it's not interesting for me, then it's not gonna be interesting for them."

One significant manifestation of the idea that teachers' approaches to learning influence their approaches to teaching is that the teachers who expected much of themselves as learners also expected much of their students. For example, June's high expectations for her own work are revealed in the variety of changes she has pursued including integrating social studies and English through team teaching, creating a new course emphasizing student-driven inquiry, and using student portfolios. Through classroom observations, I found that June expected students to think analytically about readings and films and to make connections among ideas. Just as June has been willing to try assignments and activities whose outcomes are not assured, she wants her students to take risks:

> I've always been interested in seeing the classroom as being sort of a . . . mini-workshop. . . . This should be a place where you can feel safe enough to risk doing some things that you want to try

out. Who are you? What can you do? Should you only have this be a safe environment because I've [the student] always done social studies, and I know how to do a worksheet, and therefore, I can get an 85, and that's all I want? Or can you have a safe environment where you can also risk and become empowered to do things other than just what you already know how to do well?

A focus on the teacher as learner is important, but it also carries with it certain risks. For instance, students obviously do not always learn the same ways a teacher does and are not always as enthusiastic about a subject as the teacher. Also, embracing the teacher as a learner peels back the facade of the teacher as expert, both on a particular subject and on teaching and learning, and some teachers, administrators, and parents may not be understanding of teachers' decisions to admit their uncertainties and declare their position as learners.

Teacher Control

The data of this study not only reveal a connection between teacher change and teachers as learners but also suggest that teachers' readiness and willingness to change are related to their sense of control over classroom happenings and over themselves as teachers. I use the word *control* in two overlapping ways; the first is the idea of being in charge or exercising authority, and the second is the idea of having a handle on something, feeling capable and sure of oneself. Teacher control as it is explored here encompasses numerous issues besides classroom management (probably the most common use of the term) including control over teaching methods, subject matter, and curriculum; control over the rate of change in one's courses; and even control over one's will to pursue opportunities, make priorities, and take risks. As part of the notion of teacher centeredness, all these kinds of teacher control seem to be important for teachers to change and improve.

Control in the Classroom

Teachers in this study maintained control in the classroom in a variety of ways and used this control to aid their efforts to improve. First, they used control over student behavior not only to accomplish routine class activities but also to try new things. Davis High's staff development facilitator, Olivia Banks, made me aware of this issue in one of our first conversations when she postulated that new, young teachers are not likely to be trying innovative strategies in the classroom, because they are "just overwhelmed by the students. . . . They just need some way to get some control in their classrooms. They use worksheets a lot because it is a way to keep some order." Lisa (in her third year as a teacher) and Gene (in his fourth year) partially confirmed Olivia's observation. Both of them felt that their teaching had improved as they had learned "how to handle kids more," as Gene put it. Many teachers' comments suggested that controlling student behavior is not primarily about "sitting on" students and keeping them still, but rather, getting to know them, learning how to relate to them, and figuring out what they need so that they can learn. Ella recognized the need for control in the classroom to try new labs or other lessons. She explained,

> I've never been afraid of losing control. Because if I lost control, I would admit it. I would stand in front of students and [say], "Look folks, this is out of hand. Let's regroup. Let's figure out what we're gonna do. I mean, we can't do this, because everybody's talking or . . . . What's a better way of doing this?"

Teachers also seek control over the methods (e.g., class discussions, questioning, assignments, labs, long-term projects) they are using to teach a lesson or concept, but this does not mean that a teacher is always certain how new methods will play out in the classroom. Instead, the teachers in this study seemed more likely to attempt something new if they felt they had "safe-guards" in place to make it work. Ella emphasized that she does not "take risks without planning"; teachers who are "afraid of losing control," she said, "don't have the one, two, three, four of how to implement this stuff."

Ted Wyatt (a teacher in the ESL program) discussed how he had not tried something new because he had not felt that he had control over the methods. Although he had taken a series of workshops on cooperative learning during the previous year, and he said that he was excited about using this approach, he also said that he was hesitant to do so because he had not yet resolved how to grade cooperative projects: "They didn't really address that [grading] very much in the workshop. So that's something that I still need to look at and need to get some more information on, maybe some more ideas, before I use it a lot." Lisa talked about wanting to use more technological resources and creative materials, but she admitted that she was not yet ready. She believed she would eventually reach the point in her work where she could say, " 'Okay, I've got all this under control and now I wanna get to the good stuff.' I feel like I haven't even hit the good stuff," she observed.

Teachers who are trying new things also have a sense of control over the subject matter and courses they teach and the curriculum they are expected to use or that they have developed. A number of teachers suggested that having this control allowed them to experiment more with new ways of teaching that curriculum. After she had taught advanced placement American history for a few years, June felt she was gaining some control: "By 3 years, you kind of know the material, and then you can start to play around with it." Experience has also given Fran enough control over her English courses that she can diverge from the traditional curriculum. In her efforts to teach literature, for instance, Fran no longer begins with the assumption that all students should be exposed to a certain set of classics; instead, she takes into account the gender, race, and background of readers (her students) when choosing books, and she allows students much more freedom to make their own selections. Having control over subject matter and curriculum, however, does not preclude the postmodern recognition of knowledge as culturally and contextually dependent, and of course content as slippery and shifting rather than a set of fixed truths. This kind of teacher control, as I understand it, involves having enough familiarity with one's courses and content specialty to recognize and incorporate varied interpretations and to be able to make changes in the curriculum that reflect the fluid nature of knowledge.

The data of this study point to one more kind of teacher control in the classroom. Discussions with some of the teachers indicate that it is helpful to balance stability and tradition in one's teaching with innovation and risk and thus control the rate of change. Fran's teaching, which combines new approaches such as community service projects with more conventional instruction such as punctuation quizzes, exemplifies this kind of control. Also, both Karen Valusek (a math teacher) and Ella believed that there is still a place for teacher lecture despite their efforts to incorporate more discovery and cooperative learning experiences. The data suggest that controlling the rate of change and mixing old and new practices benefits the teachers by allowing them to minimize the risks involved with change, focus their change efforts on pressing problems, take the time to polish their use of a new practice, and ensure that their practices remain consistent with their goals.

Control Over Self

Control over self, as well as control in the classroom, influences teachers' readiness for and approaches to change. Teachers need to hold certain teacher-centered behaviors and attitudes that result in the kind of self-discipline that enables change. For example, teachers need to feel a sense of power or efficacy in their work. Typically, the term *efficacy* is used in educational literature to refer to teachers' sense of success in reaching and teaching students (e.g., Wasley, 1990; Yee, 1990), but I am broadening this meaning to include teachers' belief that they have the power to change what they perceive as problematic. Olivia, for example, compared her own approach to change with the perspectives of teachers in the school whom she perceived to be avoiding change:

> I think it's paralysis more than anything else. How do you get them to believe that they have power? And I think that's been the key to my success as a teacher. I never believed for a moment that I was not the most powerful person on earth. Probably half arrogantly and half with a sense of humor that if I didn't do it, it wasn't gonna get done, so, "Get out of my way," and, you know, "Close the door, and let's design a class that's effective and healthy for kids."

Many of the teachers in my study exhibited a belief in their own power to make change happen. June said that she felt "secure" at the school so that the risks of change did not daunt her much, and Ella emphasized that in her work she was "not a follower": "I'm not afraid to do things that nobody else is doing."

Some teachers demonstrated their sense of efficacy through a willingness to fight for what they wanted and needed for improvement. They seemed to believe that just about any support, materials, time, or space that they required could be had if they were creative or insistent enough. For instance, when Fran decided that students needed to produce a school newspaper, she looked for a way to get computers into her classroom. I asked Fran how she had procured her six computers and two printers. "I just badgered people," she recalled. She worried that other teachers were jealous of her computer setup, but contended, "They haven't fought for them, and I don't feel sorry for people who don't . . . fight for stuff and . . . speak up."

Fran, Karen, June, and Olivia all maintained and acted on a sense of efficacy—a belief that their efforts toward improvement were worth it and that if they fought for what they wanted, they would somehow get it. These teachers, however, were clearly in positions from which they could be insistent and expect a response: They were known to be good teachers by others in the educational system. They were all fairly experienced teachers, and they were all involved in special efforts (such as university projects or state-level mentoring) that recognized their excellence as teachers. Not only might such recognition have encouraged an attitude of confidence and empowerment (an internal sense of power), but it may have allowed them to wield a certain amount of external power in the school and/or district.

Teachers who change also demonstrate control over their own will. They need the will to face down their fears and to find the energy and time to do the work of change. Many teachers talked about the fear and risk associated with change when they did not know how it was going to turn out. Olivia believed that teachers fear change because "nobody knows what that change will look like at the end," and Ted admitted that he avoided changes because of his "familiarity with doing it the way I've done it in years past." Of course, conserving some stability in one's teaching is important for all teachers, and maintaining some practices that are "meaningful and familiar" can allow teachers to take risks in other areas of their teaching. When a fear of the unknown prevents a teacher from making any improvements, however, some control over self is required to meet the ongoing need for change.

Teachers also admitted that change takes extra work and extra time, which they did not always want to give. Gene explained that at first he did not want to take students on a physics field trip because "it seems like a lot of work. It's that sort of thing, you know. I can't help it, I'm human." June admitted that helping students locate materials for her more creative assignments "takes tremendous time," and she revealed that she spends many weekends and parts of most holidays and breaks doing library research for her classes. Despite the challenges posed by the fear, work, and time that can accompany change, most of the teachers in this study had decided to practice a kind of control over self that compelled them to swallow their fear, take on the work required, and make the time necessary to improve. As Gene said, "I sort of force myself to do it anyway."

Taking on the challenges of change and practicing control over self is facilitated by the teachers' sense of security and confidence. Olivia used the term *security* to denote a sense of purpose in one's work and surety about one's abilities: "It's a little chutzpah, it's belief in yourself." In contrast, she observed that "if you're insecure, you're going to use the [course] book as your bible, which is the least inspiring text, and you're not going to stray from the known." Similarly, Karen observed that teachers differ in their feelings of "comfort." She compared teachers in her math project who were "trying here and there with new lessons" to others who "just scoop up everything and just run with it." Closely linked to a sense of security as a teacher is a feeling of confidence, which also relates to whether one feels in control in the classroom. My analysis suggests that self-confidence, readiness for change, and success with change are intertwined and mutually reinforcing. Confidence seems to have been both an instigator and result of change for Ella, who laughingly shared, "I was always very confident. I'm even more confident now."

A final issue related to control over self is control in one's personal life. One aspect of this is teachers' ability to take care of themselves and get their personal needs met so that they can concentrate on improving their work lives. In observing the lives and work of other teachers, Olivia has come to believe that teachers who seek excellence in their work "have happy personal lives." A second aspect of this control is the ability to prioritize the many commitments of work and home life. Teachers realize that to have the time and energy for change, they may have less time and energy for other activities in their lives. Understandably, teachers are more and less willing to make the work of change a priority, depending, for example, on whether or not they are married or have young children at home.

Conclusion

Valuing teachers' voluntary, ongoing changes in practice is one way of empowering them in the process of educational improvement. For high school teachers who want to do more to change their practice, and for those in schools who want to assist teachers in this process, the findings of this study encourage teachers to focus on their own needs to learn and be in control while also focusing on their students' needs to learn and gain some control in their own work and lives. Those outside of classrooms—policymakers, administrators, and staff development specialists—who endeavor to foster educational change and who espouse the importance of empowering teachers in this process need to consider altering their usual question to teachers, "How can we include and make use of you in our educational reform efforts?" to "How can you include and make use of us in your educational reform efforts?" With support that they deem necessary, teachers may be able to increase their sense of power to create change. They will then be able to use teacher-centered behaviors and attitudes to take a more central role in decisions about and action toward educational improvement in their classrooms and schools.

Note

1. Consistent with my promise of confidentiality, all names of institutions and persons have been changed.

References

Ball, D. L., & Rundquist, S. S. (1993). Collaboration as a context for joining teacher learning with learning about teaching. In D. K. Cohen, M. W. McLaughlin, & J. E. Talbert (Eds.), *Teaching for understanding: Challenges for policy and practice* (pp. 13-42). San Francisco: Jossey-Bass.

Bogdan, R. C., & Biklen, S. K. (1992). *Qualitative research for education: An introduction to theory and methods* (2nd ed.). Boston: Allyn & Bacon.

Chenoweth, T., & Kushman, J. (1993, April). *Courtship and school restructuring: Building early commitment to school change for at-risk students.* Paper presented at the annual meeting of the American Educational Research Association, Atlanta, GA.

Cohen, D. K. (1991). Revolution in one classroom (or, then again, was it?). *American Educator, 15*(2), 16-32, 44-48.

Cohen, R. M. (1991). *A lifetime of teaching: Portraits of five veteran high school teachers.* New York: Teachers College Press.

Cohn, M. M., & Kottkamp, R. B. (1993). *Teachers: The missing voice in education.* Albany: State University of New York Press.

Cuban, L. (1990). A fundamental puzzle of school reform. In A. Lieberman (Ed.), *Schools as collaborative cultures: Creating the future now* (pp. 71-77). New York: Falmer.

DeVault, M. L. (1990). Talking and listening from women's standpoint: Feminist strategies for interviewing and analysis. *Social Problems, 37*(1), 96-116.

Fullan, M. G. (1991). *The new meaning of educational change.* New York: Teachers College Press.

Glaser, B., & Strauss, A. L. (1967). *The discovery of grounded theory: Strategies for qualitative research.* Chicago: Aldine.

Kadel-Taras, S. (1996). *Always a better way: Making sense of teacher change.* Unpublished doctoral dissertation, Syracuse University, Syracuse, NY.

Kahaney, P. (1993). Afterword: Knowledge, learning and change. In P. Kahaney, L. Perry, & J. Janangelo (Eds.), *Theoretical and critical perspectives on teacher change* (pp. 191-200). Norwood, NJ: Ablex.

Lieberman, A., & Miller, L. (1991). Revisiting the social realities of teaching. In A. Lieberman & L. Miller (Eds.), *Staff development for education in the '90s: New demands, new realities, new perspectives* (pp. 92-109). New York: Teachers College Press.

Louden, W. (1991). *Understanding teaching: Continuity and change in teachers' knowledge.* New York: Teachers College Press.

Richardson, V. (1990). Significant and worthwhile change in teaching practice. *Educational Researcher, 19*(7), 10-18.

Richardson, V. (1994a). Conducting research on practice. *Educational Researcher,* 23(5), 5-10.

Richardson, V. (Ed.). (1994b). *Teacher change and the staff development process: A case in reading instruction.* New York: Teachers College Press.

Rud, A. G., Jr., & Oldendorf, W. P. (Eds.). (1992). *A place for teacher renewal: Challenging the intellect, creating educational reform.* New York: Teachers College Press.

Schofield, J. W. (1989). *Black and white in school: Trust, tension, or tolerance?* New York: Teachers College Press.

Stephens, D., Gaffney, J., Weinzierl, J., Shelton, J., & Clark, C. (1993). *Toward understanding teacher change* (Tech. Rep. No. 585). Champaign: University of Illinois at Urbana-Champaign, College of Education, Center for the Study of Reading.

Strauss, A. (1987). *Qualitative analysis for social scientists.* Cambridge, UK: Cambridge University Press.

Wasley, P. A. (1990). *Stirring the chalkdust: Three teachers in the midst of change.* Providence, RI: Brown University, Coalition of Essential Schools.

Wideman, R. (1991). *How secondary school teachers change their classroom practices.* Unpublished doctoral dissertation, University of Toronto.

Wilson, D. E. (1988, March). *Writing projects and writing instruction: A study of teacher change.* Paper presented at the annual meeting of the Conference on College Composition and Communication, St. Louis, MO.

Wilson, S. M., Miller, C., & Yerkes, C. (1993). Deeply rooted change: A tale of learning to teach adventurously. In D. K. Cohen, M. W. McLaughlin, & J. E. Talbert (Eds.), *Teaching for understanding: Challenges for policy and practice* (pp. 85-129). San Francisco: Jossey-Bass.

Wolk, R. A., & Rodman, B. H. (1994). *Classroom crusaders: Twelve teachers who are trying to change the system.* San Francisco: Jossey-Bass.

Yee, S. M. (1990). *Careers in the classroom: When teaching is more than a job.* New York: Teachers College Press.

9 Adaptive Teacher Beliefs for Continued Professional Growth During Postmodern Transitions

M. Jayne Fleener

Pamela G. Fry

M. Jayne Fleener is Associate Professor and Mathematics Education Certification Chair, Instructional Leadership and Academic Curriculum at the University of Oklahoma. Her primary research focuses are on educational dynamics, teacher development, and beliefs. She has published articles on student and teacher beliefs about mathematics education using metaphor analysis, chaos and learning organization theory, and the nature and role of dialogic communities for teacher change.

Pamela G. Fry is Associate Dean in the College of Education at the University of Oklahoma. Her primary research interests are in professional teacher preparation and development in the contexts of language and culture. She has published articles on metaphor and the analysis of teaching.

ABSTRACT

This chapter outlines the social, political, scientific, and economic factors of and tensions between modernity and postmodernity. The modernist tradition is compared with a postmodernist perspective of an adaptive and interdependent world culture. Educational reform efforts are discussed grounded in this climate of paradigmatic change. Within this context, the complex interplay among beliefs, practices, and reflection is addressed related to Combs's effective personal theories of teachers. A model of teacher reflectivity is presented that represents an important aspect of teachers' struggles within these changing social realities and serves as a process to ensure continued professional growth and adaptation.

It is no coincidence that the 1990s seem to be the age of reform. Politically, we see economic and social changes dominating the news. As a social institution, schools are similarly caught up in debates about school restructuring and educational reform. School prayer, basic skills development, national curricular standards, and school-to-work are just a few of the major issues facing a concerned public and professional educators. Struggles with transforming schools involve questions of needed changes in teacher preparation and the proliferation of professional development models for continued teacher growth.

Is our personal and social angst resulting from the preoccupation with social, economic, and political changes merely a consequence of "millennium madness," or are we truly entering into a new age of social and political interdependencies that requires an examination of and changes in our social and political institutions and policies? How are schools affected and how must they adapt to these changes? What is the role of teacher professional development in helping teachers adjust to and survive this climate of change and uncertainty? Ultimately, what role can teacher professional growth play in the improvement of education for our children?

This chapter will outline both the social, political, scientific, and economic factors that suggest we are indeed entering into a very different era in human social development and how teachers can successfully adapt to those changes. The modernist tradition, which has predominated our institutional and personal relationships as well as influenced our individual belief systems for the past 300 years, will be compared with a postmodernist perspective of an adaptive and interdependent world culture. Educational reform efforts will be discussed within this climate of paradigmatic change. In particular, teacher preparation and teacher development, as a continuum of professional teacher growth, will be described. Finally, teacher change and teacher beliefs will be explored and a model of teacher critical decision making for reflective growth and adaptive change will be presented as an important aspect of teachers' struggles within the changing social realities. The role of teacher beliefs and the need for professional development models that account for the social, political, economic, and technological tensions of early 21st-century society will be delineated and the need for more constructive models of professional development and growth will be argued.

Age of Modernity

Transition to the Modern Perspective

The modern perspective came about as social, political, religious, and scientific revolutions replaced medieval forms of government and religious control. The modern perspective represents "social emancipation" from the "particularism, paternalism and superstition of premodern times" (Hargreaves, 1994, p. 25). The transitory period between premodernism and modernism is known as the Renaissance or Age of Awakening, when the rights, responsibilities, and capabilities of the individual became paramount. The 16th century marks the beginning of the era known as the Enlightenment, often characterized as the Age of Reason because of its emphasis on individual rationality. Turner (1990, quoted in Hargreaves, 1994) summarized the rise of modernity this way:

Modernity arises with the spread of western imperialism in the sixteenth century; the dominance of capitalism in northern Europe . . . in the early seventeenth century; the acceptance of scientific procedures with the publication of the works of Francis Bacon, Newton and Harvey; and preeminently with the institutionalization of Calvinistic practices and beliefs in the dominant classes of northern Europe. (pp. 24-25)

Dramatic changes in social, political, economic, scientific, and technical cultures marked this transition from the premodern to modern world, suggesting a fundamental shift in worldviews. The basic tenets of the modern perspective, described below, reveal that the world that was created with this paradigmatic shift is indeed the world in which most of us have lived.

Cornerstones of Modernity

The rejection of the authority and mysticism of the medieval church, the rise of new forms of governance structures and economic bases, and the emphasis on the rights of individuals characterized the transition from the premodern era to the modern era. From these beginnings, the modern perspective is grounded in three fundamental beliefs, which are the basis for our own society and the development of the Industrial Age. These are the beliefs in (a) individual rationality, (b) social progress, and (c) universal truths. Each of these cornerstones of modernity will be described below.

Individual Rationality

Individual rationality, as a cornerstone of the modern perspective, has ramifications for the role of the individual in society, the purpose of social systems, the power of the intellect, and the predictability and regularity of nature. Descartes' *cogito* ("I think, therefore I am") placed the human intellect as the final determiner of that which is certain. As the basis of all knowledge, belief in the primacy of individual rationality empowered humans with the ability to reason and discover truths about the nature of reality. Discoveries by Isaac Newton suggesting uniformity, regularity, and predictability of planetary motion further gave credence to the perspective that through rational deliberation, humans could discover the inner workings of nature.

The emphasis on the intellect in the modern era had ramifications for all aspects of social and intellectual life. The faith in the human intellect "celebrated the individual as opposed to established authority . . . the supremacy of reason, of the individual, and of individual freedom . . . Protestantism in religion, self-expression in the arts, [and] experimentation in science" (Elkind, 1995, p. 9).

The picture of the universe as a giant clock is the dominant metaphor for the modern perspective. This perspective implies that humans can understand the mechanics of reality, as the clock maker understands the mechanics of a clock by taking the clock apart, studying the pieces, and putting it back together again. Mechanical time, in fact, became more than a metaphor for scientific inquiry during the Industrial Revolution. Time itself took on a new meaning within our social, economic, and political institutions (Capra, 1982). Mechanical time, unlike cosmic time, was to be controlled, measured, and further delineated into finer and finer increments. Like the clock maker, in a mechanical universe we not only have the means of understanding our reality by studying its pieces but of defining and fixing it as well. As we pull our universe apart to understand its components, we are empowered to replace the broken parts and fix the clock to our specifications; thus, we are mandated to control our environment for individual, social, and political progress.

Implicit in this worldview is the belief that rational progress of social institutions will ultimately contribute to more freedom for the individual. Thus, individual rationality not only is the basis for the modern perspective, but it is toward the vision of further freeing the individual from social, economic, and natural constraints that individuation is important. As argued by David Harvey (1989, quoted in Hargreaves, 1994),

> The scientific domination of nature promised freedom from scarcity, want, and the arbitrariness of natural calamity. The development of rational forms of social organization and rational modes of thought promised liberation from the irrationalities of myth, religion, superstition, [and] release from the arbitrary use of power. (pp. 25-26)

Social Progress

The power of the intellect to both discover the inner workings of nature and free the individual from social and natural constraints, as described above, is intimately connected to the second cornerstone of the modernist perspective, namely, the belief in social progress. Social progress is "the idea that society and the lot of individuals within that society are gradually improving" (Elkind, 1995, p. 9). The growth in scientific knowledge and advances in technological innovations during the Industrial Era are indicators of this belief. The relationship between individual rationality and social progress is summarized by Hargreaves (1994): "Modernity rests upon the Enlightenment beliefs that nature can be transformed and social progress achieved by the systematic development of scientific and technological understanding, and by its rational application to social and economic life" (p. 25).

Universal Truths

Scientific rationalism and the power of the intellect to discover the inner workings of the universe similarly led to the belief in universal truths. Scientific and social theories as articulations of universal truths predominate the modern perspective. By removing the perspective of the scientist and using objective, verifiable, replicable modes of inquiry, these truths, according to the modern perspective, are discoverable. Thus, through disinterested, value-free inquiry, universal truths can be uncovered. The epistemological stance of modernity, therefore, is one of positivist inquiry.

Postmodernity

Origins of Postmodernity

The basic tenets of the modernist perspective were severely challenged in the early part of the 20th century with discoveries in quantum physics. Operating within the clockwork metaphor, the modernist perspective provided an approach to understanding based on the belief that one could examine the basic building blocks of a system to understand the system itself and how it works. Thus, the agenda for quantum physicists early in the 20th century was to understand quanta, the subatomic particles that make up our world. Knowing about the nature of quanta as the basic "things" of reality would reveal, from the modernist perspective, underlying truths about reality. What was discovered, however, was that quanta are not things at all. As described by Garmston and Wellman (1995):

In the quantum world, thingness gives way to a conception of a world composed of energy, a world in which subatomic particles appear as waves of probability. These are not probabilities of *things,* but rather are probabilities of *interconnections.* . . . In the quantum world, elementary matter loses its thingness by displaying two identities. It can appear as particles—localized points in space, or it can appear as waves—energy spread over an area of fixed volume. . . . The wave packet contains two complementary aspects of one existence. These two aspects cannot, however, be studied at the same time. . . . Quantum matter is influenced by the very act of observation. To observe and measure is to make a choice. In such choice making, the observer joins the system being observed. (p. 8)

These discoveries marked a significant break with the modernist perspective that elements of a system can be studied separately from the system. Similarly, the certainty of knowledge and the belief in objective scientific inquiry were challenged by these discoveries in quantum physics to the extent that, before he died, Einstein confessed quantum physics must be wrong, for "God does not play dice with reality" and quantum reality cannot be mere probabilistic relationships.

The Tension of the Late 20th Century

Linearity, predictability, and objectivity of inquiry were confounded by the discovery of nonlinearity, uncertainty, irregularity, interconnectivity, and subjectivity in the quantum world. If scientific rationalism and the modernist perspective cannot answer questions about the basic building blocks of matter, what are the implications for other areas of knowing? Can we continue to tout the tenets of individualism, social progress, and universal truths in a rapidly changing world full of contradictions, interdependence, contextual relativity, and uncertainty?

The tension between the modernistic and postmodernistic perspectives is found in the social, economic, and political realms as well. We, as a world society, are confronted with an uncertain future, interdependent world economies, political upheaval, rapid technological innovations, and the proliferation of information. Within these contexts, schools too are found to be in a precarious position of redefining a reality of which we are not certain.

Perhaps most important for educational reform efforts, in general, and for teacher professional development, in particular, is not only a realization of the shifting paradigms that mark the end of the 20th century but the contradictions and tensions created by living in these "interesting times" of changing worldviews. Hargreaves (1995) cites five contextual paradoxes in particular that schools must face during these turbulent times:

1. Many parents have given up responsibility for the very things they want schools to stress.
2. Business often fails to use the skills that it demands schools produce.
3. More globalism produces more tribalism.
4. More diversity and integration is accompanied by more emphasis on common standards and specialization.

5. Stronger orientation to the future creates greater nostalgia for the past.

Schools in the United States today evolved during a time of industrialization and immigration and are based on modernistic principles. The changing roles of schools and teachers during this transitory period of confused values and shifting perspectives must be examined within the context of an understanding of the origins and goals of schools in a time of modernistic technocracy.

Adaptive Personal Beliefs

The tension between the modernist and postmodernist perspectives affects teachers as "the teacher's role expands to take on new problems and mandates, . . . creating senses of overload . . . [as] old missions and purposes begin to crumble . . . and strategies teachers use, along with the knowledge base which justifies them, are constantly criticized" (Hargreaves, 1994, p. 4).

Within this context of shifting paradigms, rapid change, technological innovation, information overload, and social pressure, adaptive teacher beliefs are vital to accommodate paradox, cooperate with transition, and prepare for changes necessary for surviving the future. This section of the chapter will address belief structures especially adaptive to the modernity-postmodernity tension.

Combs (1982) suggests six characteristics of an effective personal theory of teaching. He claims personal theories must be

1. Comprehensive
2. Accurate
3. Internally congruent
4. Personally relevant
5. Appropriate to the tasks confronted
6. Open to change

These categories will be used to examine the nature of beliefs and the role systems of beliefs play in individuals' adaptation to the modernity-postmodernity tension and in the eventual restructuring that schools will find necessary to accommodate changes in our social, economic, scientific, and world cultures.

Comprehensive Beliefs

Persons with comprehensive belief structures successfully deal with the complexities of change demanded by the incongruities, uncertainties, and tensions of postmodernist society. Similarly, comprehensive beliefs are necessary for flexible teaching. Without a comprehensive system of beliefs, teaching becomes "flat" or routinized as teachers are forced to adopt strategies that minimize complexity rather than deal with the realities of complexity. In Glickman's (1985) view,

> *The only alternative for a teacher in a complex environment who cannot adjust to multiple demands and is not being helped to acquire the abilities to think abstractly is to simplify and deaden the instructional environment.* Teachers make the environment less complex by disregarding the differences between students, by establishing routines and instructional practices that remain the same day after day and year after year. (p. 52, italics in original)

Given the rapid changes in society's demographics and the amount of information generated in a postmodernist era, the implication for teacher development is clear and urgent: Teachers need support in their efforts to develop comprehensive belief systems.

Accurate Theories

An accurate theory of teaching, according to Combs (1982), must be based in critical reflection for an individual to interpret and assess actions. Although Combs did not address the multiple realities of complex societies, this aspect of effective systems of teacher beliefs addresses the mismatch among perceptions, assumptions, and actual roles teachers and education play in our society. For example, the well-known comparison of schools to factories is commonly used but does not reflect the role schools must play in a postmodernist society. Students cannot be perceived as "products" for society to "consume," nor can the antiquated notions that, as "raw materials," students can be "standardized" to ensure "product quality" and reflect "managerial efficiency" continue to be used to judge the effectiveness of schools. Through the reflective process, teachers' personal beliefs must be examined in view of the needs and changes of our postmodernist framework. Unconscious, often unquestioned beliefs are open to scrutiny for teachers through their own professional efforts to develop a picture of teaching and education that more accurately reflects the realities of our complex and rapidly changing society.

Internally Congruent Systems of Belief

In addition to accurately reflecting our social realities, an effective belief system needs to be internally consistent yet flexible as new ideas are constructed from critical reflection of experiences. Furthermore, congruent beliefs serve an individual in various contexts. For example, if one believes that the development of autonomy is a primary goal of schooling, it is likely that the same person will value autonomy as a goal for his or her students as well.

Personally Relevant Belief Systems

Lack of meaning and sensemaking is a characteristic of our society trapped between the changing paradigms of modernity and postmodernity. Effective belief systems, in addition to reflecting and recognizing the realities of our times and being internally congruent, must be personally relevant. If a belief system is personally relevant, a teacher understands those beliefs, and those beliefs are meaningful within that individual's situation. The beliefs provide a personal frame of reference from which one interacts with the world and reflects and constructs new ideas.

Beliefs Appropriate to Tasks

For a personal belief system to be appropriate to tasks, not only must it be comprehensive in nature but one must be able to use it to make clearly understood and appropriate choices for any given context. Thus, despite the multiplicity of perspectives and the tensions existing for teachers in schools from a variety of sources, there are courses of action that can be judged as making the most sense in a given situation. Combs's (1982) notion of "beliefs appropriate to tasks," therefore, implies a systematicity, interdependence, and connectivity of beliefs and actions related to values, previous interactions, and decisions. Combs states, "Beliefs in a personal theory do not exist in a jumbled mass. They are organized in terms of value and relevance and may result in vastly different choices" (p. 9). For example, teachers who value student autonomy may also recognize the need and time for teacher authority while maintaining respect for the dignity of students. The choices made by teachers with an effective personal belief system are based on an understanding and exploration of possibilities within relevant contexts. Myopic commitment to practices or values without recognizing the particularity of demands within specific contexts are not aspects of an effective teacher belief system.

Open to Change

An effective personal system of belief includes mechanisms for recognition of and adaptive change through positive feedback from the environment. Whereas negative feedback, like static on the radio, is to be controlled for and ignored, positive feedback encourages change to the system as the organism adjusts to its environment (Gleick, 1987). With regard to teacher change, as Combs (1982) notes, personal theory must accommodate new meanings yet is not "willy-nilly with every new theory that appears on the horizon" (p. 9). Although your beliefs may remain stable through time, adaptations to related strands of those beliefs change with experiences and reflection.

Adaptive Model of Teacher Reflectivity

The common thread among the six interrelated aspects of an effective personal belief system is critical reflection. Critical awareness leads to personal and larger social change, necessary factors to adapt to and survive during this period of change. Freire (1973) refers to "conscientization" as the "development of the awakening of critical awareness" (p. 19). Praxis, action with reflection, constitutes the process of conscientization. Through conscientization, teachers may enact and modify their individual belief systems or theories of teaching, may experience and nurture professional autonomy and adaptive behavior necessary for developing interpersonal and collective relationships, and may ultimately transform schools in the postmodern society yet to come.

Using the concept of conscientization, a model of adaptive teacher reflectivity was developed as shown in Figure 9.1.

In this model, critical reflection is a core process of adaptive teaching, which includes these three continuous and interrelated components:

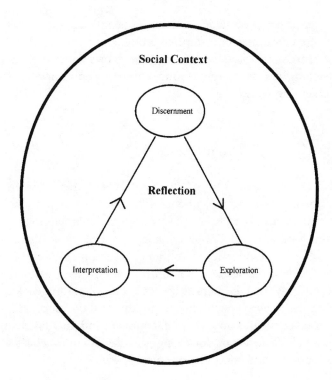

Figure 9.1. Model of Adaptive Teacher Reflectivity

1. Discernment: focusing on a phenomenon
2. Exploration: engaging in action, testing theories, and collecting information
3. Interpretation: understanding perceptions gained from discernment and exploration, generating theories, and adaptation to contexts

The process, a mechanism to develop critical awareness, allows for contextual teaching; teaching that recognizes and reacts sensitively to the complex dimensions of every classroom. As depicted in the model, the reflective process occurs within a social context that influences one's thinking and can be influenced by the reflective individual or group of individuals to form a collective conscientization. Collective conscientization, a "critical mass," is necessary to effect authentic, systematic change in schools (Hixsom, 1993).

The key to continued professional growth is insights into how to better enable teachers for continued and adaptive professional growth. Through the process of conscientization, teachers may develop adaptive personal theories of teaching necessary for dealing with the contradictions and conflicts of a changing world.

Significance

Hargreaves (1994) likens most professional development models to 12-step programs for recovering alcoholics. Effective classroom management, incorporation of new technologies or teaching methodologies, or curriculum development and implementation projects typically make teachers consumers of innovation. Programs designed to "empower" teachers to be "curriculum leaders" or to direct their own professional development similarly treat teachers as horses led to water (and we know how that story ends). These approaches to professional development are disrespectful of teachers and do little to encourage fundamental change of attitudes and beliefs necessary for changes in classroom practices and adaptation to changing and contradictory worldviews.

> Even the most well-intentioned change devices that try to respect teachers' discretionary judgments, promote their professional growth and support their efforts to build professional community are often self-defeating because they are squeezed into mechanistic models or suffocated through stifling supervision. . . . Professional development can be turned into bureaucratic control, mentor opportunities into mentor systems, collaborative cultures into contrived collegiality. In these ways, many administrative devices of change . . . take the heart out of teaching. (Hargreaves, 1994, p. 3)

Putting the "heart" back into teaching requires understanding the centrality of teacher beliefs and the interconnectedness of beliefs, actions, and reflectivity. The model of adaptive teacher reflectivity recognizes this complex interplay among beliefs, actions, and reflectivity as well as the influences of the social context. As a model of adaptive change, the relationship to current tensions between modern and postmodern paradigms is especially pertinent.

This model is not intended as a prescription for surviving the current struggles in education, nor does it imply a vision of the future that we cannot anticipate. Rather, the model is intended as an articulation of critical praxis at a time when the ground on which we are standing not only is constantly shifting but may, in fact, be dissolving. How better can we prepare for an uncertain future than by recognizing the importance of the conscientizing process for teachers as professional growth and potential change?

The challenge of restructuring in education and elsewhere is a challenge of abandoning or attenuating bureaucratic controls, inflexible mandates, paternalistic forms of trust and quick system fixes in order to hear, articulate and bring together the disparate voices of teachers and other educational partners. (Hargreaves, 1994, p. 260)

References

Capra, F. (1982). *The turning point: Science, society, and the rising culture.* New York: Bantam.

Combs, A. W. (1982). *A personal approach to teaching: Beliefs that make a difference.* Boston: Allyn & Bacon.

Elkind, D. (1995, September). School and family in the postmodern world. *Phi Delta Kappan, 77*(1), 8-14.

Freire, P. (1973). *Education for critical consciousness.* New York: Seabury.

Garmston, R., & Wellman, B. (1995). Adaptive schools in a quantum universe. *Educational Leadership, 52*(7), 6-12.

Gleick, J. (1987). *Chaos: Making a new science.* Harmondsworth, UK: Penguin.

Glickman, C. D. (1985). *Supervision of instruction: A developmental approach.* Boston: Allyn & Bacon.

Hargreaves, A. (1994). *Changing teachers, changing times: Teachers' work and culture in the postmodern age.* New York: Teachers College Press.

Hargreaves, A. (1995). Renewal in the age of paradox. *Educational Leadership, 52*(7), 14-19.

Harvey, D. (1989). *The condition of postmodernity.* Oxford: Basil Blackwell.

Hixsom, J. (1993). Staff development in an urban school: The importance of context. *Journal of Staff Development, 14*(1), 54-55.

Turner, B. S. (1990). Periodization and politics in the postmodern. In B. S. Turner (Ed.), *Theories of modernity and postmodernity.* London: Sage Ltd.

IN SEARCH OF DEMOCRACY: REFLECTIONS

Elaine Jarchow

Chapter 7 by Reitzug and O'Hair makes us think that they may be right about a new mind-set that sees democratic schools as the real world. Without such a mind-set, teachers involved in renewal and restructuring may continue to struggle. The authors, after sampling 20 schools (elementary, middle, and high school) in six states, describe these struggles as five in number. Teachers must struggle to find time to involve themselves in restructuring, and they must also struggle to communicate their beliefs in meaningful ways. The need to make sense of and control the amount of information received causes a third struggle. Because teachers must connect their discussions and commit-tee work to classroom practice, they often experience frustration. Finally, teachers must struggle to follow renewal work with action.

Reitzug and O'Hair make sense from their findings by suggesting implications for career-long teacher education. Teachers must learn to throw off the mantle of individualism and don one of connectedness. Such action, according to the authors, could result in overcoming the struggle through the pursuit of democratic ideals of inquiry, discourse, equity, authenticity, and leadership.

I wonder if these democratic ideals can be applied equally to struggles in elementary, middle, and secondary schools. For example, do secondary teachers need to "find time" in the same way that elementary teachers do? Do they engage in similar kinds of inquiry? Does a middle school teacher have unique communication and connectedness needs? In spite of these questions, I conclude with the authors that a new mind-set could result in energized democratic schools.

In Search of True Change

Chapter 8 by Kadel-Taras truly provides insight into teacher change by examining when, why, and how teachers change their practices. Through her examination of nine public high school teachers, she provides us with wonderfully insightful examples of teachers' behaviors and beliefs. She concludes that teachers change not only to address the learning needs of their students but also to benefit themselves. These teachers, then, are both teacher centered and student centered.

The author differentiates between teacher learning and teacher control. When the teachers see themselves as learners, they feel free to choose those topics that will help them to learn more. In this sense, they do benefit their students. As teachers in control, they seek to control students, methods, content, and themselves. Where they are truly successful, they can feel free to take risks. Teachers must first feel comfortable with their control over students before they can try innovative methods. Some teachers learn the joy of self-confidence, of fighting for the things they want and winning.

As a teacher educator, I wonder what we can do for preservice teachers to help them to envision a future where they are self-confident and free to take risks that may effect change. Should we "invent" risk-taking exercises to discuss in our teacher preparation courses? Should we use the case study approach to engage in discussion of risk-taking opportunities and the consequences of our actions?

In Search of the Postmodern Era

In Chapter 9, Fleener and Fry contend that K-12 schools developed during the modern period and were based on the belief that the intellect could be used to rationalize phenomena, that society would gradually improve, and that objective inquiry would lead to universal truths. These same schools and their teachers have been thrust into a postmodern world where they are forced to define a reality that is both illusive and uncertain.

The authors cite Hargreaves (1995) as the source of five paradoxes that schools must face. These include the inability of parents to endorse school values, mixed messages from business, global practices, tensions between diversity and standards, and the push-pull of past and future.

Teachers who are successful in dealing with these paradoxes must exhibit six characteristics defined by Combs (1982). If these six characteristics can be exhibited by teachers in their own personal theories of teaching, critical reflection can resolve postmodern dilemmas. Teachers must possess a comprehensive system of beliefs to make their environment less complex, and they must accurately reflect social reality with an internally congruent system of belief. Teachers must make their belief systems personally relevant and appropriate to tasks. Finally, as they receive feedback, they must adapt and be open to change.

The authors conclude their chapter by outlining a model of teacher reflectivity in which discernment (focusing on a phenomenon), exploration (engaging in action), and interpretation (understanding perceptions) work together continuously to make sense of our environment. Professional teacher development can only succeed through understanding the centrality of teacher beliefs in terms of the interconnectedness of beliefs, actions, and reflectivity.

I wonder if Fleener and Fry have tried to plan a professional development program that meets their criteria for success. If they were given 10 inservice days in a year to engage in teacher professional development, what would these days look like? Would teachers have time to reflect and to connect their beliefs and actions? Would they articulate the difficulty of using rational approaches to an irrational world?

Implications and Conclusions

What implications can we draw from our three chapters? I believe that there are five of concern to us.

1. Schools that wish to move toward democratic practice must engage staff members in positive career-long professional development. This development is not easy; it requires rigorous attention to detail. The architects of the movement must be dedicated, committed, and eager to facilitate change.

2. Connectedness is an important watchword for these who advocate lasting change. Teachers must learn to communicate in new ways, to ask important questions, and to reflect on their beliefs.

3. Teachers who wish to change must address their own learning needs as well as those of their students. Schools that offer exciting and challenging professional growth programs to their teachers will reap significant rewards in terms of teacher growth.

4. Developing teacher comfort and self-confidence can yield opportunities for teachers to try innovative methods. Offering mentors and demonstration lessons and building climates of trust can help teachers to engage in risk taking.

5. Professional teacher development programs must address the paradoxes of our time. If teachers are taught to approach all concerns with rational tools, they may be disappointed when irrational problems confront them. Teachers must learn new mind-sets as they connect their beliefs and actions through reflectivity.

As we K-12 and university teacher educators try to craft career-long teacher education opportunities, we must emphasize collaboration and cooperation. We must try innovative methods. For example, we might offer international summer seminars to teachers as well as local, domestic exchanges. If we truly believe that learning is a lifelong activity, then we must believe that teaching is one, too. Career-long teacher education must spark all of our imaginations. In *Alice in Wonderland*, Alice had this exchange with the Red Queen:

> "One can't believe impossible things," said Alice.
> "I daresay you haven't had much practice," said the Queen. "When I was your age, I always did it for half-an-hour a day. Why, sometimes I'd believe as many as six impossible things before breakfast." (Lewis Carroll, *Alice in Wonderland*)

We must engage often in thinking impossible thoughts for and with our teachers. Then our impossible thoughts can become impossible dreams and ultimately solutions to our impossible problems.

> Never measure the height of a mountain until you have reached the top. Then you will see how low it was. (Dag Hammarskjöld, *Markings*)

> You must climb the next mountain but never reach the summit. (Dennis Waitley)

References

Combs, A. W. (1982). *A personal approach to teaching: Beliefs that make a difference.* Boston: Allyn & Bacon.

Hargreaves, A. (1995). Renewal in the age of paradox. *Educational Leadership, 52*(7), 14-19.

DIVISION IV

ENHANCING THE VALUE OF TEACHER EDUCATION PROGRAMS: OVERVIEW AND FRAMEWORK

Joanne May Herbert

Joanne May Herbert is Research Associate Professor at the University of Virginia. She teaches courses in foundations, curriculum, and instruction. For the past decade, she has written and produced videocases for use in teacher education programs. Most recently, she has helped develop and teach a case-based, Internet-based course for teachers and school administrators. She has written widely on teacher preparation, teacher evaluation, and curriculum and instruction. She is also coauthor of a foundations text for beginning teachers.

The most recent wave of reform aimed at enhancing the value of teacher education programs began in 1983 with the publication of *A Nation at Risk* (see Bell, 1993). The so-called "rising tide of mediocrity" in U.S. public education stimulated many different and often conflicting attempts to improve both the quality of the people who would be teachers and the programs meant to prepare them for work in schools.

Recent attempts to change teacher education can be divided into three categories: what goes in (program entrance requirements), what goes on (program process or educational requirements), and what comes out (program exit requirements). In addition, as I explain below, people have also made efforts to shape the teaching force once it was in place through a variety of inservice initiatives.

One of the most common criticisms of teacher education—almost since its inception in the United States—has been leveled against the candidates themselves. Willard Waller (1932) noted that people's conceptions of teachers were marked by the belief that it was a kind of "second-choice" occupation. If you could not be an artist, you could always teach art. If you could not be a scientist or mathematician, you might teach science or mathematics. Perhaps because of this view of teaching as a fallback position or default option, teachers and the profession itself have suffered an understandable lack of prestige. The best and brightest, it is argued, gravitate toward other professions.

To remedy this situation, reformers have proposed raising teacher education entrance requirements; to wit: raise the minimum SAT score for admission and require higher GPAs from general studies taken in the early years prior to applying for admission to professional programs. The general rationale has been that higher entrance requirements would attract better students and exclude weaker ones.

Other reform efforts have been geared to changing program requirements once students are in teacher education. These have been characterized by attempts to forge closer ties to arts and sciences (often while diminishing time spent in professional coursework) and to make field experiences more an integral or prominent part of teacher education programs. "Teachers must know their content if they are going to be successful," has been one rallying cry. "Teachers need to know what life is like in the real world if they expect to function there," has been another. Such perceptions are difficult to oppose, even for teacher educators.

When enacted, these changes or "enhancements of teacher education" have placed more responsibility for educating teachers outside schools, colleges, and departments of education by moving coursework to arts and sciences and have located expectations for making and judging field experiences with elementary and secondary schools. Sometimes these changes have been accompanied by requirements to lengthen programs to 5 or even 6 years, or by making it mandatory to complete a bachelor's degree in 4 years and add a 5th year of professional studies. In these instances "strengthening" teacher education programs has meant "lengthening" them. In other situations, strengthening programs has meant getting rid of them entirely or replacing them with alternative routes into teaching.

Another attempt to change the process of teacher education has been to concentrate on the accreditation of programs. The National Council for the Accreditation of Teacher Education (NCATE) has changed its focus from making summative decisions about programs to one of "development." That is, NCATE trains teams of evaluators to evaluate teacher education programs and then encourages programs that apply for accreditation to enhance their offerings to obtain certification. NCATE still touches a minority of teacher education programs, however.

States have changed licensure requirements to force changes in teacher education programs. They have relied increasingly on testing teachers before granting certification. For a time, some assessment programs were elaborate efforts to observe and evaluate teachers on the job. Most, however, relied heavily on paper-and-pencil tests to screen teachers after their formal preparation and before granting certification. Certification, or licensure as it is called in other professions, connotes minimal competence—a kind of protection for the public from the abuse of people who claim but can produce no evidence of teaching expertise. The establishment of the National Board of Professional Teaching Standards that would grant national certification—or identify the very best among the teaching force—emerged in this same period.

Some states and school districts instituted mentor programs for teachers in their first 2 to 3 years on the job. State or local education authorities identified mentors or master teachers and paid them to ease the transition for others from college or university programs into elementary and secondary schools. These programs were sometimes accompanied by "career ladder" programs meant to reward more experienced teachers for their expertise and/or their assumption of additional responsibilities. Merit pay—bonuses or raises given on the basis of someone's assessment of teaching expertise—also made a reappearance during this time period, as it does every 20 years or so. Some school districts began paying bounties or signing bonuses to teachers in particular areas of need.

Within the past 3 to 5 years "enhancing teacher education" has also been defined at least in part by the degree to which technology is infused into programs. States and programs have added "technology standards" for teachers and pressed for increased access to technology for both teachers and children. The traditionally low-tech view of teaching as "chalk talk" has given way to visions of using technology to allow teachers and students to acquire information that was not at their fingertips before, to share ideas with people in virtual communities who are not physically near one another, and to step into a "virtual universe" to learn about the real world (O'Neil, 1995).

In the three chapters that follow, you will see three more views of "enhancing the profession" that fall within the existing genre of change literature. Each, however, offers its own unique view of ways to improve teacher education. Zhixin Su in Chapter 10 reminds us that the examination of teacher candidates' perspectives might help us think about ways to attract and retain minority teachers in classrooms. Barbara Young in Chapter 11 reinforces the importance of examining the effect of cooperating teachers' supervision on student teachers' perceptions and experiences. And Sharon Gilbert and Jerry Hostetler in Chapter 12 argue that reflective behaviors can be enhanced to encourage people to think productively about the complexities of teaching.

References

Bell, T. (1993). Reflections one decade after *A Nation at Risk. Phi Delta Kappan,* 74(8), 592-597.

O'Neil, J. (1995). On technology in schools: A conversation with Chris Dede. *Educational Leadership, 53*(2), 6-12.

Waller, W. (1932). *The sociology of teaching.* New York: Russell & Russell.

10 Becoming Teachers

Minority Candidates' Perceptions of
Teaching as a Profession and as a Career

Zhixin Su

Zhixin Su is Professor of Education in the Department of Educational Leadership and Policy Studies and Director of the China Institute at California State University, Northridge. Her specializations are teacher education, policy, administration, foundation studies, and comparative education.

ABSTRACT

This chapter reports findings from a case study of minority teacher candidates in a major state university. The minority candidates hold markedly different views on teaching as a profession and as a career from their white peers. Whereas most of the white candidates enter teaching for traditional altruistic reasons, many minority candidates' decisions to become teachers are motivated by their awareness of the inequalities in the existing educational and social establishments. Therefore, the minority candidates have a clear and strong vision for social justice and for their own roles as change agents in the schools and society. Although the majority of candidates in the study are proud of becoming members of the teaching profession, only one third of them plan to make teaching a lifelong career. Emotional aspects would be the major cause for white teachers to leave the profession, whereas minority teachers would be more likely to leave the classroom when there are opportunities

to move into administration or do something else more rewarding. Findings from this study have significant implications for
improving the recruitment, preparation, and retention of high-
quality minority teachers for the teaching profession.

Purposes and Rationale

In recent years, teacher education reformers have argued passionately
for the necessity of pursuing both a culturally informed and a culturally
diverse teaching profession to meet the needs of an increasingly diversi-
fied student population in U.S. public schools (Darling-Hammond, 1990;
Dillard, 1994; Gay, 1990; Graham, 1987; Harberman, 1988; Hilliard, 1988;
Montecinos, 1994). A review of the existing research literature also reveals
that since the beginning of the this decade, there have been some serious
efforts to study the perspectives and experiences of minority teachers and
teacher candidates (see, e.g., Goodwin, Genishi, Asher, & Woo, 1995;
Gordon, 1994; Guyton, Saxton, & Wesche, 1995; King, 1993; Martinez &
O'Donnell, 1993; Page & Page, 1991; Yopp, Yopp, & Taylor, 1992). These
pioneering studies have shed light on the characteristics and experiences
of teachers of color and laid solid foundations for further inquiry.

The case study reported in this chapter is yet another effort to build
the knowledge base on minority teachers. Specifically, the study has been
designed to explore minority teacher candidates' family and educational
backgrounds and entry perspectives; to examine minority candidates'
basic beliefs, attitudes, and values regarding education, schooling, and the
teaching profession; and to evaluate minority candidates' socialization
experiences in teacher education.

In many ways, this case study is an extension of a large national
research project in the United States, the Study of the Education of Educators (SEE), directed by John Goodlad from 1985 to 1990, in which the
author participated as a researcher and conducted a study of the socialization of teacher candidates in the 29 selected teacher training institutions
across the nation. The national study did not focus on minority candidates
as a special subgroup, although the major report of the SEE recognizes that
the disproportionately small number of individuals from minority groups
who choose to enter teacher education programs commonly encounter
either segregation or repetition of the minority experience characterizing
their earlier schooling (Goodlad, 1990).

The case study builds on the major assumptions of the author's study of teacher socialization in the SEE and the arguments in the existing literature for the necessity to diversify the teaching profession. It takes the position that minority teachers are the crucial source of both the competence and the numbers needed to provide an adequate education not only for the rising numbers of minority youths in our cities but for all children. Indeed, understanding the characteristics, perspectives, and socialization experiences of minority teacher candidates is the key to creating and implementing more effective programs for recruiting and preparing those individuals who have the appropriate commitment and competence for careers in public school teaching.

Detailed discussions of findings on the profiles and socialization experiences of minority teacher candidates are presented in other research reports; this chapter will focus on minority candidates' views on teaching as a profession and as a career. Specifically, it will (a) examine minority candidates' conceptualization of teaching as a profession, their ideas of what makes a good teacher, and their perceptions of the status of the teaching profession; (b) describe their entry perspectives—the fundamental reasons for them to choose to enter teaching; (c) explore their perceptions of the role of teachers in school reform and social change; (d) delineate their commitment to teaching as a lifelong career; (e) discuss what they consider would be the likely reasons for them to leave teaching; and (f) contemplate the implications of these findings for further inquiry and reform.

Method and Procedures

Teacher candidates enrolled during the 1993-1994 academic year in a 1-year teacher certificate/master's degree program at a large public university in California participated in the study. Because it is a major research institute, the university has several hundred doctoral students in education, but its teacher education program enrolls only 150 to 200 candidates each year. In recent years, to meet the challenge of diversity, the program has admitted a large number of minority candidates, increasing the percentage from 20% in 1988 to 40% in the fall of 1993. The high proportion of minority students in the selected teacher education program created an ideal sample for the case study.

For data collection, both interview and survey instruments were adapted from the SEE (Goodlad, 1990; Sirotnik, 1988). The items in the survey and interview were organized around the major themes stated in the purposes of the case study. The survey was administered to all the teacher candidates toward the end of their training, and of the forms returned, 90 were from white Caucasian students and 58 were from minority students including 31 Asian Americans, 5 African Americans, 21 Hispanics, and 1 Native American. Individual interviews were conducted twice, once in the middle of the program and once near the end of the program, with the majority of the minority students in the program including 20 Asian American, 17 Hispanic, and 4 African American students, as well as 15 randomly selected students from the white Caucasian group. About half of the students interviewed were in the multiple-subject credential program for elementary school teaching and half were getting the single-subject credentials for secondary school teaching. Most of the interview questions were open ended to generate unrestricted responses and detailed descriptions of personal thoughts and experiences.

In data analysis and interpretation, descriptive statistics were applied to survey data and content analyses were employed to organize interview data (Miles & Michael, 1994; Sax, 1979). These methods were chosen because the study is primarily a descriptive, comparative, and exploratory one. Information gathered from the participants has been merged to identify themes and perspectives common in all as well as in different ethnic groups and to offer a comparative analysis of minority and white students' characteristics, perspectives, and experiences. In addition, comparisons and contrasts have been made between findings from this case study and those from other relevant research. Although one cannot generalize the findings from this limited sample to minority students in all other teacher education programs, the findings are relevant to teacher education policymakers and reformers who must listen to students of color to better understand diversity and incorporate it into teacher recruitment and preparation.

Findings and Discussions

Views on Teaching as a Profession

It has been argued that the most critical issue facing U.S. education today is the professionalization of teaching (Darling-Hammond, 1985). Although U.S. teachers and teacher educators share the conviction that teaching by its very nature is a profession, the actual conditions and circumstances of teaching tend to undermine such belief, and teaching is seen by many in the public as a partial profession or pseudoprofession, resting on experiences and apprenticeship rather than on sound theories and ideas. Goodlad (1984) delineates this dilemma: "In general the practicing teacher . . . functions in a context where the beliefs and expectations are those of a profession but where the realities tend to constrain, likening actual practice more to a trade" (p. 193).

Findings from this study lend support to these observations. Participants were asked whether they considered teaching a profession and why. The overwhelming responses from both mainstream[1] and minority candidates were "yes," "definitely," and "absolutely." In this case, there were no major differences in response between minority and mainstream students or among students from different minority groups. Most believe that teaching is or should be a profession because it is a specialized human service field such as medicine and law that requires special training and certification. They also recognized the important roles teachers can play in shaping children's and youths' lives. All of them were aware that teaching has not been recognized as a profession by many in the public and that it has not enjoyed the same respect, social status, and economic compensations as some other human service professions such as law and medicine.

Most of the minority candidates in this study share with their mainstream counterparts the same perceptions of what makes a good teacher. They demonstrate a strong belief in the progressive or child-centered school of thought regarding the purpose of schools. The two major themes running through the interview data are "love of children" and "love of learning." The following comments illustrate them well:

A good teacher genuinely cares for her students, must be willing to take time out of her schedule to always be there for a student. A teacher should also be funny, entertaining, energetic, able to make learning an enjoyable experience. (Asian American student)

One who cares about the students, about their feelings, has good knowledge of the materials, and most importantly, can transmit that knowledge and promote critical and analytical skills. (Hispanic student)

To affect each and every student in some way. To present content in a way that is accessible to students. To grow professionally in knowledge about content and teaching as a profession. To be a role model and motivator to students both inside and outside the classroom. (African American student)

A good teacher should be very responsive to the needs of his or her students. A good teacher strives to be creative, patient, enthusiastic, with a love of learning. (white student)

In addition to the commonly shared belief among all the students interviewed in the child-centered philosophy regarding what a good teacher should be, minority students demonstrate an awareness of the need for them to challenge the existing curriculum in schools and the dominant culture in the society and to develop critical thinking and social reconstruction skills in their students. They see the good teacher as someone who not only cares for children and learning but also is sensitive to diversity in the schools and society and committed to improving and transforming the society. In contrast, none of the white students mentioned these concerns when they described the necessary qualities of a good teacher.

Survey data presented in Figure 10.1 indicate that when asked to express their concerns about improving the status of the teaching profession, both minority and mainstream students gave "higher teacher salaries" the highest ratings of agreement. Clearly, although most of the teacher candidates have pursued a career in teaching not for monetary reasons, they believe that the best way to improve the status of the teaching profession is for teachers to get what they deserve. All the students in this study also considered "significantly altered working conditions for teachers," "develop differentiated staffing/career opportunities," "develop leadership roles," "develop participatory management roles," "emphasize the moral and ethical basis of teaching," and "require national accreditation with high program standards for all teacher-preparing institutions" as among the most important measures to improving the status of the teaching profession. This finding is very similar to that from the SEE (Su, 1993), demonstrating a consistent and genuine concern among teachers and teachers-to-be to restructure their workplace, play a decision-making role beyond classroom teaching, revitalize the moral dimensions of teaching, and improve the quality of teacher training nationwide.

Although minority students agreed with their white counterparts on the importance of most of the measures, they differed markedly on two measures. Minority students gave "national teacher certification board" and "clear conceptual and practical argument for why teaching is a profession" relatively high ratings—5.31 and 5.56, respectively. White students rated

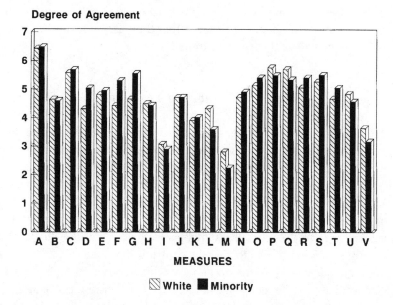

Figure 10.1. Measures to Enhance the Teaching Profession: Teacher Candidates' Perspectives

NOTE: A = higher teacher salary; B = demonstrable, scientific basis of teaching; C = significantly altered working conditions for teachers; D = national program exit-level teacher examination; E = higher program entry-level standards; F = national teacher certification board; G = clear conceptual and practical argument for why teaching is a profession; H = a master's degree in addition to the teaching credential; I = a doctoral degree in addition to the teaching credential; J = 5 years of university/college preparation; K = 6 years of university/college preparation; L = eliminate/phase out undergraduate education majors; M = eliminate/phase out all undergraduate education courses; N = develop a clear conceptual and practical argument for teaching as part art, part science, and part craft; O = develop differentiated staffing/career opportunities; P = develop leadership roles as an integral part of teaching responsibilities; Q = develop participatory management roles as an integral part of teaching responsibilities; R = emphasize the moral and ethical basis of teaching; S = require national accreditation with high program standards for all teacher-preparing institutions; T = model teacher education programs after other professional training programs in medicine, law, and so on; U = eliminate "emergency certification" options; V = develop a small cadre of "professional teachers" with the remaining force at lower levels of preparation.

them lower—4.43 and 4.66, respectively. Our findings indicate that minority teachers tend to support the establishment of some national standards for teachers more strongly than their white peers and that minority educators feel a more urgent need to clarify the arguments for teaching as a profession. Because many of the minority teachers are the first professionals in their families, it is not surprising that they aspire for a profession with high standards and clear definitions.

Reasons for Entering Teaching

Previous research on teacher socialization has identified both intrinsic or psychic rewards and extrinsic or material rewards for teaching (Lortie, 1975; Su, 1993; Yarger, Howey, & Joyce, 1977; Zimpher, 1989). In this case study, the teacher candidates were asked to rate 14 reasons for entering teaching. Figure 10.2 compares the minority and white students' entry perspectives. In general, they seem to agree on the degree of importance placed on each of the reasons, with the intrinsic rewards—"to have a personally satisfying job"; "to make a contribution to society"; "to help children and/or young adults, to be of service to others"; "like children and/or youths"; and "to work in a noble, moral, and ethical profession"—being the most important. Their views are quite similar to those found in the SEE, which surveyed nearly 3,000 teacher candidates across the nation (Goodlad, 1990; Su, 1993), and to findings in other recent studies of minority teachers (King, 1993; Page & Page, 1991).

The interview data revealed that although most of the minority and white students cited altruistic/intrinsic reasons for their decisions to enter teaching, there were some significant differences in their entry perspectives. The white students wanted to teach primarily because they liked children and believed that they could have a positive impact on individual students' lives. Some white students came to teaching for pragmatic reasons—the teaching schedule was good for the family, teaching was a reliable job. There were a few white students who had entered the teacher education program because they were not sure what they wanted to do.

In contrast, minority candidates, especially those who perceived their early school experiences as particularly or uniquely negative due to their racial status and language difficulties, demonstrated a strong awareness of the unequal educational opportunities for poor and minority children, the irrelevance of the existing curriculum and instruction for minority students, and the need to restructure schools and society. Thus, they are clearly committed to entering teaching as social change agents. For them, the rewards for teaching would not be financial but emotional and cultural. Their views represent a critical perspective seldom found in teacher education, and their voices should be heard by teacher educators and

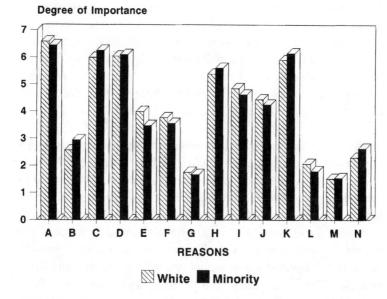

Degree of Importance

REASONS

White ▨ Minority ■

Figure 10.2. Reasons for Entering Teaching: Teacher Candidates' Perspectives

NOTE: A = to have a personally satisfying job; B = to have a high-paying job; C = to make a contribution to society; D = to help children and/or young adults, to be of service to others; E = to have more time off during the year; F = to pursue an interest in a particular subject; G = to have a backup job while pursuing another career; H = to work in a noble, moral, and ethical profession; I = to pursue an interesting career with interesting colleagues; J = to have job security and a steady income; K = I like children and/or youths; L = I didn't know what else to do with my college education; M = I didn't think there was any other career open to me; N = I was influenced by others (family, friends, etc.).

teacher candidates who do not see the responsibilities of the teacher beyond classroom or school doors.

Teachers' Role in School Reform and Social Change

Given their critical perspectives, it was not surprising that most of the minority teacher candidates believed very strongly in the necessity to restructure the existing schools and society. The African American candidates most eloquently and forcefully exposed the irrelevance of the existing school organization and curriculum for students from poor and minority backgrounds:

The minority students are not able to form a connection between life and what they are learning in schools. There are no role models for them. The existing classes are set up which are not always conducive to learning, especially with different cultural groups. It is very individual and based on competitions. The minority students are not motivated to achieve because they don't think education will get them anywhere.

When you open the textbook, mainstream histories and heritages are always validated. Columbus. Who are the presidents? Who do you see for society's standards of beauty—always white. Self-esteem problems—no pride in race and lineage. All we read about is how we were slaves, lynched, Martin Luther King was shot. It stems from the view that we are not validated in schools and the media, and I can see a student saying, "What am I going to amount to? I was a slave, and I am still being discriminated against." The books don't print the truth. We don't feel we have a place or can succeed. A lot of pride is lost very early in minority students' lives.

Standards are placed in the lap of children who have money. A lot of minority people don't have money. They have no money or people in power to make the tests. The knowledge that students are being tested on may not be their knowledge. They are not being judged on what they know, so that is why they are doing poorly. The worst teachers are often in these schools because most teachers do not want to be there.

Their descriptions confirmed the observations made by Goodlad (1990) that minorities often see little reason to succeed in an institution of schooling that they perceive to be serving the aspirations of whites. To make a difference in the lives of students from poor and minority backgrounds, most minority teacher candidates in the study expressed the wish to teach in inner-city schools:

I will go where the poor, minority populations dwell. Because there is a lot of negativity in textbooks, I will make it a point to supplement with my own knowledge to make the students feel validated. We have a great history and rich culture. I will be willing to draw from my own funds to do it. The "lone heroine"—

to attack injustice. Teachers have to take it upon themselves to solve the problem. You can't wait for the state to change texts or the district to change learning material. I will take it upon myself in one classroom. That's a start. I don't want to go to affluent schools. They don't have a need for me.

L.A. inner city. I feel that there are very capable, involved teachers in the suburbs. It is comfortable to live there. LAUSD [Los Angeles Unified School District] and other cities need new blood and more minority teachers. And people from our generation who are teaching have more insight.

Inner city of Los Angeles. Because that is the community I am familiar with and one that I am a product of. There is a definite need for dedicated teachers.

Moreover, minority students felt strongly that teachers should be change agents in the schools and the society:

Schools could be a very enriching environment for students. I would like to see teachers involved in political debates and activism to show students what is out there. Schools should be connected to the real world. Teachers should not be ambivalent about what is happening in the society because school is not isolated from society. Teaching is a profession and teachers should align themselves with causes outside of schools that affect society.

One of the main reasons I chose teaching was I wanted to be a social change agent. I affect a few students who affect their families and society.

The minority teacher candidates observed that some minority students' parents were intimidated by the school system, and they see the need for teachers to make themselves accessible not just in the school room but also in the community. Furthermore, they believed that teachers should reach out to the parents and engage in "a lot of talking and reflecting about what is important in education." They wanted to empower parents and form close alliances with the parents in educating their children.

In comparison to minority students' firm determination to work in inner-city schools, about half of the white students in our sample were hesitant about teaching in urban schools and many preferred to just go back to the suburban areas where they came from:

I would rather work in a suburb. It's where I'm from. I feel comfortable there.

A suburb in northern California. I have mixed feelings—a desire for making a difference in inner cities, and a desire to go where I've grown up and I'm comfortable.

I will work in a suburb because I do not speak a second language and I see this as a barrier in my job search in city schools.

The students' family backgrounds, upbringing, and their prior schooling experiences seem to be major determining factors here. Although the teacher education program in the study offered lectures on critical pedagogy to all the candidates, arranged for all of them to conduct some student teaching in inner-city schools, and actively advocated the need for them to go into teaching in urban schools, its efforts were clearly not sufficient to motivate all white candidates to go into teaching in these schools. In fact, most of the white students interpreted the meaning of change in schools and society as "experiments with different teaching methods," "make change in curriculum," and "help students better able to deal with societal problems." None of them mentioned the dire experiences that children from poor and minority backgrounds have in urban schools and what they could do to help these children, whereas these were the major concerns in minority candidates' responses.

Commitment to Teaching as a Lifelong Career

In many countries, such as Japan, China, and Germany, most schoolteachers enter the teaching profession as a lifelong career. They devote their whole lives to the education of the next generations. In the United States, however, the turnover rate among schoolteachers is very high, and in some cases, about half of the graduates from the teacher education programs do not even enter the teaching profession (Su, 1993). In this study, all the candidates in the program were asked whether they thought they made the right decision to become teachers. The majority of them—78% of the white students and 88% of the minority students—said yes, 21% of the white students and 12% of the minority students said that they were not sure, and 1% of the white students said no. It seems that most of these candidates had positive attitudes toward becoming teachers.

However, when asked whether they were committed to teaching as a lifelong career, only 33% of the minority students and 35% of the white students said yes, 19% of the minority students and 16% of the white students said maybe, and 48% of the minority students and 49% of the white students said no. There was almost no difference between minority and white students' responses, contrary to the conclusions from some previous studies, which found that minority teachers were significantly more negative than their white peers in their evaluation of their career choices (King, 1993; Mack & Jackson, 1990; Page & Page, 1991). Figure 10.3 indicates that among those not prepared to make teaching a lifelong career, 26% of minority students and 25% of white students planned to teach for 11 or more years, 29% of minority students and 40% of white students wanted to teach for 6 to 10 years, and the rest planned to teach for fewer than 6 years.

If we are to develop effective strategies to retain the best teachers, it is very important to discover the reasons why some future teachers are committed to teaching as a lifelong career whereas so many of their peers would want to leave teaching in a few years. According to the interview data from this study, the committed candidates, whether minority or white, tend to be idealistic and passionate about the teaching profession and they believe very strongly in the power of education to fulfill themselves and to serve others:

> Yes, of course I will make teaching a lifelong career. It is something that is more of a calling. No matter what I do, some part of me will have to teach. I have to have that type of social interaction. Only death or old age will deter me from teaching. Nothing else will discourage me. (African American student)

> I have not found anything else as fulfilling or have felt as passionate about as teaching. I will do it as long as I have that feeling. Nothing has come close. I feel like I could do it for the rest of my life. Teaching is moving towards ideas I want. I will not get out because of the money. (white student)

> I think I will commit to teaching as a lifelong career because it will always be fulfilling. I believe that teaching is at a turning point

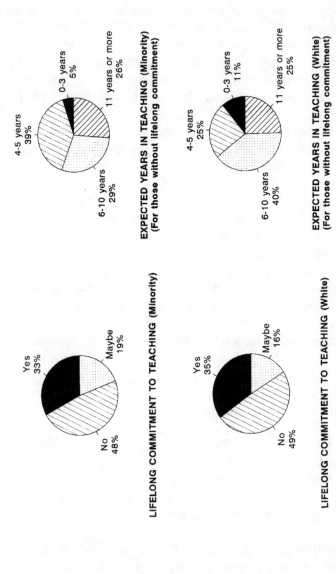

Figure 10.3. Teacher Candidates' Commitment to Teaching

and about to make major changes and that being involved during this time will be very exciting. (Asian American student)

On the other hand, those who are not committed to teaching as a lifelong career often lack such ideals and passions about the teaching profession. A typical response is as follows:

I am not ready for it. My timing is just not right. I don't think it was really for me even in the beginning. This whole year has been difficult because of that. I have other aspirations and interests I would like to experience. It is not definitive, but I am not captivated or ready to teach. I am hoping to write a little bit, live abroad, and experiment with writing.

Survey data presented in Figure 10.4 indicate similarities and differences between white and minority students when they were asked to rate the likelihood of 10 possible reasons for leaving teaching. Whereas the white students considered "emotional aspects (e.g., stress, frustration)" as the most likely causes for leaving teaching, minority students viewed "opportunity to do something else more rewarding" as the major reason to make career changes. Both white and minority candidates regarded "poor working conditions" and "administration-related problems" as the second and third most likely reasons for them to leave teaching. Moreover, minority students assigned higher ratings to "inadequate, low salary" and "no chance for advancement" than their white counterparts.

These results are consistent with findings from the interview data, which indicate that minority teacher candidates are more concerned about the low status and salary of teachers than their white peers. Moreover, some minority candidates have strong aspirations to move out of teaching into administration to effect great changes in the existing schools:

I would like to make teaching a lifelong career, but I want to fix the problems in schools. That means that I would go into administrative affairs. Nonetheless, I would still be in education. (Asian American student)

I only plan to teach for 5 to 6 years. I plan to get on and go into administration where I feel changes will happen at a higher level. They have most of the power. I teach to get experience being in the trenches. I want to move on to principal or superintendent or

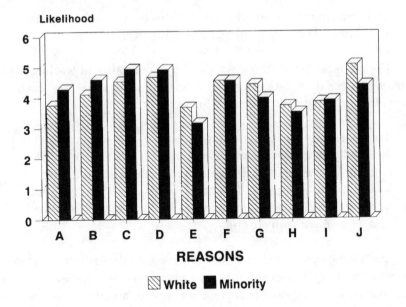

Figure 10.4. Possible Reasons for Leaving Teaching: Teacher Candidates' Perspectives

NOTE: A = inadequate, low salary; B = no chance for advancement; C = opportunity to do something else more rewarding; D = poor working conditions; E = student-related problems; F = administration-related problems; G = faculty-related problems; H = parent- or community-related problems; I = lack of respect (i.e., low status); J = emotional aspects (e.g., stress, frustration).

doing something on a level where real change can occur. (African American student)

I am not going to stay in the classroom for the rest of my life. I'm planning to move into an administrative position because of the greater possibilities to bring changes as an administrator. Teachers are very subordinate. You can do so much in the classroom, but you can do better as an administrator. (Hispanic student)

In fact, 10 of the 41 minority students interviewed expressed their wishes to become education administrators and policymakers to make changes in schools, whereas only 1 of the 15 white students interviewed desired to become a principal, and he did not consider change as a major goal in his ambition.

Conclusion

The results of this study indicate that both white and minority teacher candidates are genuinely concerned with the status of the teaching profession and they understand the dilemma facing the profession in U.S. society. Minority students are more affected than their white counterparts by the low status and poor compensations of the profession, both in making their decisions to enter teaching and in developing their plans as career teachers. Genuine efforts must be made to enhance the status and rewards of the teaching profession. Otherwise, not only will we not be able to recruit more minority teachers, but also those who are working in schools right now will leave the profession for better paying, more prestigious positions in other occupations, as some already have (Brown & Nicklos, 1989).

In conceptualizing what makes a good teacher, minority teacher candidates differ from their white peers in significant ways because of the differences in their demographic backgrounds, prior schooling experiences, and entry perspectives. Whereas the mainstream students choose to become teachers mainly for traditional altruistic reasons, minority students enter teaching with a keen awareness of the inequalities experienced by the poor and minorities. Consequently, minority students tend to perceive the good teacher as someone who not only cares for children and learning but also takes the responsibility to transform schools and society. In contrast, such social consciousness is conspicuously absent from white students' responses. Similarly, the minority candidates' perspectives on teachers' roles as change agents for schools and society are significantly different from those held by the white students. Again, the minority students recognize the inequalities in the existing educational and social establishments and see themselves as important players in restructuring schools and society. All of them are strongly committed to teaching in urban schools. The white students, on the other hand, interpret the terms *change* and *change agent* in a different light and focus more on specific curriculum and instructional reforms in the classroom. Many of them prefer to teach not in inner-city schools, but in suburban schools where they experienced their own earlier schooling.

Although the teacher education program in the study placed a special emphasis on training teachers to be social justice educators, apparently it was not very successful in raising the social consciousness of all the white teacher candidates. Because the majority of people in the teaching profession are still from the mainstream group, it is very important to develop strategies to help them become social justice educators who genuinely care for children from poor and minority backgrounds. The most powerful resource for improving the teacher education curriculum may be minority teacher candidates, who can share their past experiences and current thoughts with their white peers. In doing so, they help them understand and develop a critical perspective and a social consciousness needed for becoming change agents for the schools and society.

A difficult challenge for teacher educators is how to deal with future teachers' lack of commitment to teaching as a lifelong career. Findings from this study indicate that only one third of the prospective teachers plan to make teaching a lifelong career. Nearly half of them do not plan to do so. Because the more committed teachers tend to be more idealistic, passionate, and determined believers in the power of education to change individuals, schools, and society, a personal interview at the time of entry into teaching should help screen out or educate the less committed candidates. Minority candidates who aspire to become educational administrators to effect greater changes in schools should be encouraged. We need to have more minority representation in school administration. It is hoped that as teachers become more involved in the decision-making process in schools, minority teachers will feel equally powerful by remaining in the classroom. Ultimately, enhancing the status of teaching as a profession and improving working conditions are the keys to retaining good teachers, both minority and mainstream, in teaching as a lifelong career.

Note

1. In this chapter, *mainstream* and *white* are used interchangeably to mean *white Caucasian.*

References

Brown, W., & Nicklos, L. (1989). Recruiting minorities into the teaching profession: An educational imperative. *Educational Horizons, 67*(4), 145-149.

Darling-Hammond, L. (1985). Valuing teachers: The making of a profession. *Teachers College Record, 87*(2), 205-218.

Darling-Hammond, L. (1990). Foreword. In M. E. Dilworth, *Reading between the lines: Teachers and their racial/ethnic cultures* (Teacher Education Monograph No. 11, pp. vii-viii). Washington, DC: ERIC Clearinghouse on Teacher Education.

Dillard, C. (1994). Beyond supply and demand: Critical pedagogy, ethnicity, and empowerment in recruiting teachers of color. *Journal of Teacher Education, 45,* 9-17.

Gay, G. (1990). Achieving educational equality through curriculum desegregation. *Phi Delta Kappan, 72*(1), 56-62.

Goodlad, J. I. (1984). *A place called school.* New York: Macmillan.

Goodlad, J. I. (1990). *Teachers for our nations' schools.* San Francisco: Jossey-Bass.

Goodwin, L. A., Genishi, C., Asher, N., & Woo, K. (1995, April). *Asian American voices: Speaking out on the teaching profession.* Paper presented at the annual meeting of the American Educational Research Association, San Francisco.

Gordon, J. (1994). Why students of color are not entering teaching: Reflections from minority teachers. *Journal of Teacher Education, 45,* 346-353.

Graham, P. A. (1987). Black teachers: A drastically scarce resource. *Phi Delta Kappan, 68*(8), 598-605.

Guyton, E., Saxton, R., & Wesche, M. (1995, April). *Experiences of diverse students in teacher education.* Paper presented at the annual meeting of the American Educational Research Association, San Francisco.

Harberman, M. (1988). Proposals for recruiting minority teachers: Promising practices and attractive detours. *Journal of Teacher Education, 39*(4), 38-44.

Hilliard, A. G. (1988). Reintegration for education: Black community involvement with black schools. *Urban League Review, 11*(1, 2), 251-271.

King, S. H. (1993). Why did we choose teaching careers and what will enable us to stay? Insights from one cohort of the African American teaching pool. *Journal of Negro Education, 62*(4), 475-492.

Lortie, D. C. (1975). *Schoolteacher.* Chicago: University of Chicago Press.

Mack, F. R., & Jackson, T. E. (1990, February). *High school students' attitudes about teacher education as a career choice: Comparison by ethnic/racial group.* Paper presented at the annual meeting of the Association of Teacher Educators, Las Vegas, NV.

Martinez, R. R., & O'Donnell, J. (1993, April). *Understanding the support systems of Hispanic teacher candidates: A study through in-depth interviews.* Paper presented at the annual meeting of the American Educational Research Association, Atlanta, GA.

Miles, M. B., & Michael, A. (1994). *Qualitative data analysis.* Thousand Oaks, CA: Sage.

Montecinos, C. (1994). Teachers of color and multiculturalism. *Equity and Excellence in Education, 27*(3), 34-42.

Page, J. A., & Page, F. P., Jr. (1991). Gaining access into academe: Perceptions and experiences of African American teachers. *Urban League Review, 15*(1), 27-39.

Sax, G. (1979). *Foundations of educational research.* Englewood Cliffs, NJ: Prentice Hall.

Sirotnik, K. A. (1988). Studying the education of educators: Methodology. *Phi Delta Kappan, 70*(3), 241-247.

Su, Z. (1993). The study of the education of educators: A profile of teacher education students. *Journal of Research and Development in Education, 26*(3), 125-132.

Yarger, S. J., Howey, K., & Joyce, B. (1977). Reflections on preservice preparation: Impressions from the national survey. *Journal of Teacher Education, 28*(6), 34-37.

Yopp, R. H., Yopp, H. K., & Taylor, H. P. (1992). Profiles and viewpoints of minority candidates in a teacher diversity project. *Teacher Education Quarterly, 19*(3), 29-48.

Zimpher, N. (1989). The RATE project: A profile of teacher education students. *Journal of Teacher Education, 40*(6), 27-30.

11 Theoretical Orientation to Reading and Student Teaching Placement

Three Case Studies in Match and Mismatch Contexts

Barbara N. Young

Barbara N. Young is Assistant Professor in the College of Education, Department of Educational Leadership, at Middle Tennessee State University. Teaching duties include courses such as educational psychology, effective teaching and methods, and managing the classroom for instruction.

ABSTRACT

Studies of what happens to student teachers during student teaching are vital and must be conducted to examine the effect of cooperating teachers' supervision on student teachers' perceptions and experiences. Is college instruction in methods classes "washed out" by student teaching experience because of the strong dichotomy existing between practical theory and traditional classroom practice? Does the practicum experience serve to merely "socialize" the prospective teachers into established patterns of school practice relating to curriculum and instruction? This chapter presents research examining perceptions of three student teachers and transactions occurring between these student teachers and respective cooperating teachers when pairs held the same theoretical orientation and when they held conflicting orientations to the reading process. Conclusions are addressed in terms of interpretation of data. Suggestions for future research and emergent questions concerning the practicum experience in general and the student teacher/cooperating teacher relationship in particular are presented.

Statement of the Problem

Research on teacher education programs indicates that content learned during preservice coursework may be forgotten as a result of the interactions, anxieties, and particular experiences that occur during student teaching (Hoy & Rees, 1977; Yee, 1969). Although the student teaching experience is evidently the most influential component of the teacher education program, and the influence of the cooperating teacher is extremely significant, little attempt is made to select cooperating teachers based on specific criteria. Generally, cooperating teachers are held to criteria such as having 3 to 5 years of successful teaching experience, the building principal's recommendation, and a master's degree. At present, the traditional practice of arbitrarily pairing a student with a cooperating teacher is still the norm in most student teaching situations across the country (Goodlad, 1991). Recent research indicates this common practice must be examined for possible changes if the practicum experience is to be made more effective (Goodlad, 1991; Holmes Group, 1990).

Specifically, there is a need for "research strategies that [will] enable the penetration of the complex and interrelated world of field-based experiences" (Zeichner, 1980, p. 52). Most research done in this area has relied too heavily on statistical data (Carter, 1993; Tabachnick & Zeichner, 1984). As a result, the research has oversimplified and ignored many complex factors present in the transactions and context of the field experience (Carter, 1993; Feiman-Nemser, 1983). Also, this research did not comprehensively take into account the complexities present in the interactions between student teachers and cooperating teachers, nor did it fully address questions concerning the significant influence of particular cooperating teachers on student teachers and resulting effects, if any, of the transactions between the pair (Hoy & Rees, 1977).

Studies done by Zeichner and Tabachnick (1981) have suggested that college instruction in methods is "washed out" by student teaching experience because of the strong dichotomy existing between practical theory and traditional classroom practice. Other research has raised serious questions about the benefits of the student teaching practicum and notes that the student teaching experience merely serves to "socialize" the prospective teachers into established, ineffective patterns of school practice relating to curriculum and instruction (Zeichner, 1980). As a result, studies of what really happens to the student teacher during the practicum experience are vital, and the narrow assumptions of the empirical-analytic paradigm of most studies must be replaced or supplemented by the inclusion of authentic, qualitative data that are embedded in the daily interactions and can only be gathered through naturalistic inquiry methods (Carter, 1993; Lincoln & Guba, 1985).

Studies comparing student teachers' attitudes with attitudes of their cooperating teachers unanimously report significant changes in student teachers' attitudes in the direction of those of cooperating teachers (McShane-Bechner & Ade, 1982; Yee, 1969). Although student teachers' classroom actions, such as verbal behavior or instructional methods, are significantly affected by the cooperating teacher, and cooperating teachers are perceived by student teachers as the most influential aspect of the entire practicum experience (Friebus, 1977; Yee, 1969), the traditional practice of arbitrarily pairing a student teacher with a cooperating teacher is still the norm in most student teaching situations across the country (Goodlad, 1991). Research directed to examination of the transactions that occur between student teachers and their cooperating teachers may shed significant light on the student teaching experience (Friebus, 1977; Yee, 1969). As a result of such research, data supporting careful, rather than random or arbitrary, pairing of student teachers with cooperating teachers may be obtained.

Research Design

Because theoretical orientation to reading is built on different theoretical foundations concerning the nature of knowledge, it follows that materials and delivery, or curriculum and instruction, differ in the classroom depending on which approach the teacher employs (see Table 11.1). Therefore, it is reasonable to question the extent to which student teachers are affected when their orientation is similar to or in conflict with the one being implemented within the classroom by their cooperating teachers.

To gain insight into these areas, the researcher used several data contexts, methods, and sources. Data consisted of observational field notes, transcribed audiotaped conference conversations, typed transcripts

TABLE 11.1 Basic Assumptions of the Technical and Reflective
Approaches and Orientations

Assumptions About	Approach	
	Technical	Reflective
Orientation	Behavioristic, mechanistic, bottom-up, outside-in	Humanistic, organismic, top-down, inside-out
Paradigm	Scientific, quantitative techniques	Naturalistic, qualitative techniques
Inquirer/subject	Independent	Interrelated
Nature of truth statements	Generalizations, focus on situations	Working hypothesis, focus on differences
Reality	Convergent, singular, fragmentable	Multiple, divergent, interrelated
Knowledge	Lawlike, generalizable to all situations	Socially constructive, time and context sensitive
Student	Passive, standardized needs, prior histories neglected	Active, interests and needs vary, prior histories important
Teacher	Deliver standardized curriculum using predetermined techniques	Make decisions on goals, content, and methods
Curriculum	Predetermined, standardized, broken into discrete skills	Flexible, based on needs and interests of students
Reading instruction	Phonics	Whole language

SOURCE: Guba and Lincoln (1981), Smith (1990).

of reflective journals, reading course overviews, lesson plans, unit plans, children's work samples, Theoretical Orientation Reading Profile questionnaires, and interviews (see Tables 11.2 and 11.3).

The following questions framed the study:

TABLE 11.2 Data Contexts, Methods, and Sources

Context	Data-Gathering Method	Source
Primary/naturally occurring transactions	Observational field notes Audiotaped conferences	Primary
Artifacts/products of transactions	Reflective journals Reading course overviews Lesson plans, unit plans Children's work samples	Primary
Cued responses	TORP[a] questionnaires Interviews	Secondary

SOURCE: Burk (1989), Patterson (1987).
a. Theoretical Orientation to Reading Profile (DeFord, 1979).

TABLE 11.3 Data Phases, Collection Sequence, Contexts, and Sources

Phase	Collection Sequence	Sources
1. Week 1 of student teaching	1. TORP[a] questionnaires 2. Initial interviews	Secondary Secondary
2. Weeks 2-9 of student teaching	1. Observational field notes 2. Audiotaped conferences 3. Reflective journals 4. Midpoint interviews 5. Reading course overviews 6. Lesson plans, unit plans 7. Children's work samples	Primary Primary Primary Secondary Primary Primary Primary
3. Week 10 of student teaching	1. TORP questionnaires 2. Final interviews	Secondary Secondary

a. Theoretical Orientation to Reading Profile (DeFord, 1979).

1. Does the student teacher appear to experience any positive or negative effects as a result of a matched-pairing placement with a cooperating teacher with regard to theoretical orientation to the reading process?

2. Does the student teacher appear to experience any positive or negative effects as a result of a mismatched-pairing placement with

TABLE 11.4 Student Teacher Pairing and Theoretical Orientation

		Theoretical Orientation	
Pair	Grade	Student Teacher	Cooperating Teacher
1/Mismatch	1	Phonics	Whole language
2/Match	2	Phonics	Phonics
3/Mismatch	3	Whole language	Phonics

TABLE 11.5 Theoretical Orientation to Reading Profile (TORP) Scores

			Score	
Pair		Phase	Student Teacher	Cooperating Teacher
1	Mismatch	1	61^a	127^b
1	Mismatch	3	84^c	—
2	Match	1	67^a	65^a
2	Match	3	55^a	—
3	Match	1	117^b	59^a
3	Match	3	120^b	—

NOTE: TORP: DeFord (1979).
a. Phonics orientation.
b. Whole language orientation.
c. Skills orientation.

a cooperating teacher with regard to theoretical orientation to the reading process?

The decision was made to focus this study on three pairs of student teachers/cooperating teachers, two mismatched pairs in relation to theoretical orientation to the reading process and one matched pair (see Table 11.4). For ethical reasons, student teachers and cooperating teachers were not purposely matched or mismatched. Random, arbitrary pairing was assigned as usual. However, following student teaching placement, pairs of student teachers and cooperating teachers were administered the Theoretical Orientation to Reading Profile (TORP; DeFord, 1979) to determine which pairs would be selected for the study. After potential pairs were identified through TORP scores (see Table 11.5), three specific pairs were chosen due to logistics and grade-level considerations in addition to TORP scores (see Tables 11.4 and 11.5). Pairs were contacted in person and asked about participating in the study. All agreed. The same three student teachers identified in Phase 1 were again administered the TORP in Phase 3 to ascertain possible theoretical orientation shift (see Table 11.5).

Conclusions: Pair 1 Mismatch

As profiled by the TORP, Student Teacher 1 and Cooperating Teacher 1 were mismatched (see Tables 11.4 and 11.5). The student teacher's initial score on the TORP indicated a phonics orientation, and the cooperating teacher's score indicated a whole language orientation. Although the student teacher professed a belief in the whole language orientation practiced by the cooperating teacher and presented within the student teacher's university methods classes, when given control over instructional focus, the student teacher employed instructional techniques, materials, and methodology for teaching reading in keeping with a phonics orientation. The cooperating teacher, on the other hand, had a whole language orientation and had implemented instruction for the teaching of reading in accordance with this philosophical belief system (see Table 11.1).

Because the three orientations—phonics, skills, and whole language— are presented as operating on a continuum, there are points of overlap in instructional practices, particularly in areas of proximity to another orientation. That is, the phonics and skills orientations tend to share practices, as do the skills and whole language orientations, but there is little or no sharing between typical phonics instructional focus and whole language. As a result, the student teacher's final TORP score probably would not be expected to change so completely that it reflected a whole language orientation. However, the student teacher's final TORP score change from phonics to skills indicated movement along the language continuum in the direction of her cooperating teacher's whole language orientation beliefs and practices.

As a result of Pair 1's ongoing dialogue concerning lesson planning and instructional strategies, the cooperating teacher and student teacher were able to address their differences in relation to theoretical orientation, and the cooperating teacher was able to offer guidance for lesson modification. The student teacher accepted these suggestions, saw them as "fun," and successfully implemented many of them. Encouraged by the cooperating teacher, the student teacher's lessons involved more literature, became more holistic, and involved more discovery learning.

Cooperating Teacher 1 offered constructive criticism in a positive manner; provided feedback, guidance, and support; and created an overall atmosphere or context in which the student teacher felt encouraged and supported. Throughout the student teaching experience, the actions and attitude of the cooperating teacher were aimed at facilitating and guiding the student teacher. As a result, the student teacher was able and willing to experiment and take risks. The inquirer concluded that the student teacher did not appear to experience any significant negative effects as a result of her mismatched-pairing placement with regard to theoretical orientation to the reading process. In fact, positive effects were recorded and commented on by the student teacher in her reflective journal:

> I found my student teaching experience a wonderful learning experience. My cooperating teacher was wonderful. We got along extremely well because we had a lot in common. We both enjoy incorporating whole language activities into the classroom. Not only was she my cooperating teacher, she was also a good friend. I could not have been any happier with my teacher. I will miss her and my students a great deal.

Although Pair 1 held diametrically opposing theoretical orientations to the reading process, with no overlap, their mismatched-pairing placement did not produce negative effects in the student teacher. Rather, it produced positive effects due to the personality traits of the cooperating teacher such as openness, empathy, helpfulness, supportiveness, creativity, a nurturing manner, understanding, encouragement, a positive attitude, and kindness. As a result, the inquirer concluded that this particular mismatch (i.e., phonics student teacher/whole language cooperating teacher), in and of itself, did not cause the student teacher to experience negative effects.

This suggested to the inquirer that the personality traits of the cooperating teacher (e.g., openness, empathy, helpfulness, supportiveness, creativity, a nurturing manner, understanding, encouragement, a positive attitude, kindness), in addition to the belief system or theoretical orientation, were equally important as to whether the student teacher viewed the student teaching experience as negative or positive.

Conclusions: Pair 2 Match

As profiled by the TORP, Student Teacher 2 and Cooperating Teacher 2 were matched in regard to theoretical orientation (see Tables 11.4 and

11.5). The student teacher's initial score on the TORP indicated a phonics orientation as did the TORP score of the cooperating teacher. When given control over instructional focus, the student teacher employed instructional techniques, materials, and methodology for teaching reading in keeping with a phonics orientation. The cooperating teacher also had implemented instruction for the teaching of reading in accordance with this philosophical belief system (see Table 11.1). On the second administration of the TORP, the student teacher scored even lower, which indicated a movement in theoretical orientation more decidedly in a phonics orientation and that her initial belief system became even stronger as she put theory into practice. Also, it suggested that the cooperating teacher's beliefs and practices reinforced the belief system of the student teacher.

As a result of Pair 2's ongoing dialogue concerning lesson planning and instructional strategies, the cooperating teacher was able to offer guidance, support, encouragement, and creative ideas for lesson modification. The student teacher accepted these suggestions, welcomed the teacher's intervention and guidance, and often commented on their similarities in theoretical orientation, attitudes, expectations, and actual implementation of instruction. By the 10th and final week of the student teaching experience, Student Teacher 2 was developing lessons much like those of her cooperating teacher.

Cooperating Teacher 2 offered constructive criticism in a positive manner; provided feedback, guidance, and support; and created an overall atmosphere or context within which the student teacher felt encouraged and supported throughout the student teaching experience by the actions and attitude of the cooperating teacher. As a result, the student teacher was able and willing to experiment and take risks. The inquirer concluded that the student teacher did not appear to experience any significant negative effects as a result of her matched-pairing placement with regard to theoretical orientation to the reading process.

In fact, positive effects were recorded and commented on by the student teacher in her final reflective journal entry:

> As my student teaching experience comes to an end, I feel happy but also very sad. I look back on all of the things that happened to me, the experiences, the influence of my cooperating teacher, and the children, and I smile. I think that I had a great student teaching experience. I had great children and I had a great teacher. Sometimes I think I learned more in my student teaching than in any class I had in college.

Pair 2 appeared to be in harmony from the first week through the last week of the practicum experience. Although Pair 2 held the same theoretical orientation, and they agreed on methodology, materials, and instructional implementation and had similar expectations with regard to the teaching of reading, the student teacher's positive perception of her cooperating teacher involved more than theoretical orientation similarity. For example, the student teacher repeatedly referred to her cooperating teacher's "positive attitude," willingness to "discuss and brainstorm" ideas with her, supportiveness, encouragement, and kindness. As a result, the inquirer concluded that this particular match (i.e., phonics student teacher/ phonics cooperating teacher), in and of itself, did not cause the student teacher to experience positive effects.

As in Case Study 1, this suggested to the inquirer that the personality traits of the cooperating teacher (e.g., openness, empathy, helpfulness, supportiveness, creativity, a nurturing manner, understanding, encouragement, a positive attitude, kindness), in addition to the belief system or theoretical orientation, were equally important as to whether the student teacher viewed the student teaching experience as negative or positive.

Conclusions: Pair 3 Mismatch

As profiled by the TORP, Student Teacher 3 and Cooperating Teacher 3 were mismatched in regard to theoretical orientation (see Tables 11.4 and 11.5). The student teacher's initial score on the TORP indicated a whole language orientation, and the cooperating teacher's score indicated a phonics orientation. Because their scores clustered on opposite ends of the theoretical orientation continuum, little or no sharing of theory between phonics and whole language orientations would exist. That is, they viewed the reading act and the teaching of reading very differently (see Table 11.1).

Initially, the student teacher felt obligated to follow the same basic routines, employ the same methodology, and make use of the same instructional materials that her cooperating teacher had established in accordance with her phonics orientation. As a result, the student teacher unwillingly implemented a phonics approach under the guidance and direction of her cooperating teacher. Although the student teacher "wanted to make some changes," she soon realized that doing so would prove to be "difficult." As she noted in numerous reflective journal entries, Student Teacher 3 expressed her views about the teaching of reading and a desire for change in relation to instructional implementation. She also expressed frustration, anxiety, sadness, disappointment, concern, anger, and discouragement as she interacted with her cooperating teacher and worked within her cooperating teacher's model of instruction.

Later, when Student Teacher 3 assumed total, unsupervised control over instructional planning early in the student teaching experience, she was able to implement a more holistic and integrated approach to reading instruction than her initial instruction. As evidenced in data collection, when the student teacher realized that the cooperating teacher did not intend to monitor her student teaching in any manner whatsoever, the student teacher took over. She began making reading instruction, and other subject areas, more varied and integrated. Reading instruction was given a new format, with different guidelines, structural organization, and materials and methodology. In the opinion of the inquirer, as soon as the student teacher felt it was possible, she tried, as much as it was feasible within her placement site, to implement integration of reading, writing, listening, and speaking with other subjects and to address the individual needs of her learners through her instructional organization and implementation. As a result of this quite "different" approach to instruction, the student teacher seemed more at ease and less stressed.

The student teacher's final TORP score was higher than her first score. This score indicated a movement in theoretical orientation even more decidedly in the direction of a whole language orientation and away from that of her cooperating teacher's beliefs and practices. This final TORP score suggested that the student teacher's initial belief system became stronger as she put theory into practice and witnessed the phonic decoding method of teaching reading in practice. This finding was confirmed by the student teacher herself as she stated: "I think I have become even more convinced that a literature-based program is interesting and exciting to the students and I love teaching with books. . . . I can't wait to try it in my own classroom" (final interview).

As a result of this pair's minimal contact concerning lesson planning and instructional strategies, the cooperating teacher and the student teacher did not address their differences in relation to theoretical orientation. Due to her mostly inactive role, the cooperating teacher was not perceived by the student teacher as offering support, guidance, constructive criticism, or encouragement. According to the student teacher, the brief exchanges with her cooperating teacher were neither positive in tone nor did they contain suggestions concerning materials or methods of instructional implementation. In fact, the student teacher perceived contact with her cooperating teacher as negative. The student teacher said that the cooperating teacher's input was stifling her creativity and opportunity to experiment.

Cooperating Teacher 3 did not offer constructive criticism in a positive manner, and she did not provide guidance, feedback, support, or encouragement for the student teacher. The cooperating teacher created an overall atmosphere or context in which the student teacher felt frustrated, anxious, saddened, discouraged, disappointed, and angry throughout the student teaching experience due to the actions and attitude of the cooperating teacher. As a result, the student teacher made use of strategies such as "strategic compliance" or "strategic redefinition" (Lacey, 1977), meaning she maintained a veneer of conformity to gain a favorable evaluation. However, she continued to maintain her original perspectives and put them into practice whenever the cooperating teacher's absence allowed her to do so. The inquirer concluded that the student teacher did appear to experience negative effects as a result of her mismatched-pairing placement.

Student Teacher 3's final reflective journal entry, unlike the final journal entries of the other two student teachers, did not voice appreciation or gratitude for her cooperating teacher's guidance and/or for the student teaching experience itself. Rather, she said:

> As my time in this classroom comes to an end, I hate to leave these kids. My classroom will be less rigid and structured. . . . I have arranged with Ms. _ [cooperating teacher] to return to this classroom for a few hours each week to read to the kids and listen to them read. I'm looking forward to it. . . . I want my own classroom and students and all the hard work that goes with being a positive teacher.

Like Pair 1, Pair 3 held diametrically opposing theoretical orientations to the reading process with no possible overlap in their theories. Unlike the student teachers from Case Studies 1 and 2, who were pleased with their student teaching placements, the Case Study 3 student teacher was displeased. Although the Case Study 1 student teacher also had a mismatched-pairing placement with a cooperating teacher that held a diametrically opposing orientation, Student Teacher 1 did not report her student teaching experience as being negative as did Student Teacher 3.

As a result, the inquirer concluded that this particular mismatch (i.e., whole language student teacher/phonics cooperating teacher), in and of itself, did not cause the student teacher to experience negative effects. Furthermore, the student teacher's overall perception of her cooperating teacher seemed to play a major part in whether the student teacher perceived the student teaching experience as negative or positive.

In these three case studies, certain personality traits of the cooperating teachers, in addition to their belief systems or theoretical orientations, appeared to be important factors in determining whether the student teachers viewed their practicum experiences as negative or positive. As a result, the inquirer concluded that the combination of direction of the mismatch in theoretical orientation in Case Study 3 (i.e., student teacher/whole language orientation; cooperating teacher/phonics orientation) and the personality traits of the cooperating teacher contributed significantly to the Pair 3 student teacher experiencing negative effects during student teaching.

Implications for Teacher Education

This study has generated a number of emergent questions and areas for future research for those who study the elementary student teaching experience in general and the student teacher/cooperating teacher relationship in particular.

For example, should observation and analysis of a cooperating teacher's interaction pattern precede any assignment of a student teacher, and should the screening process in effect for cooperating teacher selection be other than or in addition to a master's degree, building principal's recommendation, and 3 to 5 years of successful teaching experience regardless of theoretical orientation?

Taking into account interaction patterns and student teacher perceptions, it may be that a cooperating teacher should be carefully selected on the basis of motivation to be a teacher educator as well as on instructional expertise. Furthermore, theoretical orientation identification of the student teacher and purposeful matching/mismatching of the pair as a part of the student teacher's placement process has emerged as significant. Therefore, the question of whether "practice" preservice practicum/tutorial experiences should be controlled for orientation match/mismatch to ensure student teachers' exposure to other orientations before they are assigned to student teaching becomes relevant. Also, should student teachers' input in regard to placement with particular cooperating teachers be included in the placement process?

Given the impact of theoretical orientation on the teaching of reading in particular and the student teaching experience in general, should education programs plan teacher education courses such as reading methods courses with theoretical orientation in mind? Should the student teacher be instructed to behave based on what he or she believes, his or her theoretical orientation, or should the student teacher behave more like the belief system of the cooperating teacher?

If the student teacher is matched or mismatched in regard to theoretical orientation, how is his or her theoretical orientation affected by the match or mismatch, and is the effect, if any, a long-term one? Most significantly, the question as to whether the student teacher has a qualitatively different student teaching experience when the student teacher is reinforced by the theoretical orientation of the cooperating teacher than when the student teacher and cooperating teacher hold different theoretical orientations should be researched, and implications for teacher education should be addressed.

If there is a significant relationship between theoretical orientations and certain psychological characteristics, how does this affect the interaction practices of, and potential as, teacher educators of potential teachers? Are specific theoretical orientation/psychological characteristics matches more conducive to a positive/negative student teaching experience than other theoretical orientation/psychological characteristics matches? Should student teacher and cooperating teacher be purposely matched/mismatched with regard to theoretical orientation/psychological characteristics?

Areas of Future Research

Several areas of future research have emerged from this study. Researchers may want to consider the following.

• Design more studies such as this one to add to the database of subjective realities concerning interactions between student teachers and cooperating teachers.

The naturalistic paradigm, with its multiple, divergent, interrelated view of reality, presents authentic, qualitative data that are embedded in daily interactions of individuals and can only be gathered through naturalistic inquiry (Bogdan & Biklen, 1992; Carter, 1993; Lincoln & Guba, 1985). As a result, more qualitative case studies that retain the holistic and complex characteristics of real-life events comprising social phenomenon would deepen our understanding of student teacher/cooperating teacher interaction patterns and the student teaching experience.

• Design longitudinal studies to address whether theoretical orientation change during student teaching is internalized by student teachers or has a carry-over effect to first-year teaching practices.

Although such studies have been done on theoretical orientation change (attitudinal change) and resistance to theoretical orientation change (attitudinal change), few studies address whether this change is internalized by the student teacher or has a carry-over effect to first-year teaching practices. At present, there is a lack of residual effect studies and more research is indicated.

• Expand the research to include additional student teacher/cooperating teacher pairs in other geographic areas.

This study examined three student teacher/cooperating teacher pairs in the same mid-Tennessee county school district. The schools were located in a small- to medium-size city. All of these student teachers were educated at the same university and were influenced by a similar set of circumstances and group of individuals. By including student teacher/cooperating teacher pairs in other geographic regions, it would be possible to look at the experiences of student teachers acting under different circumstances and having been influenced by different groups of educators.

• Study the opportunities offered in university classes to preservice and inservice teachers to question and discuss different methodologies and the underlying theories.

Teacher educators should be willing and prepared to examine their own professed and demonstrated theories. In addition, university classes such as reading methods and language arts methods classes should provide information concerning belief systems—theoretical orientations—and the corresponding methodologies. If preservice and inservice teachers are more knowledgeable about their beliefs and how these beliefs guide their practices, they will then be better able to evaluate their instructional approaches in light of pertinent research to find out why certain methods are better than others and what methodology fits which theoretical orientation.

• Examine the possibility of allowing preservice teachers to have opportunities to give direction to their field experiences.

The cooperating teacher is "viewed as their most significant professional helper" in this monumental first venture into the "real world" of the student teacher's chosen profession—the classroom. Rather than random placement of student teachers with cooperating teachers by the student teaching office, potential preservice teachers could be prepared and encouraged to examine existing classroom practices and interaction patterns of potential cooperating teachers in light of their own developing belief systems—their theoretical orientations. They should have the opportunities to discuss, compare, and examine their own theories and practices with those of the cooperating teacher, preferably with the cooperating teacher, prior to the student teaching experience. As a result, the student teacher would gain some control over the most significant aspect of teacher preparation and the most important event in the life of the preservice teacher rather than being passively controlled by it.

• Examine the possibility of making a more informed decision about student teacher placement and institute a screening process for selection of a cooperating teacher.

Given that the cooperating teacher tends to exert a substantial influence on the student teacher, some conclude that the cooperating teacher is the most powerful socialization agent in the development of teaching style by the student teacher. Research has indicated a marked convergence of styles (i.e., interaction patterns), theoretical orientation, and instructional implementation in relation to certain pairings between cooperating teacher and student teacher (May, 1990; Zevin, 1974). Educators who want the student teacher to explore various patterns, methodologies, and styles of teaching may want to make more informed decisions about student teaching placement based on things such as observation and analysis of a cooperating teacher's interaction patterns, theoretical orientation identification, motivation to be a teacher educator, instructional expertise, and certain psychological characteristics.

• Design studies to investigate the relationships between a teacher's stated theoretical orientation and reading and personality traits.

In view of the findings of this study, the inquirer concluded that in these particular case studies, certain personality traits of the cooperating teachers, in addition to their belief systems or theoretical orientations, appeared to be equally important as to whether the student teachers viewed their student teaching experiences as negative or positive. As a result, the inquirer further concluded that the combination of the mismatch (student teacher/whole language orientation; cooperating teacher/phonics orientation) and the personality traits of the cooperating teacher contributed significantly to the student teacher experiencing negative effects during her student teaching experience. Therefore, additional research to determine if certain personality traits are associated with particular orientations to the reading process is indicated.

- Design more studies that investigate the affective effects and behavioral effects on the student teacher both during and after pairing of student teacher and cooperating teacher with regard to affective factors such as theoretical orientation and personality traits.

As Puckett and McClam (1990) note, most of the studies on student teaching supervision are written from the perspective of the college supervisor or the cooperating teacher, leaving out the student teacher. Studies that do include the perspective of the student teacher focus on roles and duties, leaving out the qualities of effective supervisors. Also, studies dealing with the student teaching experience usually do not examine what happens to the student teacher after the student teaching experience.

With the widespread push to reform public education and teacher education programs, the demand is great for a body of knowledge to shed light on the complex world of the student teachers and their interactions with their cooperating teachers. Studies investigating affective effects and behavioral effects, both during and after the student teaching experience, in regard to theoretical orientation/personality traits-pairing placement, are indicated.

References

Bogdan, R., & Biklen, S. (1992). *Qualitative research for education: An introduction to theory and methods* (2nd ed.). Boston: Allyn & Bacon.

Burk, J. (1989). Six case studies of preservice teachers and the development of language learning theories (Doctoral dissertation, Texas A&M University, 1989). *Dissertation Abstracts International, 51,* 01A.

Carter, K. (1993). The place of story in the study of teaching and teacher education. *Educational Researcher, 22,* 5-12, 18.

DeFord, D. (1979). *A validation study of an instrument to determine a teacher's theoretical orientation to reading instruction.* Unpublished doctoral dissertation, Indiana University.

Feiman-Nemser, S. (1983). Learning to teach. In L. Shulman & G. Sykes (Eds.), *Handbook of teaching and policy.* New York: Longman.

Friebus, R. (1977). Agents of socialization involved in student teaching. *Journal of Educational Research, 70,* 263-268.

Goodlad, J. (1991). Why we need the complete redesign of teacher education. *Educational Leadership, 49*(3), 4-6, 8-10.

Guba, E., & Lincoln, Y. (1981). *Effective evaluation.* San Francisco: Jossey-Bass.

Holmes Group. (1990). *Tomorrow's schools: Principles for the design of professional development schools.* East Lansing, MI: Author.

Hoy, W., & Rees, R. (1977). The bureaucratic socialization of student teachers. *Journal of Teacher Education, 28*(1), 23-26.

Lacey, C. (1977). *The socialization of teachers.* London: Methuen.

Lincoln, Y., & Guba, E. (1985). *Naturalistic inquiry.* Beverly Hills, CA: Sage.

May, F. (1990). *Reading as communication: An interactive approach* (3rd ed.). Columbus, OH: Merrill.

McShane-Bechner, R., & Ade, W. (1982). The relationship of field placement characteristics and students' potential field performance abilities to clinical experience performance ratings. *Journal of Teacher Education, 23*(2), 24-30.

Patterson, L. (1987). Responses to socio-psycholinguistic composition instruction in a secondary school classroom: Toward a transactional stance for teacher researchers (Doctoral dissertation, Texas A&M University, 1987). *Dissertation Abstracts International, 48,* 12A.

Puckett, K., & McClam, T. (1990, Summer). Qualities of effective supervision. *Teacher Educator, 26*(1), 2-8.

Smith, M. (1990). A study of the socialization of student teachers with whole language perspective. (Doctoral dissertation, Indiana University, 1990). *Dissertation Abstracts International, 52,* 03A.

Tabachnick, B., & Zeichner, K. (1984). The impact of the student teaching experience on the development of teacher perspective. *Journal of Teacher Education, 35,* 28-36.

Yee, A. (1969). Do cooperating teachers influence the attitudes of student teachers? *Journal of Educational Psychology, 60*(4), 327-332.

Zeichner, K. (1980). Myths and realities: Field-based experiences in preservice teacher education. *Journal of Teacher Education, 31*(6), 45-49, 51-55.

Zeichner, K., & Tabachnick, B. (1981). Are the effects of university teacher education "washed out" by school experience? *Journal of Teacher Education 32*(3), 7-11.

Zevin, J. (1974, April). *In the cooperating teacher's image: Convergence of social studies student teachers' behavior patterns with cooperating teachers' behavior patterns.* Paper presented at the annual meeting of the American Education Research Association, Chicago. (ERIC Document Reproduction Service No. ED 087 781)

12 The Effect of Hypermedia on Reflectivity as Perceived by Students in an Early Field Experience Course

Sharon L. Gilbert

Jerry Hostetler

Sharon L. Gilbert is Associate Professor in the faculty of Curriculum and Instruction, Southern Illinois University at Carbondale. She is the coordinator of a teacher education center and pursues academic research in technology and teacher education, student teacher thinking, and reflective judgment. She created and produced interactive videodisc courseware, "The Study of Teaching," for early field experience students at SIUC in 1991, and she continues to refine the content and technology while using the product for instruction.

Jerry Hostetler is Director for Instructional Support Services at Southern Illinois University at Carbondale and also serves on the graduate faculty in the College of Education. He consults with university faculty in the development and production of multimedia, distance learning, and Web-based instruction. He developed the technology to deliver an award-winning (Authorware Academic Excellence Award) interactive videodisc program for library instruction.

ABSTRACT

The interactive multimedia project reported here was originally designed in 1991 to enhance the development of reflectivity in early field experience students providing access to real class-rooms varying in grade level, content, teaching method, multicultural representations, and settings (urban, suburban, and rural). The 1996 edition used laserdisc, QuickTime movies of teacher and professor interviews, and other elaborations such as "hot words" and video examples of concepts. Findings from the embedded tracking program and exit interviews indicate that reflective behaviors were enhanced.

The early field experience course, Education 310, contains various components designed to support reflectivity. In this report, we are particularly interested in the students' perceptions of how the hypermedia experience enhanced the development of reflectivity and complemented other activities of the course.

The interactive videodisc (IVD) project was developed to enhance the reflective teaching model on which the first field experience course is built. It provides learning opportunities that are intended to stimulate the development of reflective thinking. Research about teacher education, adult learning theory, active learning theory, and about hypermedia as a learning environment provide the theoretical basis for the IVD project.

Theoretical Bases

Research in teacher education suggests that propositional knowledge acquired in academic settings does not transfer well to practical settings (e.g., Cognition and Technology Group at Vanderbilt, 1990). Practical knowledge (Sternberg, 1996) or strategic knowledge (Shulman, 1986) entails not only knowing what you need to know but also knowing when and how to use that information. During early field experiences, novices engage in teacher watching that conveys no sense of technique or of reasons for choosing content and strategy. It does not require consideration of multiple and competing principles or precedents, a necessary step for developing strategic knowledge. Most knowledge acquired in teacher preparation programs is propositional or case-specific knowledge, which often remains disconnected from the "messy context" of the realities of life in classrooms (Lampert & Ball, 1990).

Adult learning theory suggests that adults prefer to participate as much as possible in classroom activities (Eison & Moore, 1980) working with others on problems or sharing relevant experiences in discussion (Claxton & Murrell, 1987). Such active participation in classroom activities contributes to learning and improves its retention (Darkenwald & Merriman, 1982). Active learning theory (Meyers & Jones, 1993) also involves key elements of talking, listening, reading, writing, reflection, and discussion, which represent many of the activities preferred by adult learners. Active personal engagement with content is more likely to enhance learning about the complexities of teaching (Cognition and Technology Group at Vanderbilt, 1990; Meyers & Jones, 1993).

Studies of hypermedia also support the use of this strategy. The nonlinear capabilities of hypermedia systems allow instant and variable path access to information, which creates experiences for preservice teachers that are closer to thinking, feeling, and making judgments like a teacher (Lampert & Ball, 1990; Risko, 1991). Hypermedia makes it possible to revisit scenes several times, move quickly and easily through multiple perspectives, or hold several perspectives simultaneously (Cognition and Technology Group at Vanderbilt, 1990; Lampert & Ball, 1990; Risko, 1991).

According to Kozma (1994), most of the existing research on interactive video using laserdisc technology focuses on its use in a self-instruction setting, not classroom instruction. Risko (1991) discovered that the use of videodisc-based case methodology, a delivery system similar to the IVD, resulted in active engagement and generative learning. Nix (1990) and Spiro and Jehng (1990) each reported that students developed confidence via increased metacognitive awareness triggered by the use of hypermedia cases.

Although hypermedia learning environments may be used for individual study, a major advantage of this environment is its ability to create shared learning contexts (Risko, Yount, & Towell, 1992). Copeland and Decker's (1996) study suggests that video-mediated cases, in which groups of three students discussed the video case, do have a positive effect in stimulating more thoughtful meaning making by preservice teachers.

Project Description

Project Technology

Students are involved actively in learning the content presented in the IVD project through observing, reading, writing, thinking and problem solving, talking, and discussion. They view the interactive multimedia materials individually or in groups of three or four. Groups are created by convenience, that is, students signed up for a 2-hour use time depending on their personal schedules. They were encouraged to form groups because we believed that the discussion and interaction among students of varying backgrounds, ages, experiences, and educational levels would provide multiple viewpoints and offer opportunities for expanding individuals' ways of thinking about teaching and learning. A tracking system built into the computer program gives information about how long and how often students use each of the components of the IVD materials; which components are revisited and how often and for how long; and the order of use for each of the components.

Video protocols, that is, live, unrehearsed video recordings of classroom teaching episodes, are mastered on a laserdisc. The protocols covered primary, intermediate, middle, and high school grade levels with content in mathematics, reading instruction, language arts and handwriting, a pottery-making art lesson, and Spanish. The protocols on laserdisc are easily accessed by the Hypercard program and shown on a standard color TV screen.

The video materials also included QuickTime (digital) movies of interviews of the practitioner in each episode describing his or her reflections, private knowledge, interpretations, and evaluations of the events in the language of practice. Interviews were also made with the university professors in specialized content such as mathematics education or Spanish. The professors reflected on the protocols in the theoretical language used in their courses. Thus, both practical and theoretical language was used to describe the same events.

In addition to the QuickTime movies, text screens, and graphics, other elaborations included "hot words" (links), which may be both text definitions and video examples of concepts from the text or class discussion. Concepts or professional vocabulary such as *teacher centered* or *behaviorist* became hot words identified in the main text by bold-face type. For example, if students clicked on a hot word such as teacher centered, they were immediately linked to a text screen with a written definition and the option to observe a video example illustrating the concept of teacher centeredness. Also included were a scrolling video notebook where students recorded notes and questions about the protocols, a number of options buttons and submenus for navigating the program, and printouts of the notebooks and responses to the reflective questions. A graduate student was available to provide assistance with technical problems occasionally encountered with the interactive system.

After the final examination had been taken, students participated in a semistructured, videotaped exit interview regarding their experiences and evaluations of the IVD project. The interviewers were graduate students enrolled in a research methods course; they had no connection to the course in any way.

Scope and Sequence

Four IVD lessons were developed and carefully articulated with four on-campus class meetings, the required textbook, the written assignments, and 13 full days of field observations. The written assignments included guided-observation logs; a lesson planned, taught, and followed by a postlesson reflection; and a self-evaluation of progress based on goals written at the beginning of the semester and revised throughout.

The pretest and posttest consisted of a 10-question essay test of course concepts based on a videotaped protocol (live unrehearsed classroom episode). Students responded to the questions based on their observations of the taped classroom episode.

The course had a 4-week cycle. In the first week of the cycle, students read the related textbook selections, then in groups of three or four they collaborated on the related IVD lesson. The second and third weeks of the cycle consisted of two full-day guided observations in an elementary or secondary classroom. Students were instructed to observe and write about events that were conceptually related to the IVD lesson. These concepts represented four themes: physical and psychosocial environment, classroom discipline and management, lesson design, and teaching methods. An on-campus whole-class session culminated each of the 4-week cycles.

Each of the four IVD lessons had three or four reflective questions requiring written responses. The reflective questions became more cognitively complex as the lesson progressed, beginning with relatively simple description such as "identify and describe three instances of disruption." The next reflective question asked students to "analyze the effects on teaching and learning of the classroom context you described in the previous response." The final reflective question presented students with the opportunity to take a position or evaluate the actions and events in the protocol. For example:

> Write about your agreement or disagreement with the teacher's or professor's comments. Describe alternatives and the plausible outcomes of those alternatives. Support your claims with evidence

from at least one source other than your personal experience, such as research, the textbook or on-screen information, or your campus classes.

In an IVD session, students could choose to view the video protocols, teacher and professor interviews, and digital movies. They read, discussed, and interpreted text and graphics; took notes on an on-screen scrolling notebook; or answered reflective questions in each lesson. At the completion of the lesson, they received a printout of the questions with their responses and a copy of their scrolling notebook.

During the whole-class session, the instructor guided discussion of the protocol using the students' original ideas from IVD reflective question printouts. During the discussion, both practical and theoretical professional language was clarified, multiple perspectives explored, and students shared their experiences from their classroom observations to draw relationships between their observations and the IVD protocols.

Method

Data Collection

Data were collected from the exit interviews and the embedded tracking system. All interviews were conducted by graduate students experienced in research methods, and then transcribed and analyzed for trends among the students' self-reports of their experiences with the course and perceptions of professional growth. Interviews were semistructured and consisted of questions grouped around themes of (a) personal and course goals, and overall professional growth; (b) experiences with IVDs; (c) experiences with written assignments; (d) experiences with field observations; (e) experiences with on-campus class meetings; and (f) technology. Interview data are quoted verbatim but information that might identify persons or places has been changed. (All names of students are pseudonyms.)

Embedded tracking data described how many students worked together on each of the four lessons; the amount of time spent on each question; the frequency of access and duration of use of each component, including hot words (links), review or synopsis cards, QuickTime movies, and video protocols; and the frequency of amended answers to questions after additional information had been accessed. These data were analyzed for trends and compared to students' self-reports in the interviews.

TABLE 12.1 Gender and Certification Level of Sample

	Elementary	*Secondary*	*K-12*
Males ($n = 5$)	$n = 1$ (Jeffrey)	$n = 3$ (Tim, Brian, Scott)	$n = 1$ (Charles)
Females ($n = 20$)	$n = 12$ (Barbara, Amy, Carrie, Tonya, Jill, Carla, Kellie, Kathy, Mindy, Lynn, Kim, Jennifer)	$n = 0$	$n = 8$ (Karen, Sharon, Krista, Carol, Michelle, Tria, Sue, Paula)

Sample Population

The sample reported on here consists of 25 students in three sections of the 1996 fall semester of Education 310, Introduction to Education. Five males and 20 females comprised the sample. Table 12.1 indicates distribution across content or certification area. Kindergarten through 12th grade certification presently includes special education, music, art, and physical education. Two of the 25 students were nontraditional.

Findings

We focus here on the sections of the exit interviews and embedded tracking system that produced data about the use of the IVD materials and their relationship to the development of reflection.

Exit interviews were organized around the six major themes listed above. Interview transcriptions were analyzed for comments that indicated the student perceived his or her reflectivity or other class activities had been enhanced by using the multimedia materials. Data from each source is presented in topic areas when similar areas existed (see Table 12.2).

Grouping

Grouping patterns of students, use of the IVDs indicated the size of groups varied across the four lessons. The data show that on the average

TABLE 12.2 Number and Average Use Frequency of Reflective Elements

	Protocol Video, No. of Times Used	Hot Words		Video Examples		Review Cards		Teacher QuickTime Videos		Professor QuickTime Videos	
		Total No.	Average No. of Times Accessed	Total No.	Average No. of Times Accessed	Total No.	Average No. of Times Accessed	Total No.	Average No. of Times Accessed	Total No.	Average No. of Times Accessed
IVD[a] 1	8	5	8.4	12	8.4	2	15	9	5.6	4	3.5
IVD 2	3	8	0.25	9	1.3	N/A	N/A	2	2	2	3
IVD 3	16	10	3.5	13	4.9	12	2.6	1	8	1	5
IVD 4	9	7	3.5	6	5.6	7	3.5	2	4.5	2	2

a. Interactive videodisc lesson.

students worked in pairs 46% of the time, alone 35% of the time, and in groups of three or four 25% of the time. Students indicated during the exit interviews that they worked alone often by coincidence. "I waited 20 minutes sometimes and then I just worked alone. I think I probably would have gotten more out of them [the IVDs] if I had been in a group," Sharon pointed out. "Nobody else signed up for some of the times I could go; so I worked alone twice," Tim said.

Students worked in groups almost 75% of the time. "You'd have more discussion and somebody else's point of view. Like Sharon, 19 students believed that they "got (or would have gotten) more" out of the IVDs working in a group. Mindy, and five others, disagreed: "I didn't have to worry about being fair and putting everyone's input in [by working alone]. I didn't have to feel like anyone was just sitting there getting the information and not doing anything." Jeffrey related, "I know when I'm in a group that I kind of slough off; let someone else do the work. So I worked alone."

Data from the embedded tracking system, a time-related measure of reflection, suggested that students working alone tended to spend more time and access more of the options than students working in groups. Individuals spent an average of 1 hour 10 minutes on each of the four lessons, whereas groups spent less than 1 hour. Three students (Karen and Charles, who traveled an hour to get to the university, and Sharon) complained about the additional time requirements for the class. "It was very inconvenient. I had to get a baby-sitter during the day because I work at night," Sharon said.

Elaborations

In the second edition (1996) of the IVD program, in addition to the classroom protocols, elaborations (options) that were tracked included QuickTime movies, hot words, review cards, video examples, and the option to amend responses to the reflective questions. Review cards (summaries of terms, concepts, or hot words) permitted access sections to information and video examples used in the original hot word links during the question section. Tracking data revealed that the video protocols of the classroom lessons were revisited at least once with a maximum of three times.

The students were asked during the exit interviews about each of the IVDs' special features and elaborations. Eighteen respondents lauded the special features of the laserdisc technology, such as being able to return to a protocol or a hot word virtually at will. "We watched them all a couple of times because when you're concentrating on one thing you've missed something else. So we would go back," Charles stated. Twenty students responded appreciatively to the scrolling notebook and printouts of notes, questions, and their answers. "I kept copies so I could review and look for those concepts in my observation."

Although protocols had the potential of being the most useful of all the IVD aspects, responses to them were mixed. Three quarters of the respondents held a view similar to Carla's: "It was almost like being in another classroom and seeing another teacher." Barbara's countering perspective represented the other one quarter of the students. "You don't always see what's going on on that little TV screen. If I was there I could see the whole class." Brian represented a third perspective—the views of the secondary education majors and those in particular specialties such as speech pathology or special education. "Yeah, it did [make a difference] because I'm going to be a high school teacher and it was hard to associate with the younger kids." Sharon complained, "A lot of it was whole-class management, and I only have four kids at a time in speech. So it didn't apply."

A total of 30 hot words were in the four IVDs:

5 in IVD 1

8 in IVD 2

10 in IVD 3

7 in IVD 4

The hot words were used more during the IVDs than the review cards. Hot words, such as *teacher centered* or *behaviorist*, provided text-based definitions and in some cases video examples. For instance, a video example was provided for *transitions*, showing students changing learning activities and another group changing classes. Four of the 30 hot words in the four lessons were revisited three times, including physical and psychosocial contexts, overlappingness, transitions, and cognitivist learning theories. Review cards were opened, but data show that the links to video examples were not followed from the review cards. Video examples were more often accessed at the beginning of the IVD (see Table 12.2).

The hot words generated enthusiasm among 24 of the students during exit interviews, including 2 of those who did not believe the IVDs were useful. Placing important language or concepts in bold-face type cued students to attend. Furthermore, having both text definitions and video examples of terms and concepts made learning more efficient. "While doing the video we would watch for those bold words," Tonya explained. "We could go back and see them anytime."

All QuickTime movies were teacher or professor interviews. IVD 1 contained two QuickTime movies, IVD 2 contained four, IVD 3 contained two, and IVD 4 contained four. In IVD 1, as the number of QuickTime movies increased in a lesson, the frequency and duration of time spent on the QuickTime movies decreased from a high of 19 visits (hits) to 1. Every QuickTime movie was viewed at least once, and the teacher interviews were accessed more frequently than professor interviews.

Respondents did not mention the QuickTime movies during the exit interviews unless prompted. Sixteen of the 25 students indicated they watched the teacher more often than the professor. Jennifer's use of the classroom teacher and professor was representative of most of those who said they accessed the QuickTime movies. "We'd do our answers to the questions and then check with the teacher to see if we were on the right track." Kathy indicated a unique perspective, "We watched the first teacher one and disagreed with her. So we just didn't watch any more teacher ones. I guess thinking about it now, we should have just looked to see if they would give us a different idea." Professor interviews were not highly valued or commented on.

The reflective questions and responses in each of the four lessons were required to be printed out and handed in to the instructor. Options to return to reflective questions and to amend their responses were provided within each IVD. Once a response to a question had been written, that field was locked so that the original response could be amended but not changed. Tracking data revealed that students returned to the reflective questions about twice as often as they amended the responses.

No interview data exist about response amending; however, students did discuss the reflective questions in general. Sue's and Amy's comments are typical. "They made you look at the classroom, seeing those examples and writing about them just helped me," Sue remarked. Amy responded, "The questions probed for . . . the concepts you were supposed to be picking up and pulled those out of you."

Reflectivity

Ten of the 25 students described a transfer of ideas from the IVDs to analysis in their observations. For example, Brian reported that he developed the habit of checking how a classroom was arranged after he had worked on the IVD dealing with physical context. Kathy added, "I'd watch the video and think of my classroom and how my teacher there was applying those concepts." Paula stated,

> A lot of times after watching the IVD, I would think about that happening in the classroom that I was in. Had I observed that? What had happened? I would go through in a sense and answer that question pertaining to that classroom.

Twenty students, such as Mindy and Krista, attributed an increased awareness of the complexity of teaching to the IVDs. "As I went through the IVDs and questions I realized that there was a lot that I really didn't know." "It helped me become more aware of things in the classroom. I would think, is this child [in the classroom] displaying this behavior or something else?"

Seventeen of these respondents believed that the IVDs also increased the number and kind of observations they were able to experience in the space of one semester. Eight students did not comment. Tonya believed, "I saw a lot of things in the IVDs that I might not have seen in my actual class experience that maybe I could find valuable later." Tim reported, "That was just a different perspective. Something that you wouldn't have gotten in the one classroom that you're observing in the whole semester." But although they felt they had gained additional experiences, three students were concerned with the lack of intimacy. Carrie expressed it as:

> When I did my own observing, after a few days I knew the students and I had an idea of their personalities. I knew the teacher personally. If she did something I couldn't understand I could ask her. But sitting and viewing it on the video, I was just so distant from it.

Four students found nothing about the IVDs useful. "I just thought having to watch the videos was just like we did in the classroom every week and there was no sense to it," Jill declared. Barbara added, "The actual experience is better than seeing it on the video."

During the exit interviews, students talked about becoming more reflective by "going back and viewing the video again" to answer the reflective questions. They described how common classroom events took on new shades of meaning. "I could even see how the seating arrangement affected the way the students interacted."

In their own words, students said being reflective means "to look back," "to look back and analyze or reexamine things that happened and think about them," "trying to figure out why." The most comprehensive response stated:

> Well, I guess in a sense it means to look back and see what you've done, how you've reacted to something. If it follows the beliefs of who it involves, you and the school. And if you should change your beliefs, you know, maybe admit that you're wrong and change something. To see if you are doing the best that you can do, or if there is something you can have to make things better.

Discussion

Educators have long believed that reflection is a desirable activity for teachers, but it is not clear what constitutes genuine reflection. There are many different versions of reflective thinking including an academic version, a social efficiency version, a developmentalist version, and a social reconstructionist version (Zeichner & Tabachnick, 1991, pp. 2-3). The teacher preparation program encourages reflective thinking, but the quality and kind of reflection is not stipulated. Reviewing the extensive literature on reflection, one realizes the varied epistemological bases underlying each frame.

Pragmatism grounds the kind of reflection that appeals to many teachers; that is, they believe in the principles that produce actions that work. But, Dewey (1965) cautioned, "to accept without inquiry or criticism any method or device which seems to promise good results" may well lead to the loss of intellectual independence among teachers. How, then, is the kind of climate created that encourages future teachers to begin the process of reflectivity in the classroom?

Twenty of the 25 students indicated they believed they became more aware of the effects on teaching and learning of the commonplace events of classrooms, events not previously noticed. Viewing several teachers in different settings extended their opportunities to think about teaching from multiple perspectives. The tendency for some students to desire a right answer may indicate that they are simply responding in pragmatic ways to conditions of limited time and pedagogical experience, or it may signal that teaching is seen as a set of isolated technical procedures, rather than as a set of values shaped by culture and by social and political contexts. Such a technological belief supporting rather than challenging observed teaching practices prevents change. Students must learn to challenge their a priori assumptions, acting on the basis of choices that are made thoughtfully (some would say rationally), and not reacting from habit. Rationality of choice, we believe, is couched in careful and critical reflection.

Writing answers to the reflective questions, although difficult and distasteful, was credited in part by the students during interviews for helping them to develop reflectivity. Describing and analyzing teaching is a precursor to uncovering broader principles of classroom action, or "local theories" (Tripp, 1987), a first step in developing one's own "theories of action" (Schön, 1983). Although the project's tasks induced greater reflection, it is yet to be seen whether these students will act with independence of thought in self-governing ways in future teaching experiences. Much research suggests that faced with the pressures of student teaching and their novice years, individuals draw on practices that are remembered and familiar rather than ones that are new and innovative.

Responses about working in groups raised questions about its use in this course and about its benefits in university classes. Most students placed value on having more than one perspective about an event, despite some complaints that accounting for multiple perspectives took too much time.

Summing up the findings, based on the self-reported perceptions and the embedded tracking data, it appears that the IVD project did enhance reflective behaviors among the participants in the three sections of Introduction to Education. Some students gave clear indications that their experiences with the IVDs led them to become curious about and question events in their observation classrooms. They indicated that these events would have probably gone unnoticed before their IVD experiences. Although we cannot say that the IVDs alone were entirely responsible for the kind of transfer of reflective behavior noted by the students, we can say with some confidence that the IVDs encouraged such behaviors. It is possible that the careful articulation of all the components of the course contributed to enhancing reflection in ways yet to be uncovered. It is also possible that those individuals who showed increased reflective behaviors would have done so in any case.

Negative comments appeared to be of three kinds. First, some students complained that the IVDs were totally useless to them. The learning styles they described represented a high level of physical activity, probably precluding learning easily from materials such as the IVDs. A second group complained of difficulties they encountered with scheduling between life events, such as parenting and working, and the IVDs. Curiously, once they had aired their complaints of lack of time and inconvenience, they proceeded to talk positively about their IVD experiences. A third group of complaints came from students who were unable to identify and tie the larger concepts of each of the IVD lessons to their particular specialty. However, they too named aspects of the lessons that they found useful after they had aired their complaints.

Recommendations

The recommendations for teacher preparation derived from this research include the following:

1. Use the capabilities of technology, such as laserdisc technology, to increase opportunities for students to experience greater variety in their observations.
2. Support the development of reflective thinking with activities that aim to help students to become independent, self-regulating teachers.
3. Explore the dynamics of small- and large-group learning as a means to develop communities of learning among our prospective teachers.

References

Claxton, C. S., & Murrell, P. H. (1987). *Learning styles: Implications for improving education practices* (ASHE-ERIC Higher Education Rep. No. 4). Washington, DC: Association for the Study of Higher Education.

Cognition and Technology Group at Vanderbilt. (1990). Anchored instruction and its relationship to situated cognition. *Educational Researcher, 19*, 2-10.

Copeland, W. D., & Decker, D. L. (1996). Video cases and the development of meaning making in preservice teachers. *Teaching and Teacher Education, 12*(1), 467-481.

Darkenwald, G. G., & Merriman, S. B. (1982). *Adult education: Foundations of practice.* New York: Harper & Row.

Dewey, J. (1965). Theory and practice in education. In M. Borrowman (Ed.), *Teacher education in America: A documentary history* (p. 51). New York: Teachers College Press.

Eison, J., & Moore, J. (1980, September). *Learning styles and attitudes of traditional age and adult students.* Paper presented at the 88th annual convention of the American Psychological Association, Montreal, Quebec.

Kozma, R. B. (1994). Will media influence learning? Reframing the debate. *Educational Technology Research and Development, 42*(2), 7-19.

Lampert, M., & Ball, D. L. (1990). *Using hypermedia technology to support a new pedagogy of teacher education.* East Lansing, MI: National Center for Research on Teacher Education.

Meyers, C., & Jones, T. B. (1993). *Promoting active learning: Strategies for the college classroom.* San Francisco: Jossey-Bass.

Nix, D. (1990). Should computers know what you can do with them? In D. Nix & R. Spiro (Eds.), *Cognition, education, multimedia* (pp. 143-162). Hillsdale, NJ: Lawrence Erlbaum.

Risko, V. J. (1991). Videodisc-based case methodology: A design for enhancing preservice teachers' problem-solving abilities. In V. Hayes & K. Campbell (Eds.), *Literacy—International, national, state, and local* (Vol. 11, pp. 121-136). Athens, GA: American Reading Forum.

Risko, V. J., Yount, E., & Towell, J. (1992). Video-based case analysis to enhance teacher preparation. In N. Padak & T. Rainski (Eds.), *Reading enhances knowledge* (pp. 87-103). Provo, UT: College Reading Association.

Schön, D. A. (1983). *The reflective practitioner.* New York: Basic Books.

Shulman, L. (1986). Those who understand: Knowledge growth in teaching. *Educational Researcher, 152,* 4-14.

Spiro, R., & Jehng, J. (1990). Cognitive flexibility and hypertext: Theory and technology for the nonlinear and multidimensional traversal or complex subject matter. In D. Nix & R. Spiro (Eds.), *Cognition, education, multimedia* (pp. 163-205). Hillsdale, NJ: Lawrence Erlbaum.

Sternberg, R. (1996, October/November). *Successful intelligences.* Presentation at the 34th annual conference of the National Association of Gifted Children, Indianapolis, IN.

Tripp, D. (1987). *Theorising practice: The teachers' professional journal.* Geelong, Australia: Deakin University Press.

Zeichner, K., & Tabachnick, R. (1991). Reflections on reflective teaching. In R. Tabachnick & K. Zeichner (Eds.), *Issues and practice in inquiry-oriented teacher education* (pp. 2-3). London: Falmer.

ADDING VALUE BY MAKING THE MOST OF WHAT WE HAVE: REFLECTIONS

Joanne May Herbert

In the overview for this set of chapters, I described some recent efforts to change teacher education. In the pages that follow, I talk specifically about the implications of research conducted by Zhixin Su, Barbara Young, and Sharon Gilbert and Jerry Hostetler.

"Becoming Teachers: Minority Candidates' Perceptions of Teaching as a Profession and as a Career"

In this chapter, Zhixin Su considers some important questions. How do teacher candidates view teaching as a profession? For what reasons do they choose to teach, and for how long do they intend to do so? What are teacher candidates' perceptions of educators' roles in school reform and social change? What are some of the reasons they might leave the teaching profession?

Among other things Zhixin Su learned from her interviews with preservice teachers was that although they viewed teaching as a profession, they were aware that teachers did not enjoy the same status and economic compensation as people in other professions. Among their recommendations for change were higher salaries, improved working conditions, opportunities for leadership roles, and participation in decision making. A number of minority candidates also suggested that the establishment of national standards for teachers would likely improve the status of teaching. No big surprises here.

Despite their concern about the low status of teaching, respondents were enthusiastic about their decision to be teachers, primarily for intrinsic reasons (e.g., the opportunity to make a contribution to society, to help children). As others have found, minority candidates were more prone to teach in inner cities than their white colleagues (Darling-Hammond & Sclan, 1996). Only the minority students in Zhixin Su's study viewed themselves as agents of change, intending to alter curriculum and instruction they perceived as irrelevant to the lives of poor and minority students.

Finally, Zhixin Su learned that only a third of the teacher candidates viewed teaching as a long-term career. Caucasian teachers thought such factors as stress and frustration would determine their longevity in the profession, and minority students considered the opportunity to do "something else more rewarding" as the primary reason for leaving teaching. As others have noted, the increase in career options for minorities has influenced the continued drain on the pool of minority teachers.

As I read this piece, I wondered about the respondents—who were they, how old were they, what gender were they? If we knew more about them, we might be better able to generalize to other "minority" respondents. The capacity to do so is important if schools are to attract and retain quality minority teachers. Zhixin Su provides another chapter in the saga of the minority teacher in U.S. public education. In doing so, she keeps our attention focused on the limited options available for increasing the pool of qualified minority teachers. These conditions will only change when genuine efforts are made to enhance the status and rewards of teaching.

"Theoretical Orientation to Reading and Student Teaching Placement: Three Case Studies in Match and Mismatch Contexts"

In this study, Barbara Young examines the effects of placing student teachers in classrooms where their philosophies about teaching reading either match or conflict with their supervising teachers' beliefs and practices. The assumption is that matches enhance performance, and mismatches inhibit performance.

Although the author does not acknowledge the literature, this study follows in the tradition established by aptitude-treatment interaction researchers of the 1960s, 1970s, and 1980s. The tradition was summarily abandoned when Cronbach and Snow (1977) concluded that the payoff was too small for the effort. They defined *interactions* by using the interaction term in analysis of variance and multiple regression, which was a common but conservative way of making judgments about differential effects of treatments on people. There are other ways of assessing differential effects as this author points out, for example, self-reports of student teachers in various situations.

For the purposes of the current study, Young examined several pieces of data: observational field notes, transcripts of conferences, students' journals, lesson plans, unit plans, and children's work samples. There did not appear to be any points of comparison between student teachers' and cooperating teachers' interpretations of events. Except for results from the Theoretical Orientation to Reading Profile (TORP), then, data were based on the student teachers' perspectives.

Several other issues here might be considered. For example, how were treatments or environments defined? It seems they were defined here primarily as the philosophical positions of others in the same situation (i.e., the supervising teachers' TORP scores). Other factors that are important but were not taken into account include a description of the context (e.g., inner-city vs. suburban setting, needs and abilities of the children in the setting, the amount of time spent in the situation).

Also, the measurement of student teachers' characteristics is important. In terms of their theoretical orientation to reading, how were scores obtained? What items comprise the questionnaire? When was it administered? What is the internal consistency of the scales? Beyond these questions, we might wonder what other personality factors, professional beliefs, or dispositions might influence one's view of a student teaching placement—for instance, information-processing style, personal history, motivation, anxiety, desire to be a teacher. The researcher suggests that "certain personality traits of the cooperating teachers, in addition to their belief systems or theoretical orientations, appeared to be important factors" (p. 211) in the student teaching context. It stands to reason that the same would be true for the student teachers themselves, so it would be useful to understand how these factors were defined operationally.

In her discussion of implications for practice, Barbara Young raises a number of questions. Should cooperating teachers be screened to determine their philosophical orientations and then placed with student teachers most like them in theory? If this is not possible, how might teacher educators prepare preservice teachers to deal with classroom contexts that do not match their personal orientations? As she anticipates the future, Young suggests that preservice and inservice teachers might learn alongside one another, investigating their theoretical orientations as they participate in university courses. Future research might also include opportunities during field placements for supervising teachers and student teachers to engage in collaborative relationships (Cochran-Smith & Lytle, 1993; Lytle & Cochran-Smith, 1990; Zeichner & Liston, 1987). In these instances, teaching might be less "a matter of monologue, but of dialogue, not a soliloquy, but a conversation" (Fishman & Raver, 1989, p. 109) that might encourage both teachers and student teachers to stretch and grow as professionals.

"The Effect of Hypermedia on Reflectivity as Perceived by Students in an Early Field Experience Course"

The authors of this chapter describe an intervention designed to involve preservice teachers in problem-solving situations. Using laserdisc technology, the researchers present students with video footage from real classrooms and, through a series of questions, stimulate viewers to apply what they have learned from assigned readings and classwork to evaluate actions depicted on film. Students work on their own or with a small group of classmates to respond to questions that are later discussed in a whole-class setting. As such, the scenarios serve as cases, or "slices of real life." According to Selma Wasserman (1994), this type of curriculum has great potential to bridge the gap between "knowing" and "knowing how":

> There is nothing cold and neutral about cases, as there is about studying a list of precepts and facts. Students cannot remain passively indifferent, merely absorbing information. Cases demand active engagement. . . . Implicit . . . is the understanding that there are no clear-cut, simple answers to the complex issues teachers face. (p. 606)

According to self-report data, the majority of students in Gilbert and Hostetler's study believed that participation in the interactive videodisc

(IVD) project helped them to think more complexly about classroom situations in the field. Most students also contended that the experience exposed them to a variety of teaching and learning situations they might not have encountered otherwise.

Tracking data suggest that students followed different paths through the IVD project, and that some students spent more time on IVDs than others. A summary of student interviews reveals students' thoughts about the utility of various components of the IVD and about the effects of working alone or in small groups to analyze classroom episodes.

As I considered the results of Gilbert and Hostetler's study, I wondered what they learned from examining students' responses to the "10-question essay test . . . based on a videotaped protocol" (p. 221) administered before and after the intervention. Did students' pre- and postscores change significantly? Was there any relationship between students' performance on the test and the amount of time spent on IVDs? Did students who worked alone on IVDs score differently from those who worked in small groups? (According to the researchers, those who worked alone used more program options than their colleagues.) How did the performance of the four students who were negative about the IVDs compare to that of students who were positive about the experience? Answers to these questions might help us think more productively about ways to shape instruction to encourage critical thinking about life in classrooms.

My View

Despite valiant efforts to improve both the practice of teacher education and how it is perceived, too little attention has been paid to changing how teacher education courses are offered or what actually goes on within a course. We have assumed that numbers of hours taken in the disciplines and in professional studies, as well as the number, placement, and sequence of field experiences, make a difference. We have often ignored, however, what teacher educators and students do while they are in these courses and placements. In different ways and in varying degrees, the authors of the chapters described above acknowledge the importance of such a focus. Zhixin Su, for example, suggests that teacher educators provide opportunities for preservice teachers to consider others' perspectives. This would encourage preservice teachers to think productively about ways to meet the diverse needs of students. Barbara Young mentions the importance of determining whether courses offer preservice and in-service teachers the chance to raise questions about different approaches to teaching reading. And Sharon Gilbert and Jerry Hostetler track students' movements as they work through hypermedia materials designed to increase students' reflectivity.

We must concentrate on helping prospective teachers get the most out of courses and placements by helping them recognize problems and opportunities in these situations. We need to help them think about situations from different points of view—perspectives other than their own. We must help prospective teachers use the knowledge they acquire in classes to take actions in classrooms with children. Finally, we must help them consider the consequences of their actions. In short, we can add value to teacher education by doing the most we can with what we have.

For me, this has meant using cases. But that is only a start. Cases are only preparation for life in schools not life itself. We need to help teachers transfer what they learn from problem solving in case work to life in schools. When we do so, we will truly be enhancing the value of teacher education by preparing teachers to continue learning from their daily activities in schools.

References

Cochran-Smith, M., & Lytle, S. (1993). *Inside/outside: Teacher research and knowledge.* New York: Teachers College Press.

Cronbach, L. J., & Snow, R. E. (1977). *Aptitudes and instructional methods: A handbook for research on interactions.* New York: Irvington.

Darling-Hammond, L., & Sclan, E. M. (1996). Who teaches and why: Dilemmas of building a profession for twenty-first century schools. In J. Sikula, T. J. Buttery, & E. Guyton (Eds.), *Handbook of research on teacher education* (pp. 67-119). New York: Macmillan.

Fishman, A. R., & Raver, E. J. (1989). "Maybe I'm just not teacher material": Dialogue journals in the student teaching experience. *English Education, 21*(2), 92-109.

Lytle, S., & Cochran-Smith, M. (1990). Learning from teacher research: A working typology. *Teachers College Record, 92*(1), 83-103.

Wasserman, S. (1994, April). Using cases to study teaching. *Phi Delta Kappan, 75*(8), 602-611.

Zeichner, K. M., & Liston, D. (1987). Teaching student teachers to reflect. *Harvard Educational Review, 57*(1), 23-48.

Index

CORWIN
PRESS

The Corwin Press logo—a raven striding across an open book—represents the happy union of courage and learning. We are a professional-level publisher of books and journals for K-12 educators, and we are committed to creating and providing resources that embody these qualities. Corwin's motto is "Success for All Learners."